Script
FELICIA DAY

Art
JIM RUGG

Colors
DAN JACKSON

Letters
BLAMBOT®'S NATE PIEKOS

Cover Art
**GEORGES JEANTY WITH DEXTER VINES
AND TARIQ HASSAN**

Back Cover Art
MATTHEW STAWICKI

D0965073

DARK HORSE BOOKS

President & Publisher
MIKE RICHARDSON

Editor
SCOTT ALLIE

Associate Editor
SIERRA HAHN

Assistant Editors
FREDDYE LINS and BRENDAN WRIGHT

Collection Designer
KAT LARSON

This story takes place before the events of Season 1 of the web series *The Guild*, created by Felicia Day.

Special thanks to the cast and crew of *The Guild*; the donors for Season 1 of *The Guild*; Kim Evey; Joss Whedon; Pat Duncan; George Ruiz; and most importantly, my parents.

NEIL HANKERSON Executive Vice President TOM WEDDLE Chief Financial Officer RANDY STRADLEY Vice President of Publishing MICHAEL MARTENS Vice President of Business Development ANITA NELSON Vice President of Business Affairs MICHA HERSHMAN Vice President of Marketing DAVID SCROGGY Vice President of Product Development DALE LAFOUNTAIN Vice President of Information Technology DARLENE VOGEL Director of Purchasing KEN LIZZI General Counsel CARA NIECE Director of Scheduling SCOTT ALLIE Senior Managing Editor CHRIS WARNER Senior Books Editor DIANA SCHUTZ Executive Editor CARY GRAZZINI Director of Design and Production LIA RIBACCHI Art Director DAVEY ESTRADA Editorial Director

THE GUILD™

This volume reprints #1–#3 of the Dark Horse comic-book series The Guild, as well as a short story from MySpace Dark Horse Presents #27.

Published by Dark Horse Books, a division of Dark Horse Comics, Inc., 10956 SE Main Street, Milwaukie, OR 97222

darkhorse.com

Library of Congress Cataloging-in-Publication Data

Day, Felicia, 1979-
The guild / script, Felicia Day ; art, Jim Rugg. -- 1st ed.
p. cm.
ISBN 978-1-59582-549-0
1. Graphic novels. I. Rugg, Jim. II. Title.
PN6727.D37G85 2010
741.5'973--dc22
2010016345

To find a comics shop in your area, call the Comic Shop Locator Service toll-free at (888) 266-4226.

First edition: December 2010

3 5 7 9 10 8 6 4 2
Printed in U.S.A.

THE GUILD™

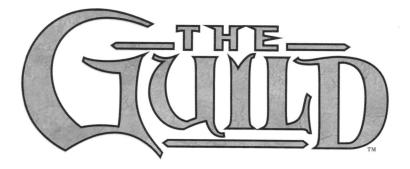

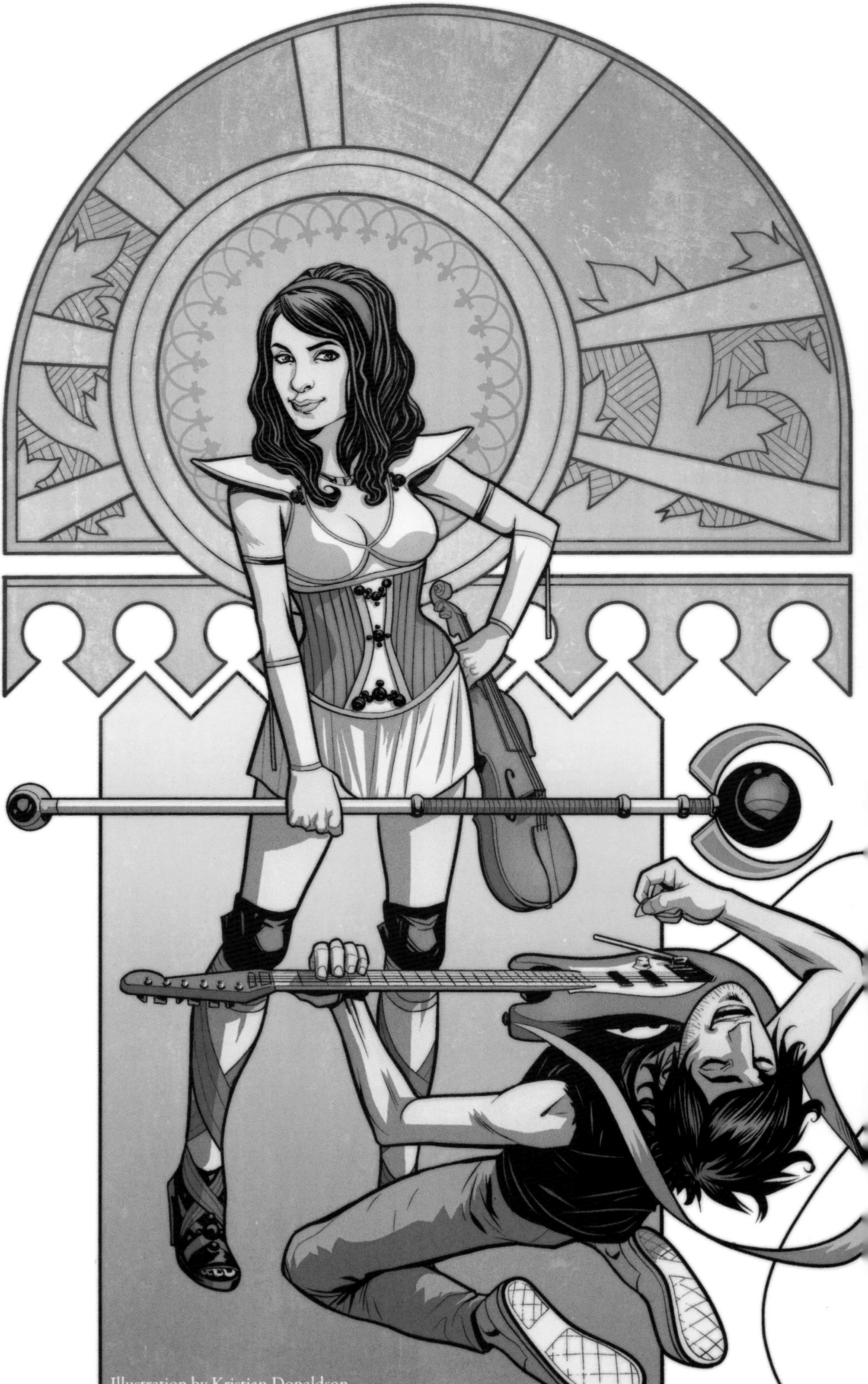

Illustration by Kristian Donaldson

INTRODUCTION

Clark Kent. Bruce Wayne. Peter Parker. Cyd Sherman?

I've been reading comic books my entire life. It all started when my dad passed his own collection off to me when I was just old enough to appreciate them. I remember taking the neatly wrapped books to my room and reading the entire stack in a single day. I enjoyed the characters, the artwork, and the authors' seemingly endless imaginations. Once I was done, I had to read more.

I figured I'd eventually tire of collecting comic books, but instead my interest in them grew as I did. As a teenager I discovered new titles while still keeping up with my old favorites. Nowadays, as an adult, a trip to my local comic shop to pick up whatever is new that week is still a Wednesday ritual. I read everything from traditional superhero to slice-of-life stories that don't include capes or powers, and I enjoy discussions with other passionate fans, even though they usually result in the most heated of arguments. I mean, why anyone would think that Godzilla could take on Charles Barkley is beyond me. (This actually exists; look it up!) Yes, I love comics.

So when Felicia Day told me that she was going to write a comic based on her web series *The Guild*, one thought came to mind.

"Awesome."

Then she said that the comic was going to be a prequel story.

"Double super awesome."

What a great team-up! (←comic-book term!) Not only were *Guild* fans going to get a brand-new story, but Felicia would be free from the restrictions that come with the show's web budgets and get to enjoy the creative freedom that only comics can provide. Now she could let Codex and the Knights of Good really shine and give fans an in-depth look inside "The Game" they play, which is something that she has only been able to reference in the web series. The end result is in fact double super awesome, and is a perfect addition to the overall *Guild* saga.

I have to admit, it was pretty exciting seeing issue #1 of this series on the shelf among all of the other titles I've grown up with. Maybe someday I'll get the chance to pass my comic-book collection down to my kids with *The Guild* in the same stack as *Superman*, *Batman*, and *Spider-Man*.

Then we can finally have that heart-to-heart, parent-to-child discussion on whether or not Vork could kick Hellboy's ass.

SEAN BECKER
Director, *The Guild* Seasons 2–4

CHAPTER 1

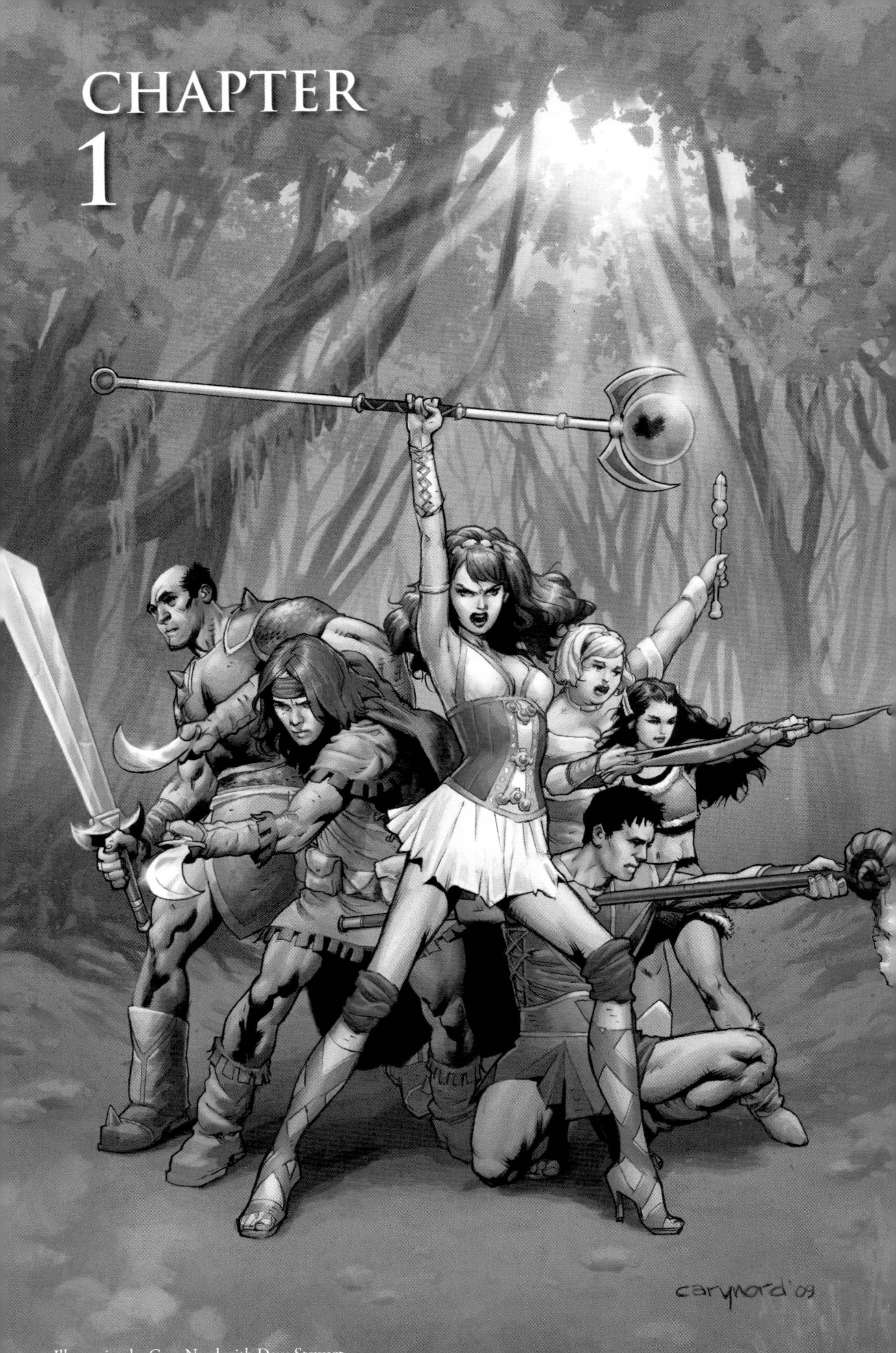
carynord'09

Illustration by Cary Nord with Dave Stewart

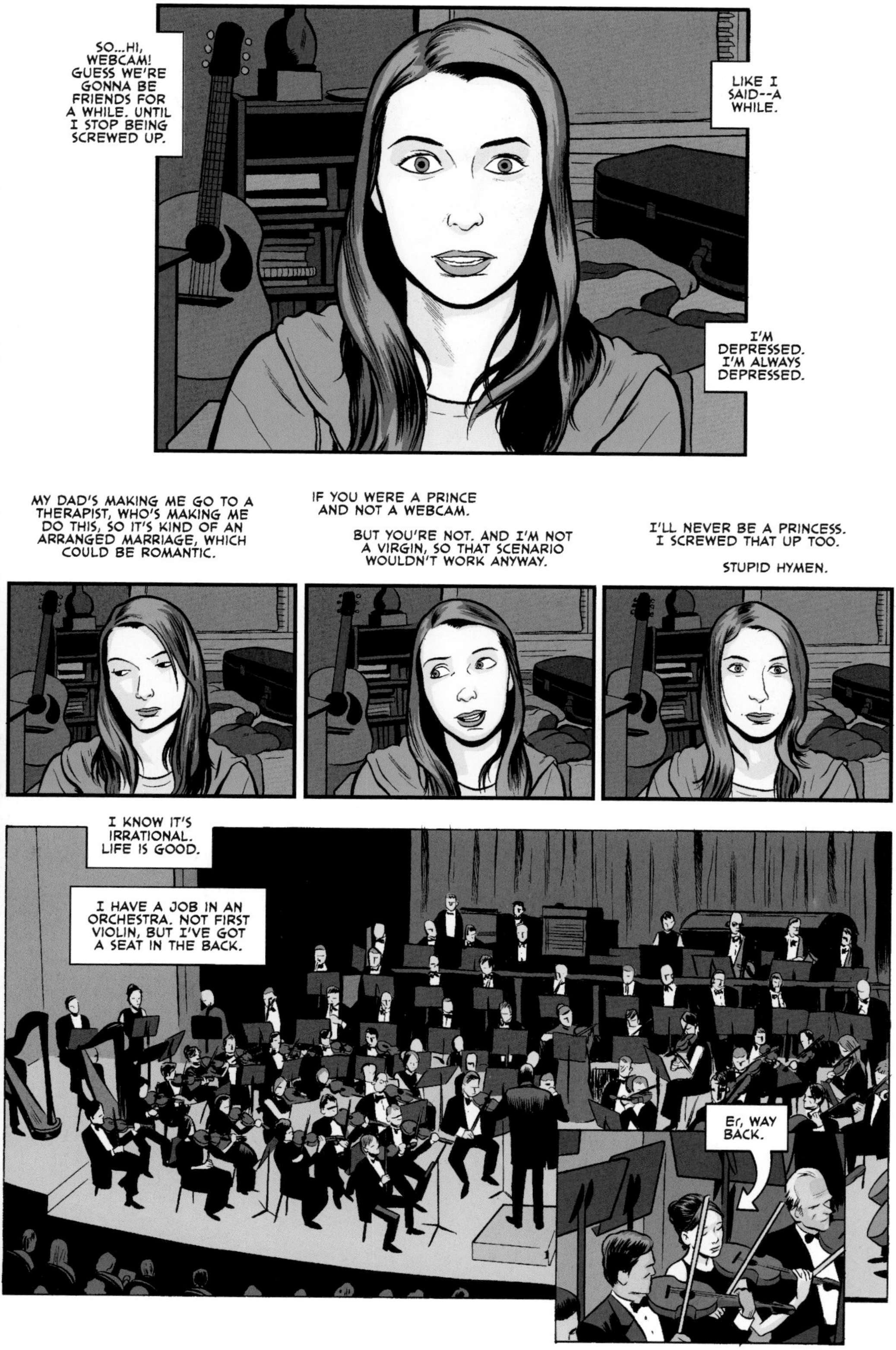
SO...HI, WEBCAM! GUESS WE'RE GONNA BE FRIENDS FOR A WHILE. UNTIL I STOP BEING SCREWED UP.
LIKE I SAID--A WHILE.
I'M DEPRESSED. I'M ALWAYS DEPRESSED.
MY DAD'S MAKING ME GO TO A THERAPIST, WHO'S MAKING ME DO THIS, SO IT'S KIND OF AN ARRANGED MARRIAGE, WHICH COULD BE ROMANTIC.
IF YOU WERE A PRINCE AND NOT A WEBCAM.
BUT YOU'RE NOT. AND I'M NOT A VIRGIN, SO THAT SCENARIO WOULDN'T WORK ANYWAY.
I'LL NEVER BE A PRINCESS. I SCREWED THAT UP TOO.
STUPID HYMEN.
I KNOW IT'S IRRATIONAL. LIFE IS GOOD.
I HAVE A JOB IN AN ORCHESTRA. NOT FIRST VIOLIN, BUT I'VE GOT A SEAT IN THE BACK.
Er, WAY BACK.

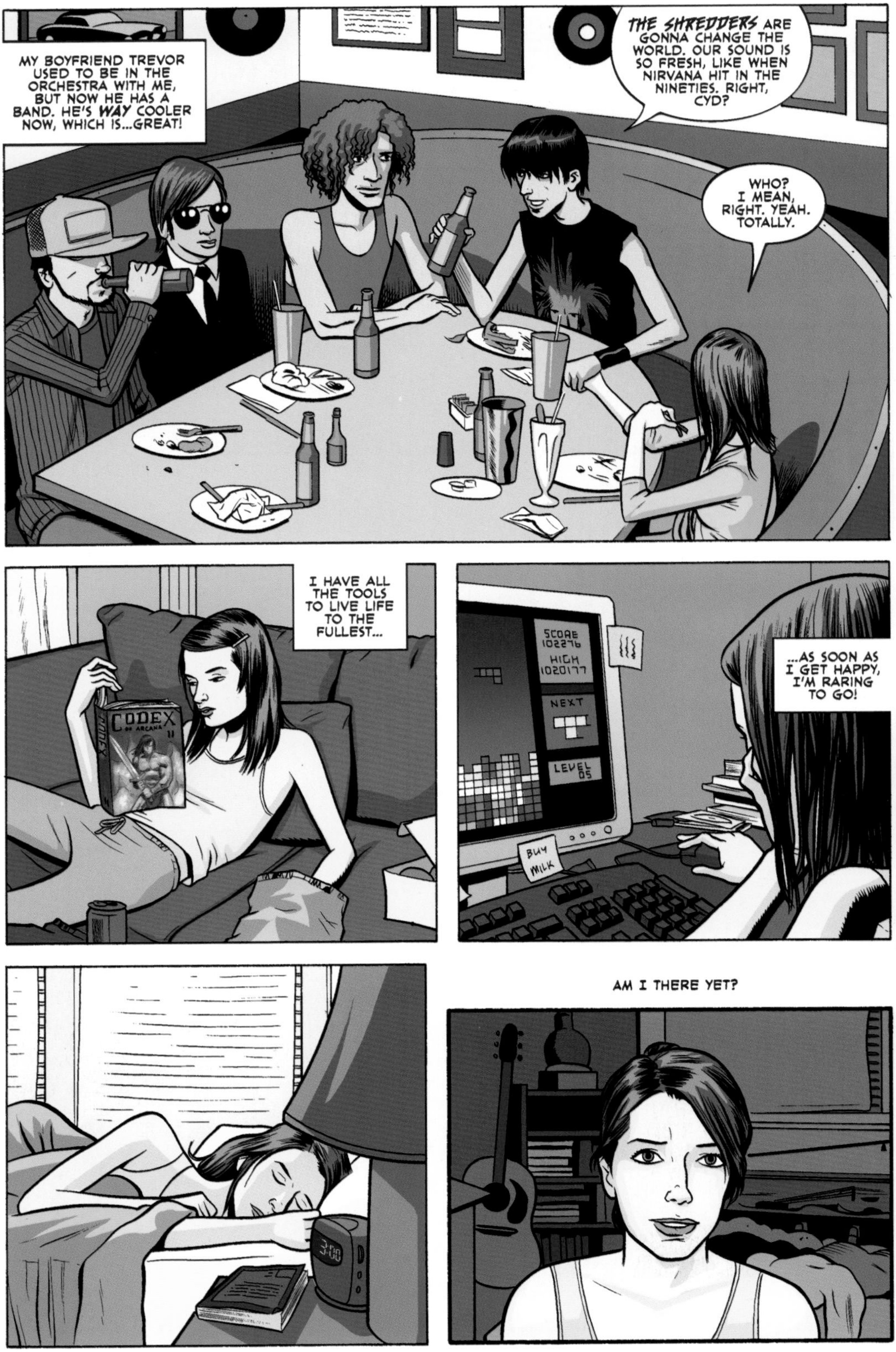
MY BOYFRIEND TREVOR USED TO BE IN THE ORCHESTRA WITH ME, BUT NOW HE HAS A BAND. HE'S *WAY* COOLER NOW, WHICH IS...GREAT!
THE SHREDDERS ARE GONNA CHANGE THE WORLD. OUR SOUND IS SO FRESH, LIKE WHEN NIRVANA HIT IN THE NINETIES. RIGHT, CYD?
WHO? I MEAN, RIGHT. YEAH. TOTALLY.
I HAVE ALL THE TOOLS TO LIVE LIFE TO THE FULLEST...
CODEX
SCORE 102276
HIGH 1020177
NEXT
LEVEL 05
BUY MILK
...AS SOON AS I GET HAPPY, I'M RARING TO GO!
3:00
AM I THERE YET?

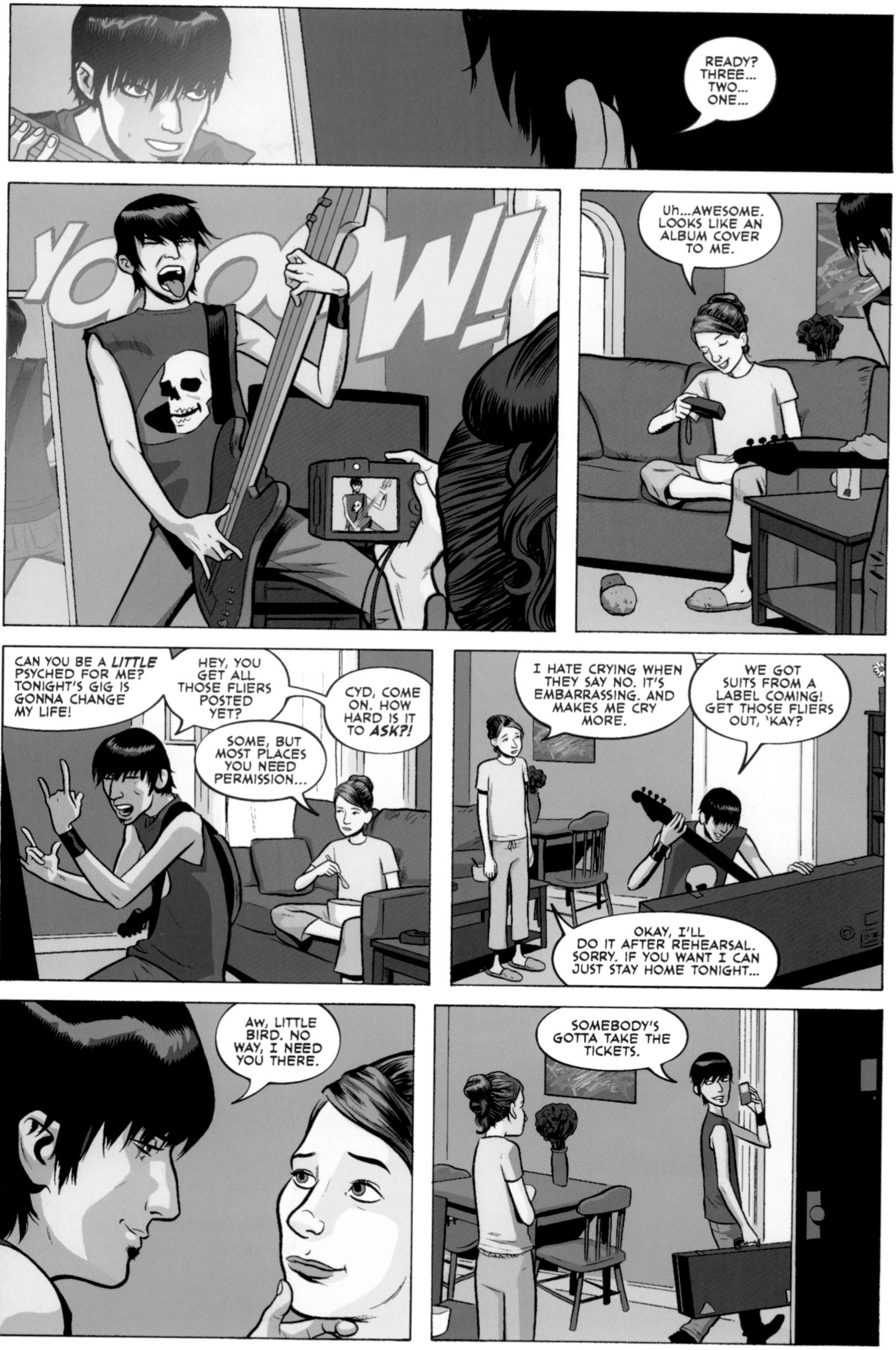
READY? THREE... TWO... ONE...
YOOOOW!
Uh...AWESOME. LOOKS LIKE AN ALBUM COVER TO ME.
CAN YOU BE A *LITTLE* PSYCHED FOR ME? TONIGHT'S GIG IS GONNA CHANGE MY LIFE!
HEY, YOU GET ALL THOSE FLIERS POSTED YET?
SOME, BUT MOST PLACES YOU NEED PERMISSION...
CYD, COME ON. HOW HARD IS IT TO *ASK?!*
I HATE CRYING WHEN THEY SAY NO. IT'S EMBARRASSING. AND MAKES ME CRY MORE.
WE GOT SUITS FROM A LABEL COMING! GET THOSE FLIERS OUT, 'KAY?
OKAY, I'LL DO IT AFTER REHEARSAL. SORRY. IF YOU WANT I CAN JUST STAY HOME TONIGHT...
AW, LITTLE BIRD. NO WAY, I NEED YOU THERE.
SOMEBODY'S GOTTA TAKE THE TICKETS.

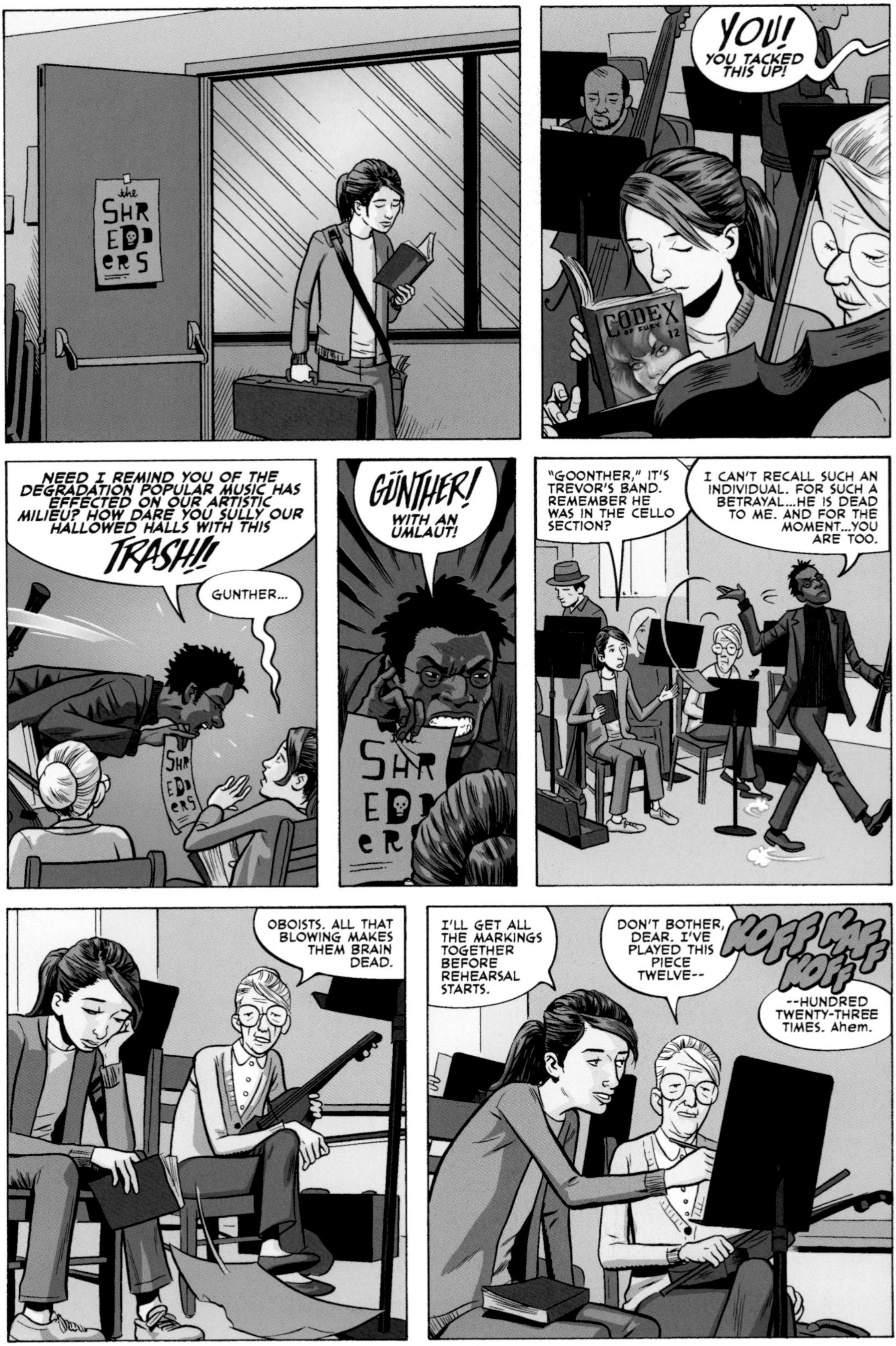
the SHR EDD ers S
YOU!
YOU TACKED THIS UP!
CODEX OF FURY 12
NEED I REMIND YOU OF THE DEGRADATION POPULAR MUSIC HAS EFFECTED ON OUR ARTISTIC MILIEU? HOW DARE YOU SULLY OUR HALLOWED HALLS WITH THIS TRASH!!
GUNTHER...
SHR EDD ers
GÜNTHER! WITH AN UMLAUT!
"GOONTHER," IT'S TREVOR'S BAND. REMEMBER HE WAS IN THE CELLO SECTION?
I CAN'T RECALL SUCH AN INDIVIDUAL. FOR SUCH A BETRAYAL...HE IS DEAD TO ME. AND FOR THE MOMENT...YOU ARE TOO.
OBOISTS. ALL THAT BLOWING MAKES THEM BRAIN DEAD.
I'LL GET ALL THE MARKINGS TOGETHER BEFORE REHEARSAL STARTS.
DON'T BOTHER, DEAR. I'VE PLAYED THIS PIECE TWELVE--
KOFF KAFF KOFF
--HUNDRED TWENTY-THREE TIMES. Ahem.

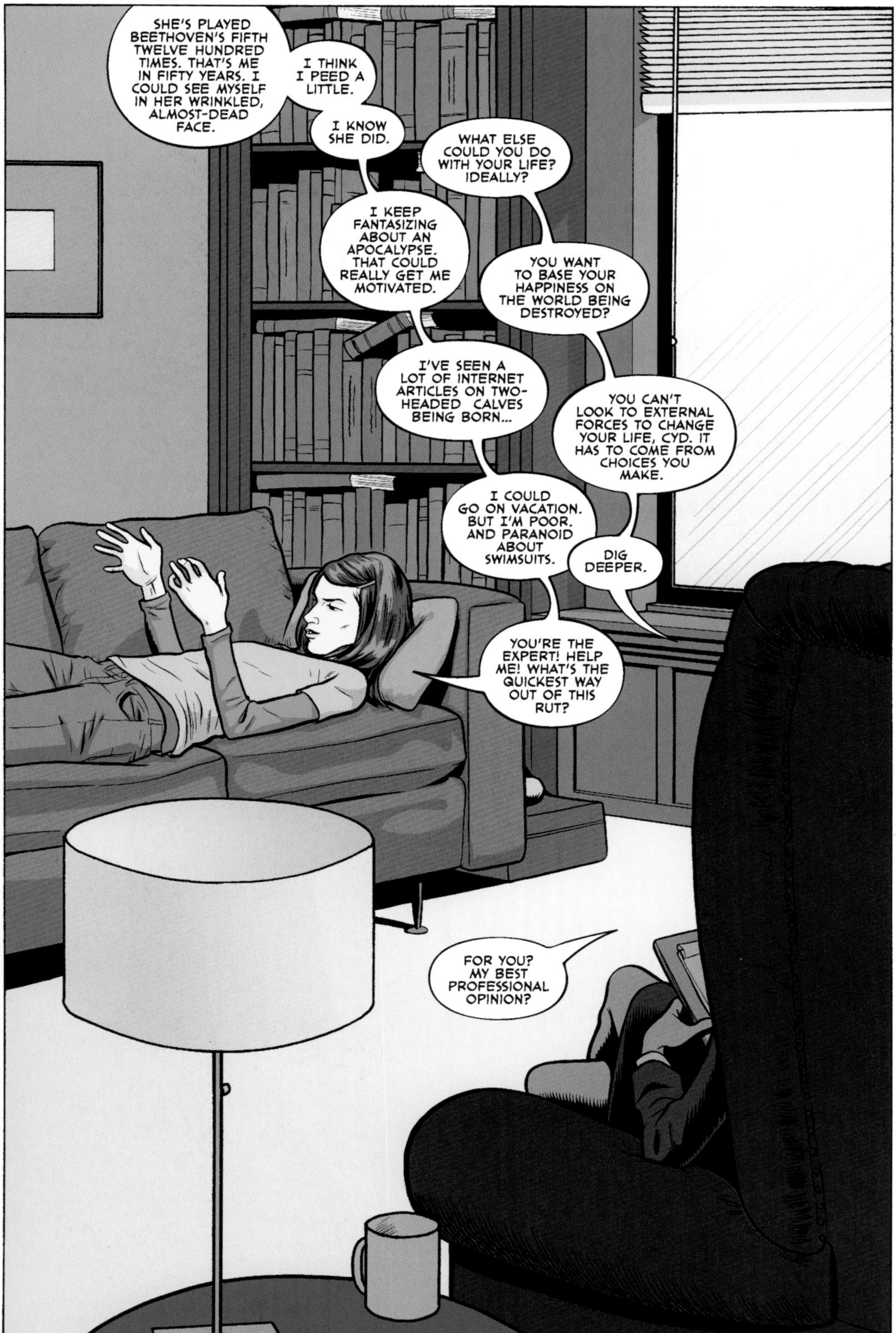
SHE'S PLAYED BEETHOVEN'S FIFTH TWELVE HUNDRED TIMES. THAT'S ME IN FIFTY YEARS. I COULD SEE MYSELF IN HER WRINKLED, ALMOST-DEAD FACE.
I THINK I PEED A LITTLE.
I KNOW SHE DID.
WHAT ELSE COULD YOU DO WITH YOUR LIFE? IDEALLY?
I KEEP FANTASIZING ABOUT AN APOCALYPSE. THAT COULD REALLY GET ME MOTIVATED.
YOU WANT TO BASE YOUR HAPPINESS ON THE WORLD BEING DESTROYED?
I'VE SEEN A LOT OF INTERNET ARTICLES ON TWO-HEADED CALVES BEING BORN...
YOU CAN'T LOOK TO EXTERNAL FORCES TO CHANGE YOUR LIFE, CYD. IT HAS TO COME FROM CHOICES YOU MAKE.
I COULD GO ON VACATION. BUT I'M POOR. AND PARANOID ABOUT SWIMSUITS.
DIG DEEPER.
YOU'RE THE EXPERT! HELP ME! WHAT'S THE QUICKEST WAY OUT OF THIS RUT?
FOR YOU? MY BEST PROFESSIONAL OPINION?

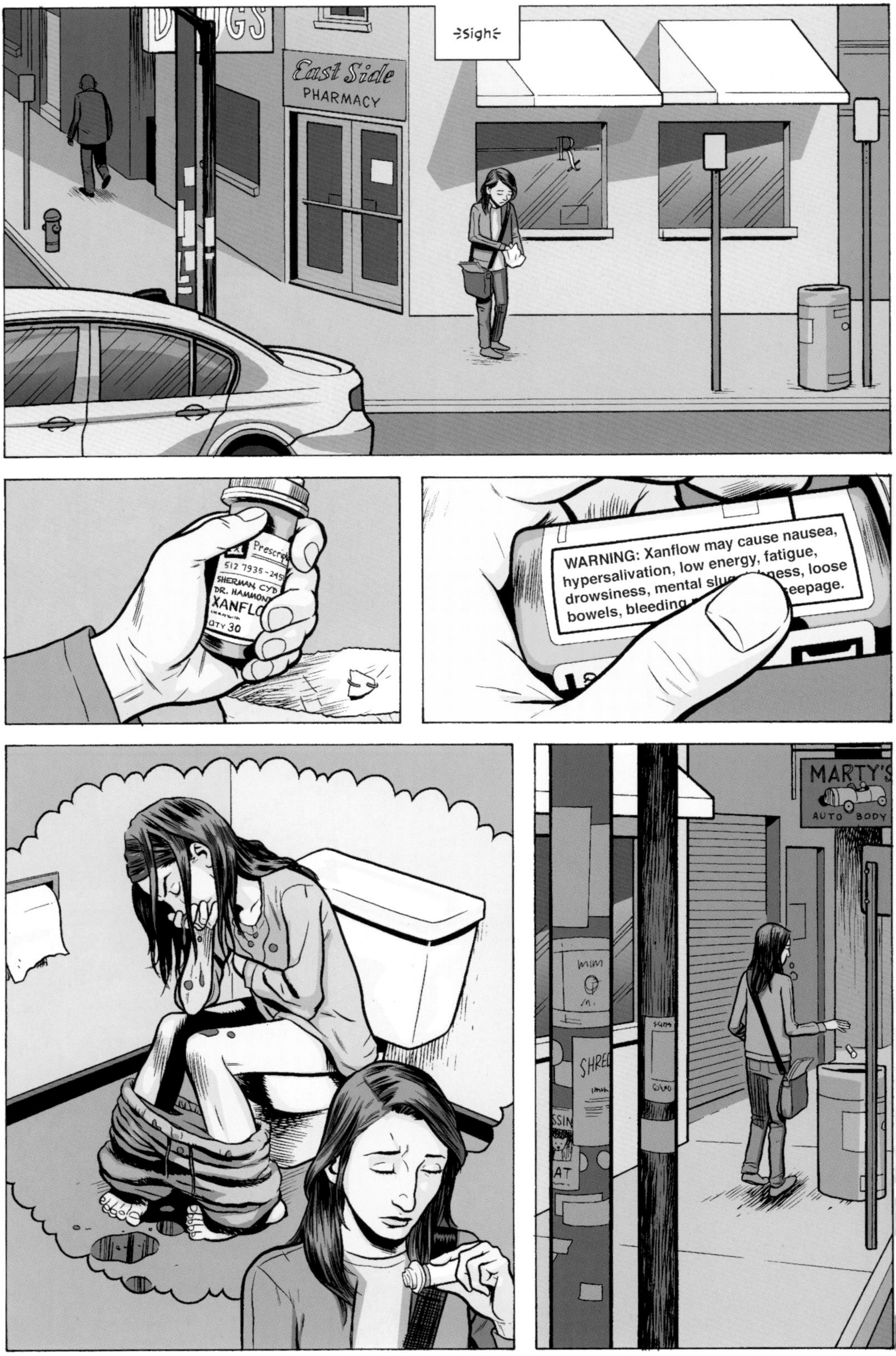
Sigh
East Side
PHARMACY
SHERMAN, CYD
QTY 30
WARNING: Xanflow may cause nausea,
hypersalivation, low energy, fatigue,
drowsiness, mental slug
loose
bowels, bleeding
eepage.
MARTY'S
AUTO BODY

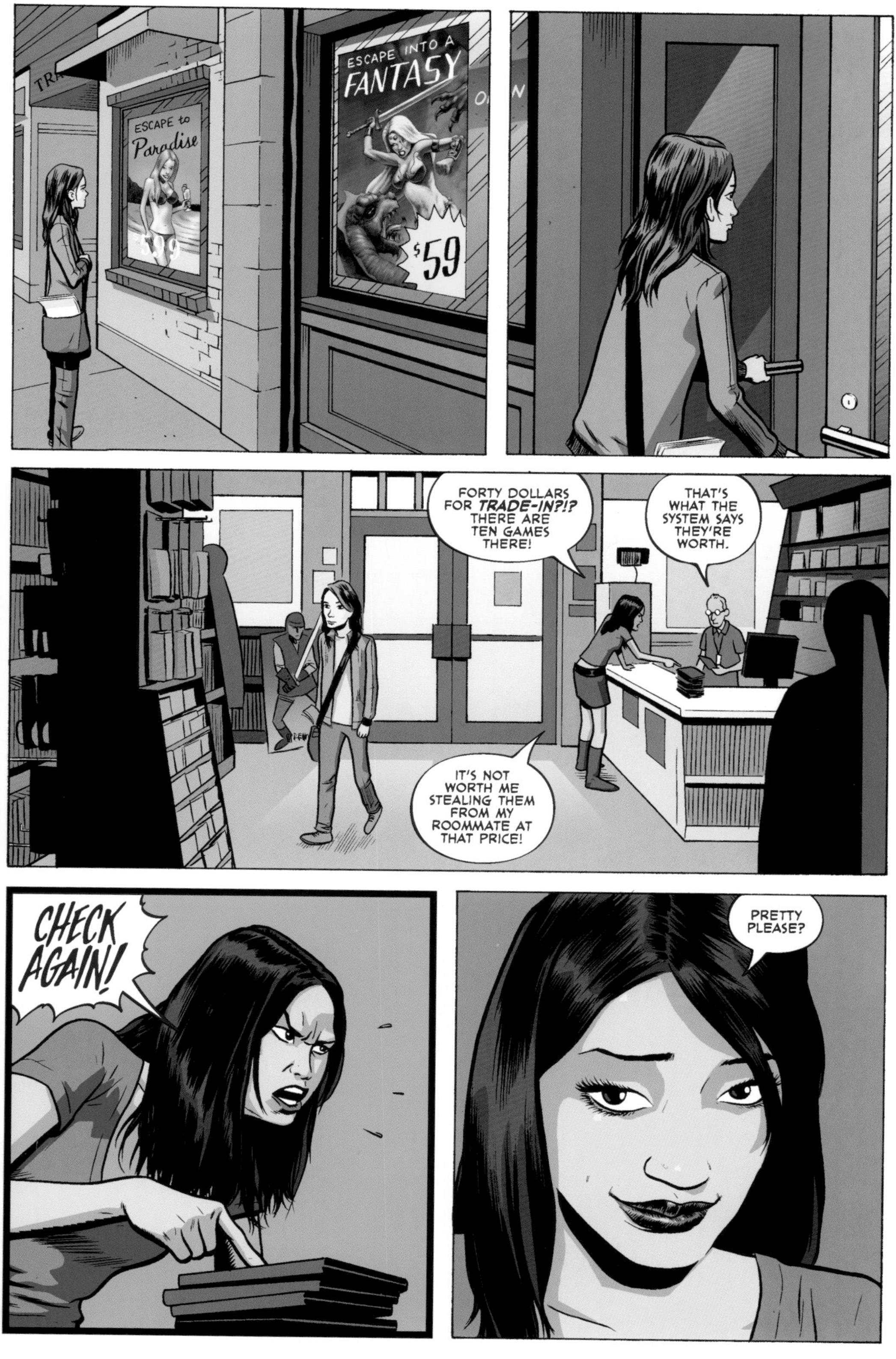
ESCAPE to Paradise
$599
ESCAPE INTO A FANTASY
$59
FORTY DOLLARS FOR TRADE-IN?!? THERE ARE TEN GAMES THERE!
THAT'S WHAT THE SYSTEM SAYS THEY'RE WORTH.
IT'S NOT WORTH ME STEALING THEM FROM MY ROOMMATE AT THAT PRICE!
CHECK AGAIN!
PRETTY PLEASE?

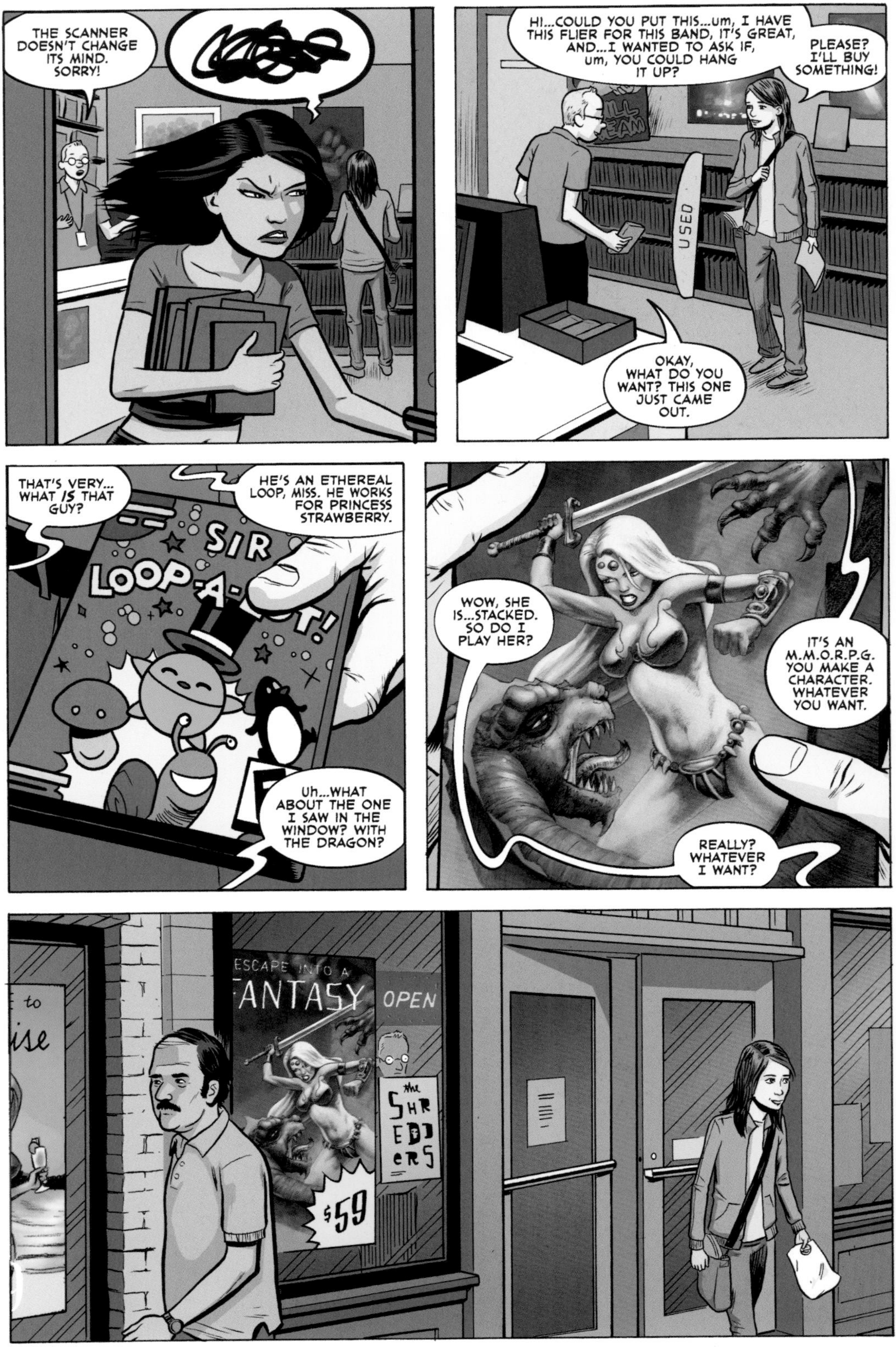
THE SCANNER DOESN'T CHANGE ITS MIND. SORRY!
HI...COULD YOU PUT THIS...um, I HAVE THIS FLIER FOR THIS BAND, IT'S GREAT, AND...I WANTED TO ASK IF, um, YOU COULD HANG IT UP?
PLEASE? I'LL BUY SOMETHING!
USED
OKAY, WHAT DO YOU WANT? THIS ONE JUST CAME OUT.
THAT'S VERY... WHAT *IS* THAT GUY?
HE'S AN ETHEREAL LOOP, MISS. HE WORKS FOR PRINCESS STRAWBERRY.
SIR LOOP-A-LOT!
Uh...WHAT ABOUT THE ONE I SAW IN THE WINDOW? WITH THE DRAGON?
WOW, SHE IS...STACKED. SO DO I PLAY HER?
IT'S AN M.M.O.R.P.G. YOU MAKE A CHARACTER. WHATEVER YOU WANT.
REALLY? WHATEVER I WANT?
ESCAPE INTO A FANTASY
OPEN
the SHREDDERS
$59

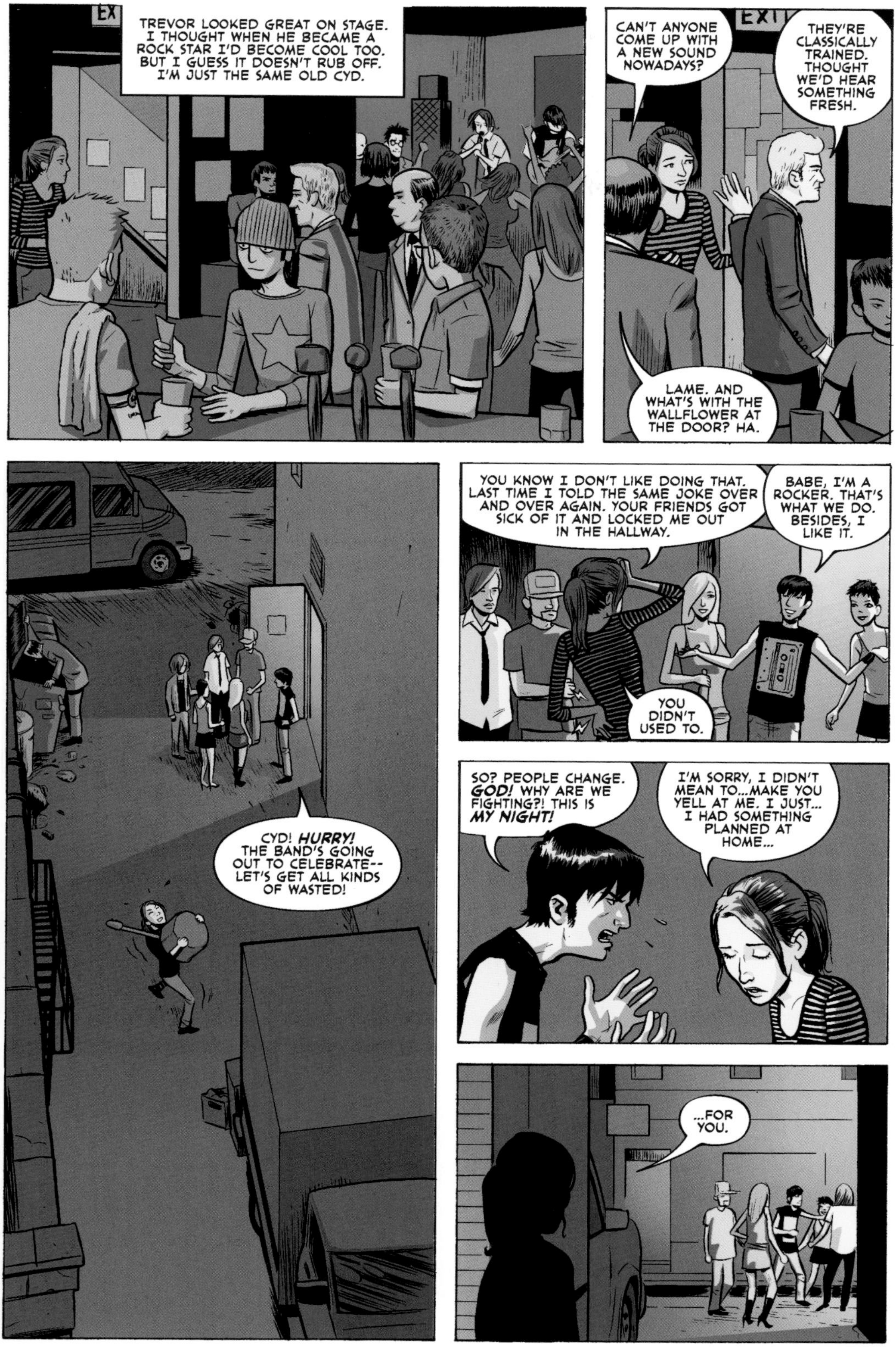
EX
TREVOR LOOKED GREAT ON STAGE. I THOUGHT WHEN HE BECAME A ROCK STAR I'D BECOME COOL TOO. BUT I GUESS IT DOESN'T RUB OFF. I'M JUST THE SAME OLD CYD.
EXIT
CAN'T ANYONE COME UP WITH A NEW SOUND NOWADAYS?
THEY'RE CLASSICALLY TRAINED. THOUGHT WE'D HEAR SOMETHING FRESH.
LAME. AND WHAT'S WITH THE WALLFLOWER AT THE DOOR? HA.
CYD! **HURRY!** THE BAND'S GOING OUT TO CELEBRATE-- LET'S GET ALL KINDS OF WASTED!
YOU KNOW I DON'T LIKE DOING THAT. LAST TIME I TOLD THE SAME JOKE OVER AND OVER AGAIN. YOUR FRIENDS GOT SICK OF IT AND LOCKED ME OUT IN THE HALLWAY.
BABE, I'M A ROCKER. THAT'S WHAT WE DO. BESIDES, I LIKE IT.
YOU DIDN'T USED TO.
SO? PEOPLE CHANGE. ***GOD!*** WHY ARE WE FIGHTING?! THIS IS ***MY NIGHT!***
I'M SORRY, I DIDN'T MEAN TO...MAKE YOU YELL AT ME. I JUST... I HAD SOMETHING PLANNED AT HOME...
...FOR YOU.

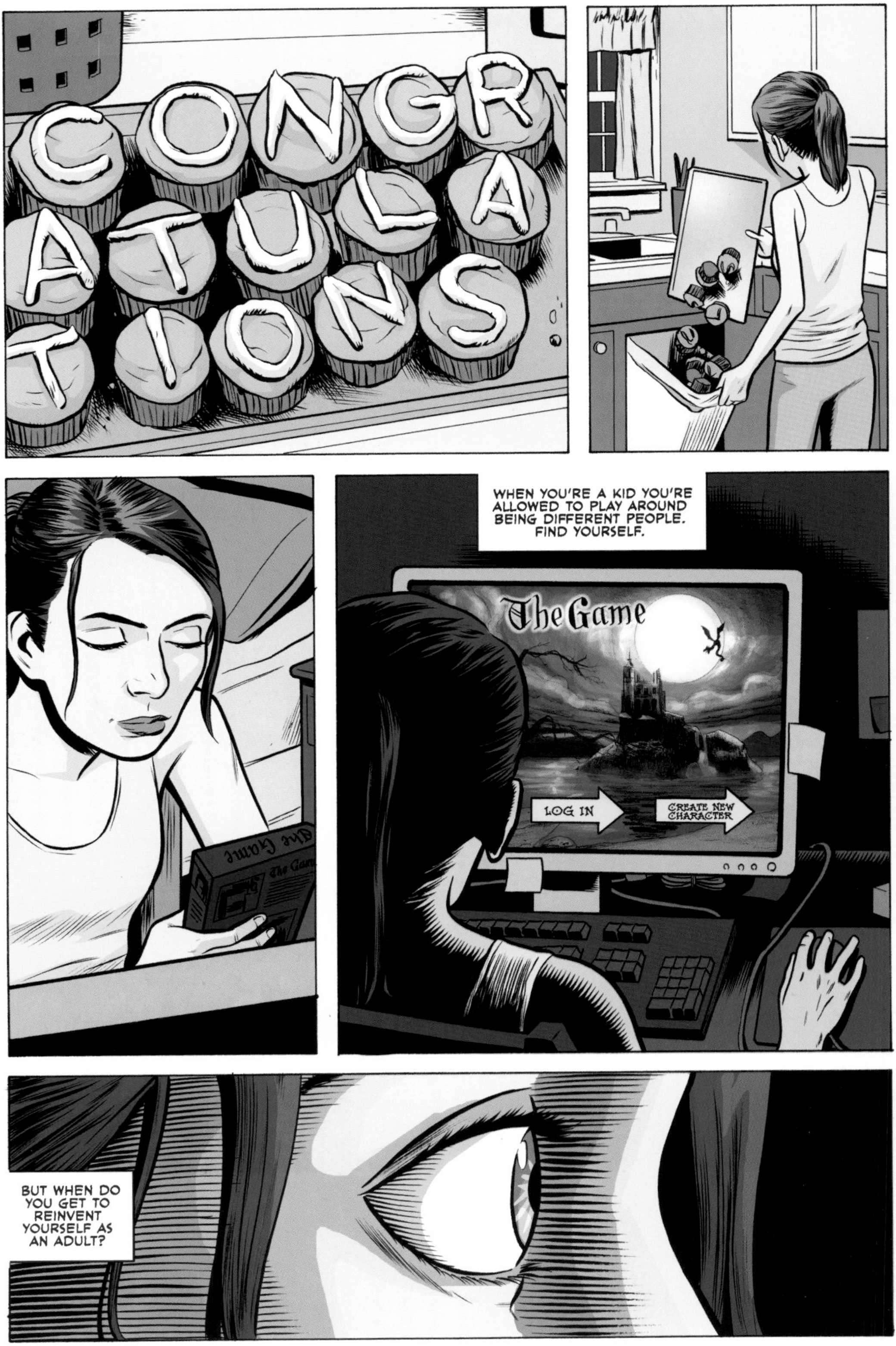
CONGRATULATIONS
The Game
The Game
WHEN YOU'RE A KID YOU'RE ALLOWED TO PLAY AROUND BEING DIFFERENT PEOPLE. FIND YOURSELF.
The Game
LOG IN
CREATE NEW CHARACTER
BUT WHEN DO YOU GET TO REINVENT YOURSELF AS AN ADULT?

IN HIGH SCHOOL I DID GOTH...

HIPPIE...

AND HIP-HOP. FOR ABOUT TEN MINUTES EACH.

BUT AFTER COLLEGE, NO ONE IS LIKE, "HEY, CYD IS DRESSED LIKE A FIFTIES WAITRESS, SO CUTE!"

FREAK SHOW.

MENTAL BREAK.

GOODBYE.

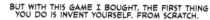

BUT WITH THIS GAME I BOUGHT, THE FIRST THING YOU DO IS INVENT YOURSELF. FROM SCRATCH.

CREATE NEW CHARACTER

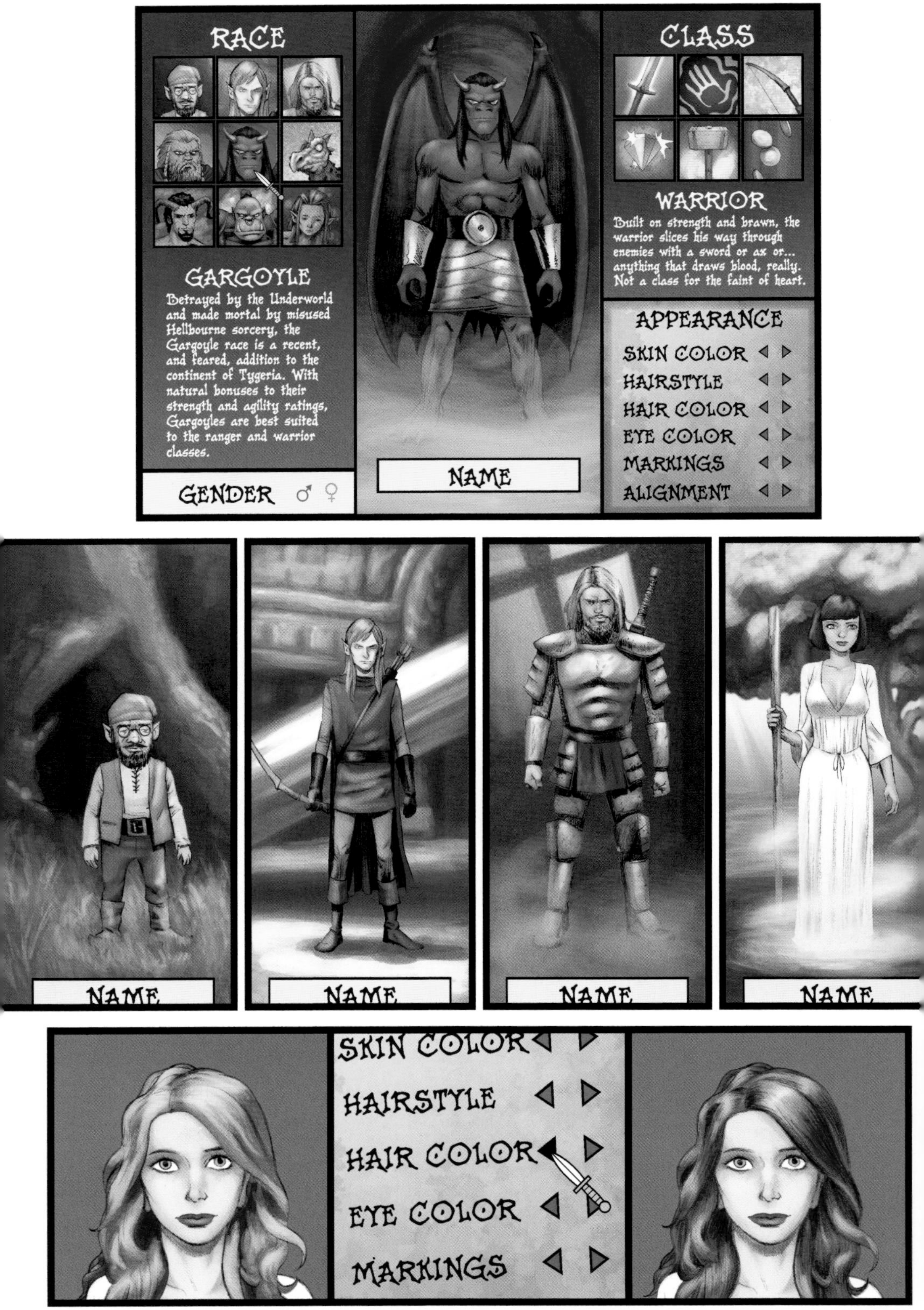
RACE
GARGOYLE
Betrayed by the Underworld and made mortal by misused Hellbourne sorcery, the Gargoyle race is a recent, and feared, addition to the continent of Tygeria. With natural bonuses to their strength and agility ratings, Gargoyles are best suited to the ranger and warrior classes.
GENDER ♂ ♀
NAME
CLASS
WARRIOR
Built on strength and brawn, the warrior slices his way through enemies with a sword or ax or... anything that draws blood, really. Not a class for the faint of heart.
APPEARANCE
SKIN COLOR
HAIRSTYLE
HAIR COLOR
EYE COLOR
MARKINGS
ALIGNMENT
NAME
NAME
NAME
NAME
SKIN COLOR
HAIRSTYLE
HAIR COLOR
EYE COLOR
MARKINGS

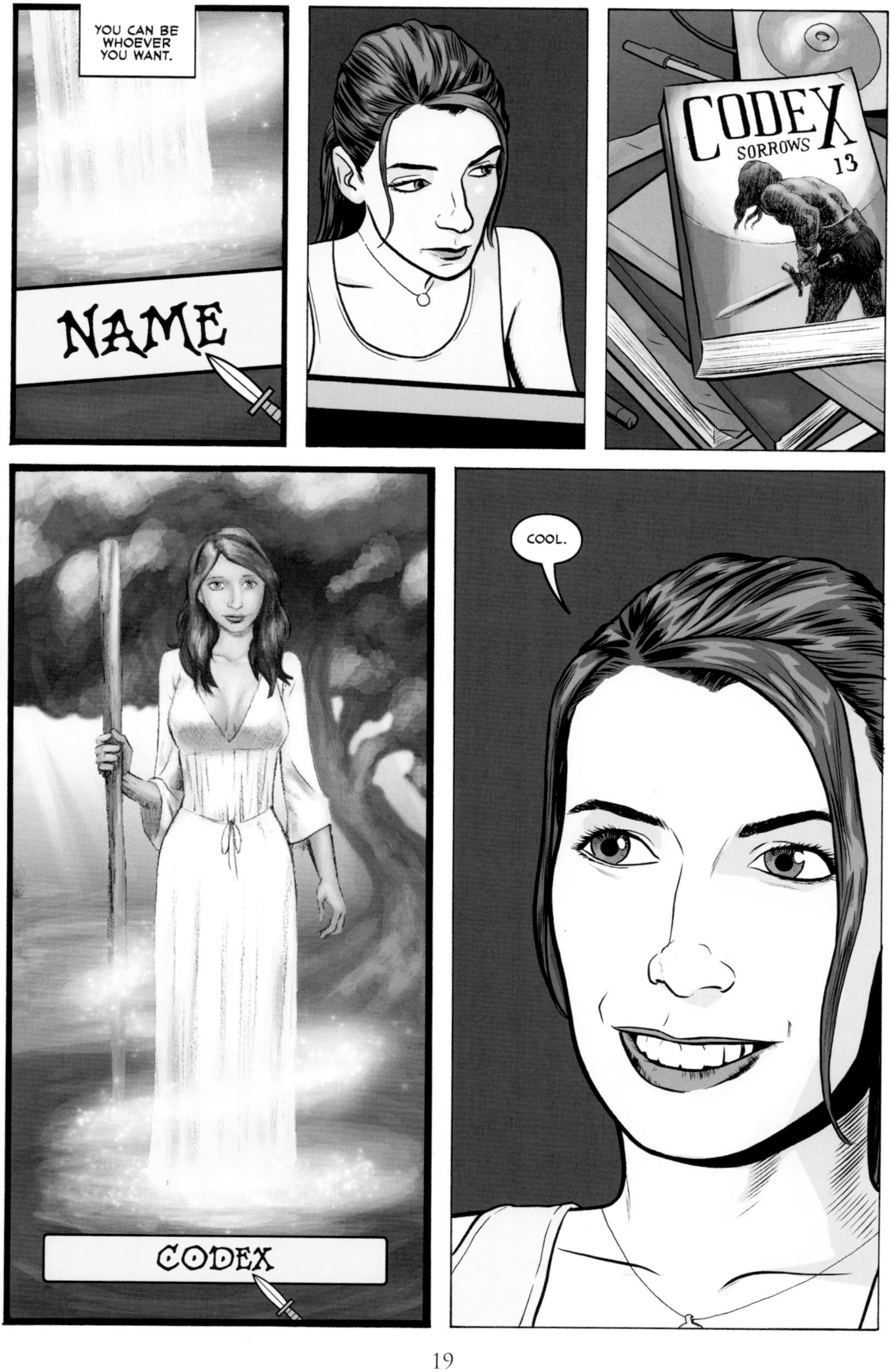
YOU CAN BE WHOEVER YOU WANT.
NAME
CODEX
SORROWS
13
CODEX
COOL.

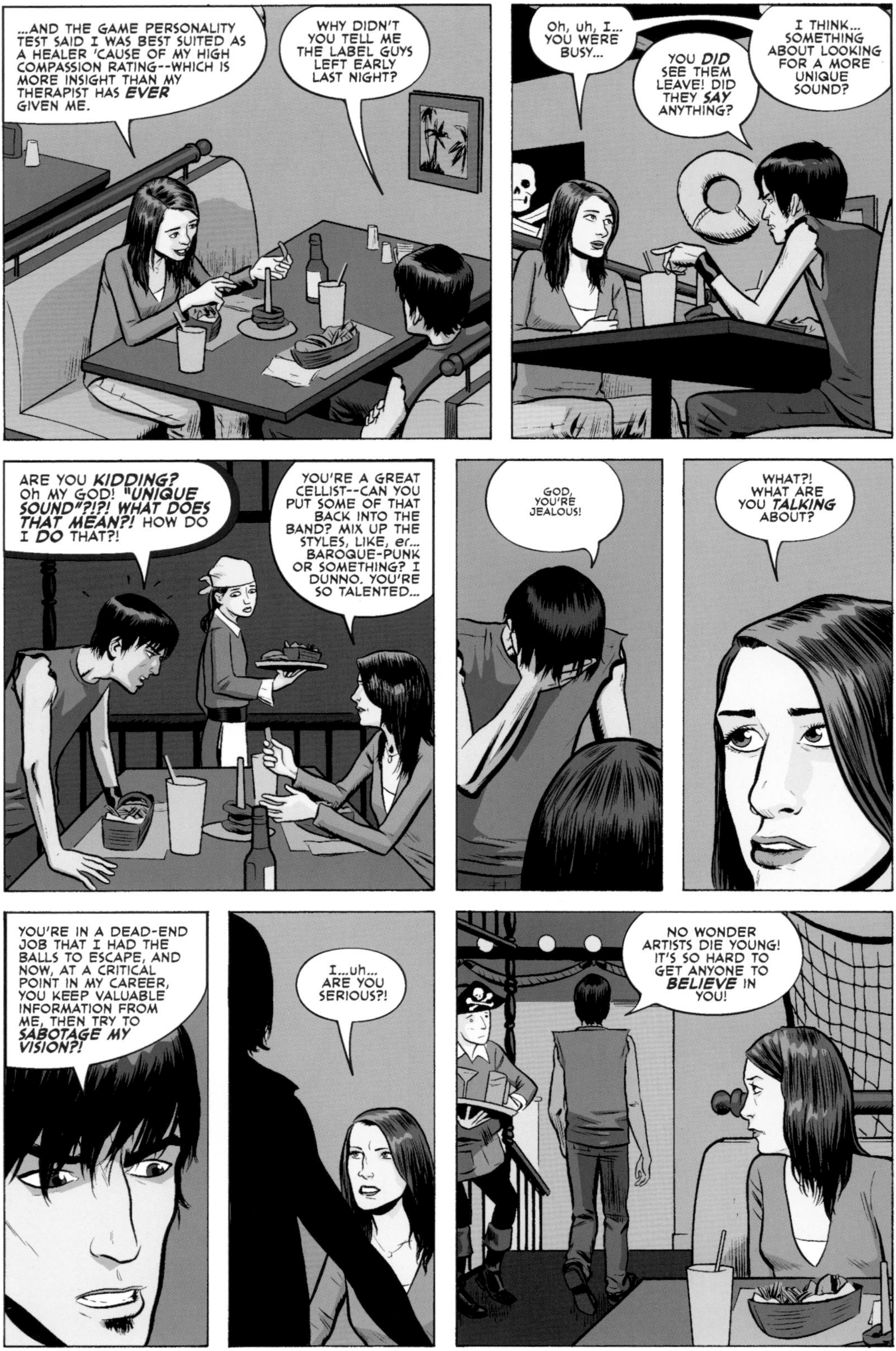
...AND THE GAME PERSONALITY TEST SAID I WAS BEST SUITED AS A HEALER 'CAUSE OF MY HIGH COMPASSION RATING--WHICH IS MORE INSIGHT THAN MY THERAPIST HAS EVER GIVEN ME.
WHY DIDN'T YOU TELL ME THE LABEL GUYS LEFT EARLY LAST NIGHT?
Oh, uh, I... YOU WERE BUSY...
YOU DID SEE THEM LEAVE! DID THEY SAY ANYTHING?
I THINK... SOMETHING ABOUT LOOKING FOR A MORE UNIQUE SOUND?
ARE YOU KIDDING? Oh MY GOD! "UNIQUE SOUND"?!?! WHAT DOES THAT MEAN?! HOW DO I DO THAT?!
YOU'RE A GREAT CELLIST--CAN YOU PUT SOME OF THAT BACK INTO THE BAND? MIX UP THE STYLES, LIKE, er... BAROQUE-PUNK OR SOMETHING? I DUNNO. YOU'RE SO TALENTED...
GOD, YOU'RE JEALOUS!
WHAT?! WHAT ARE YOU TALKING ABOUT?
YOU'RE IN A DEAD-END JOB THAT I HAD THE BALLS TO ESCAPE, AND NOW, AT A CRITICAL POINT IN MY CAREER, YOU KEEP VALUABLE INFORMATION FROM ME, THEN TRY TO SABOTAGE MY VISION?!
I...uh... ARE YOU SERIOUS?!
NO WONDER ARTISTS DIE YOUNG! IT'S SO HARD TO GET ANYONE TO BELIEVE IN YOU!

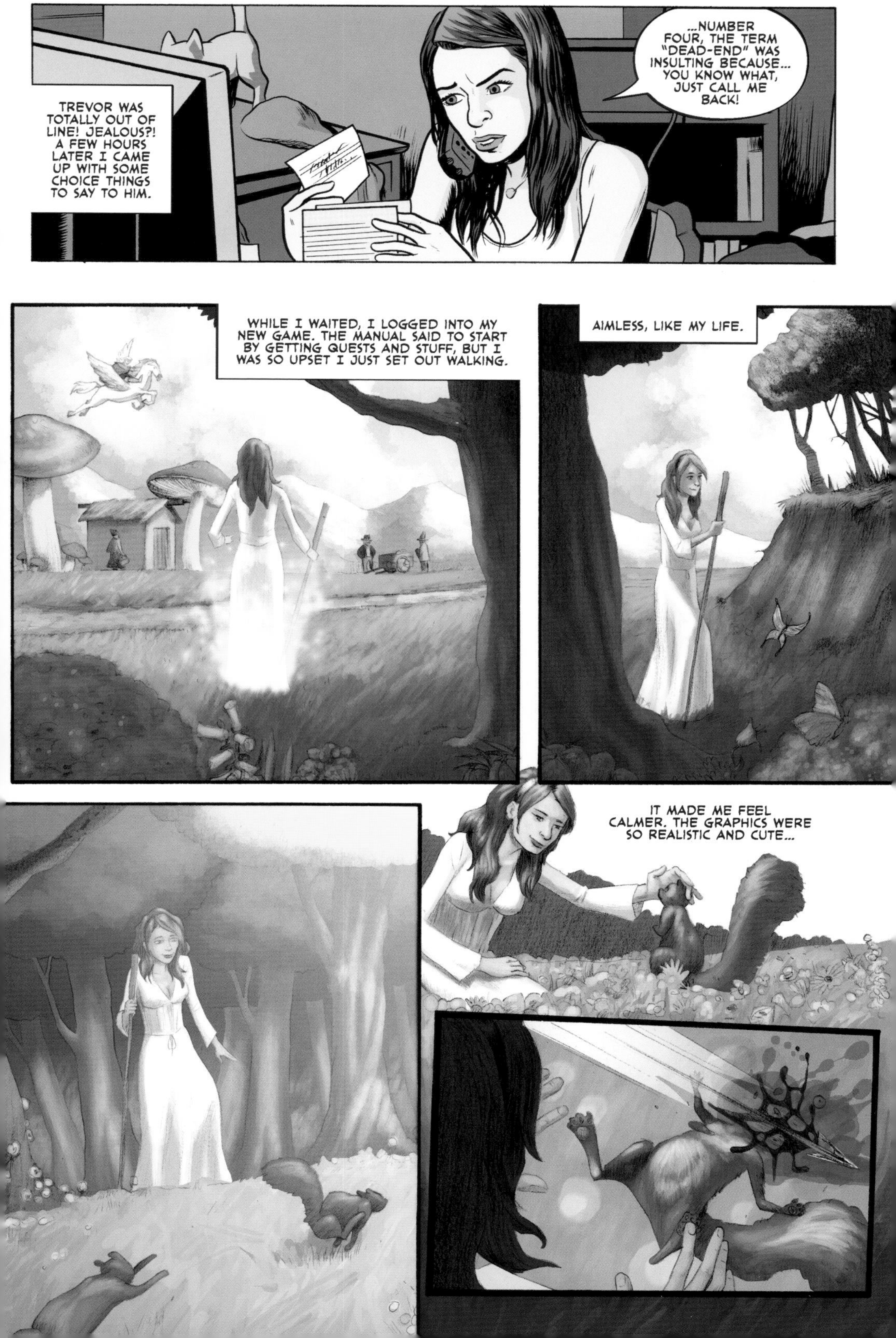
TREVOR WAS TOTALLY OUT OF LINE! JEALOUS?! A FEW HOURS LATER I CAME UP WITH SOME CHOICE THINGS TO SAY TO HIM.
...NUMBER FOUR, THE TERM "DEAD-END" WAS INSULTING BECAUSE... YOU KNOW WHAT, JUST CALL ME BACK!
WHILE I WAITED, I LOGGED INTO MY NEW GAME. THE MANUAL SAID TO START BY GETTING QUESTS AND STUFF, BUT I WAS SO UPSET I JUST SET OUT WALKING.
AIMLESS, LIKE MY LIFE.
IT MADE ME FEEL CALMER. THE GRAPHICS WERE SO REALISTIC AND CUTE...

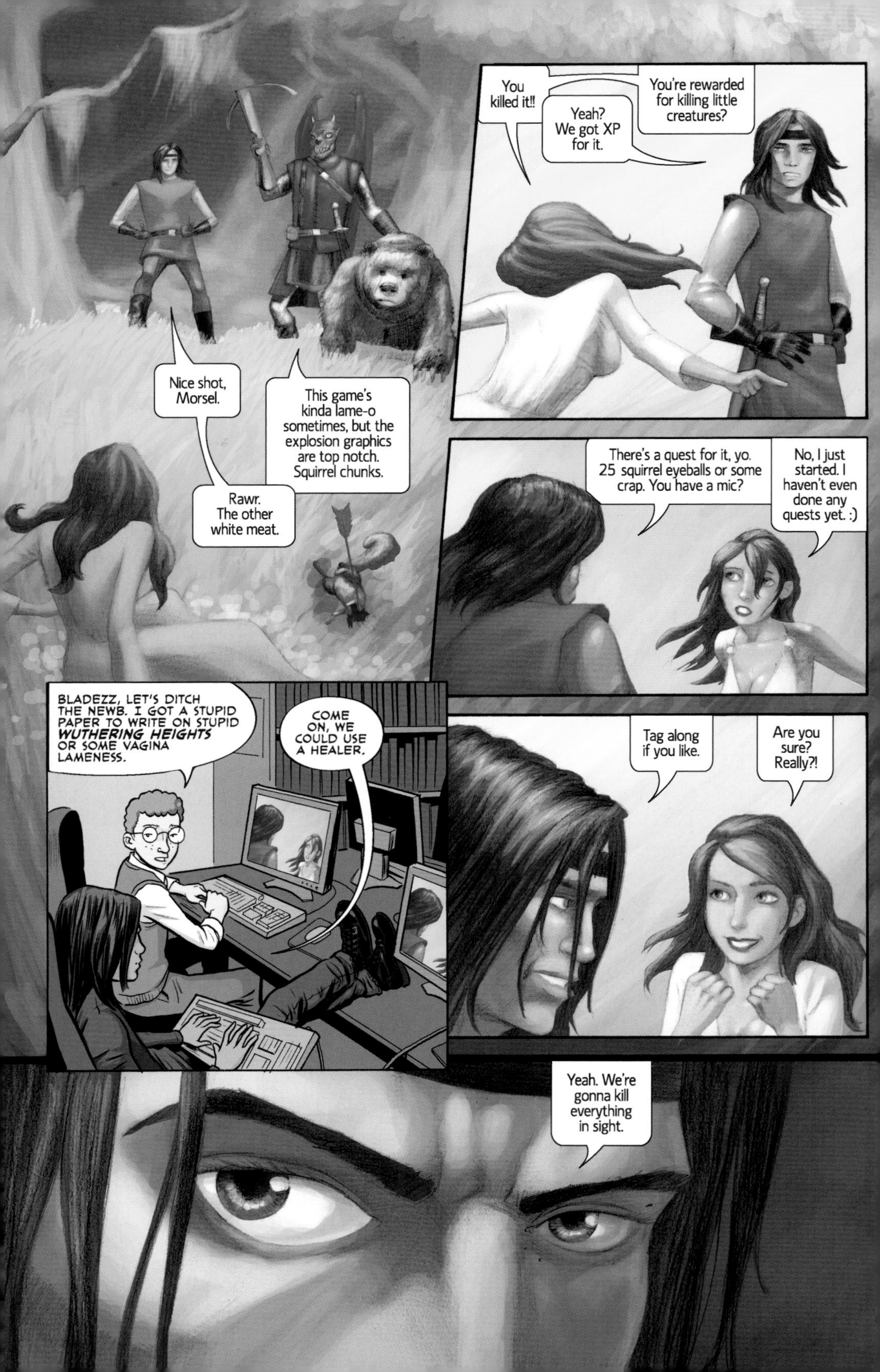

Nice shot, Morsel.
This game's kinda lame-o sometimes, but the explosion graphics are top notch. Squirrel chunks.
Rawr. The other white meat.
You killed it!!
Yeah? We got XP for it.
You're rewarded for killing little creatures?
There's a quest for it, yo. 25 squirrel eyeballs or some crap. You have a mic?
No, I just started. I haven't even done any quests yet. :)
BLADEZZ, LET'S DITCH THE NEWB. I GOT A STUPID PAPER TO WRITE ON STUPID WUTHERING HEIGHTS OR SOME VAGINA LAMENESS.
COME ON, WE COULD USE A HEALER.
Tag along if you like.
Are you sure? Really?!
Yeah. We're gonna kill everything in sight.

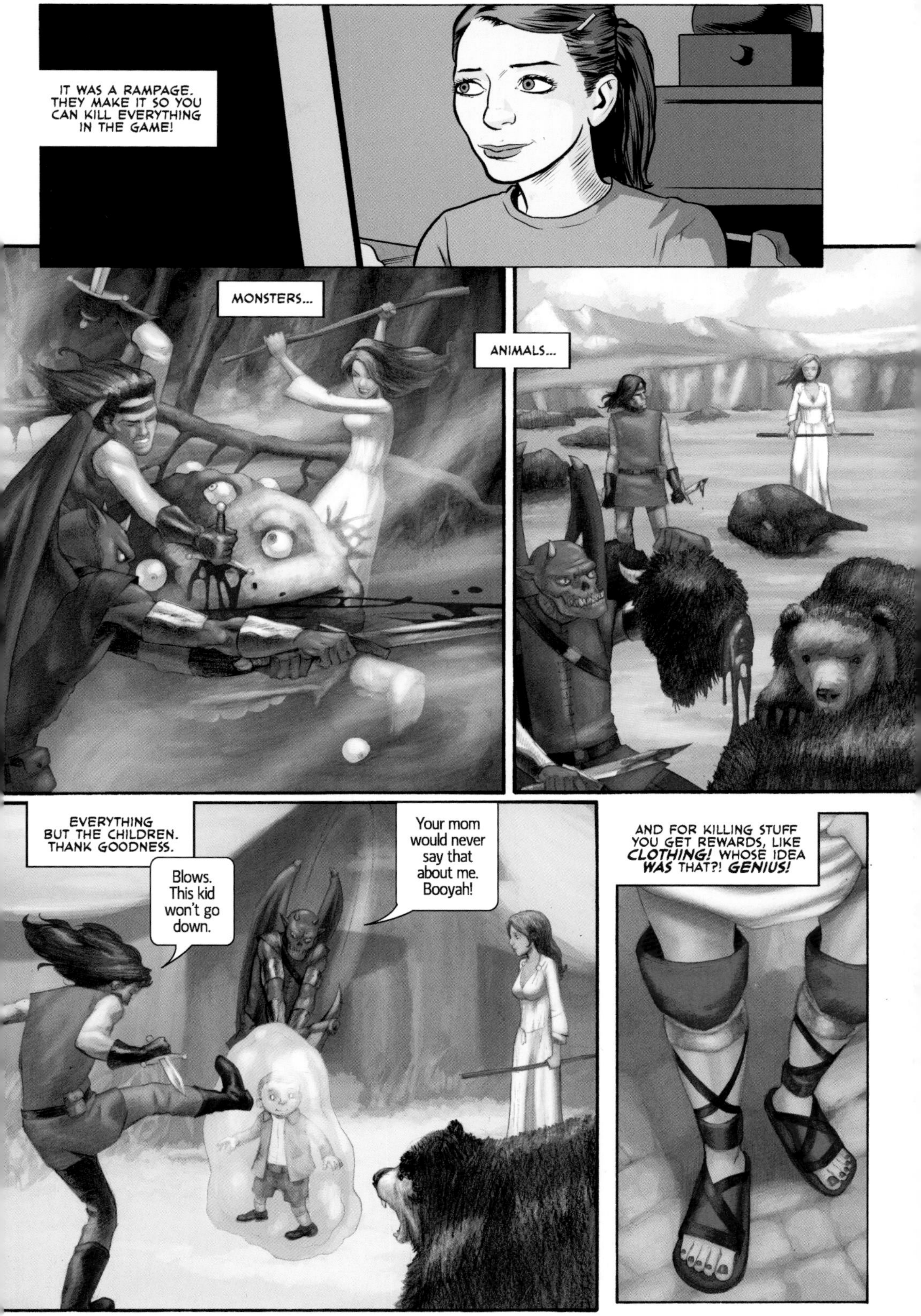
IT WAS A RAMPAGE. THEY MAKE IT SO YOU CAN KILL EVERYTHING IN THE GAME!
MONSTERS...
ANIMALS...
EVERYTHING BUT THE CHILDREN. THANK GOODNESS.
Blows. This kid won't go down.
Your mom would never say that about me. Booyah!
AND FOR KILLING STUFF YOU GET REWARDS, LIKE *CLOTHING!* WHOSE IDEA *WAS* THAT?! *GENIUS!*

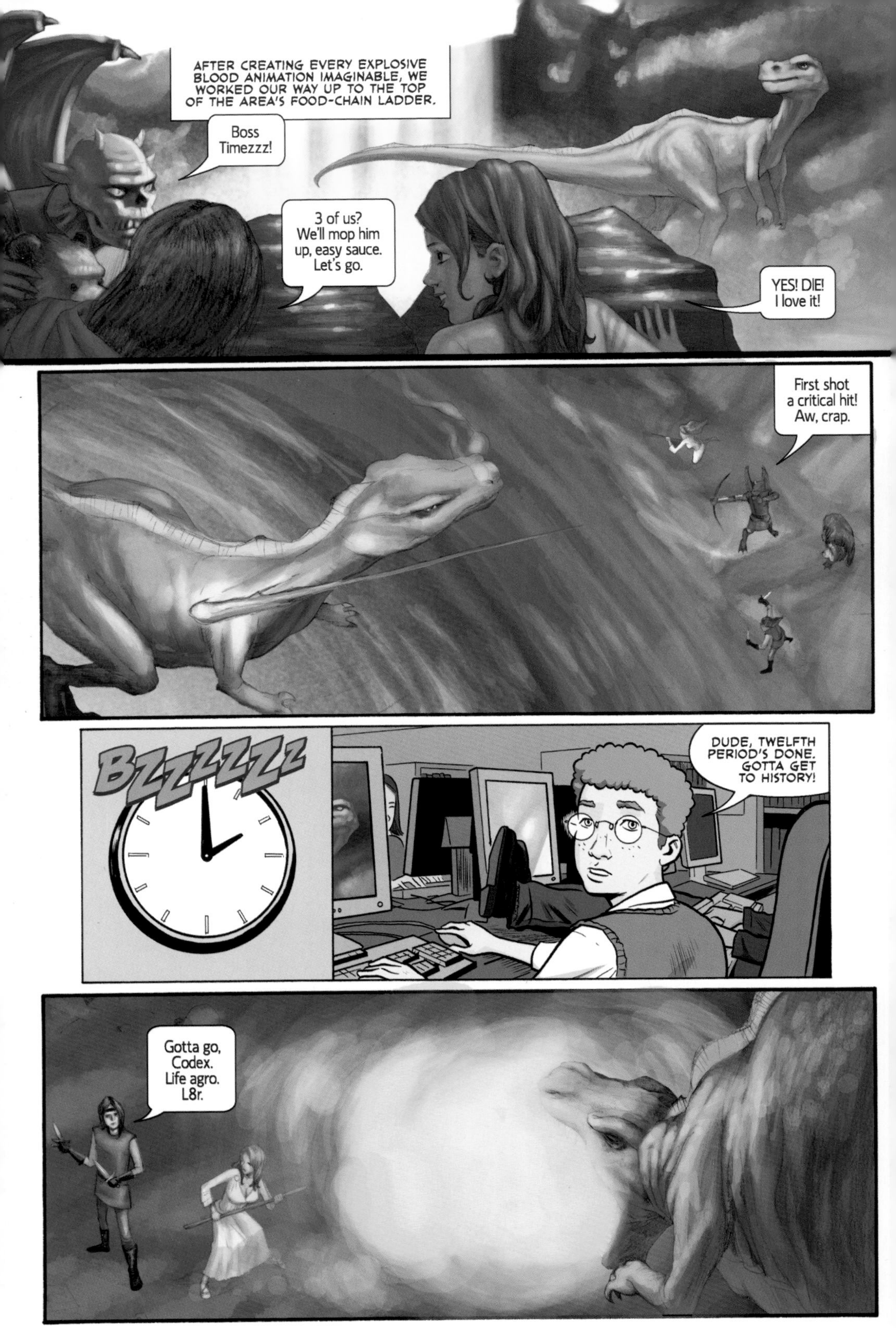
AFTER CREATING EVERY EXPLOSIVE BLOOD ANIMATION IMAGINABLE, WE WORKED OUR WAY UP TO THE TOP OF THE AREA'S FOOD-CHAIN LADDER.
Boss Timezzz!
3 of us? We'll mop him up, easy sauce. Let's go.
YES! DIE! I love it!
First shot a critical hit! Aw, crap.
BZZZZZZ
DUDE, TWELFTH PERIOD'S DONE. GOTTA GET TO HISTORY!
Gotta go, Codex. Life agro. L8r.

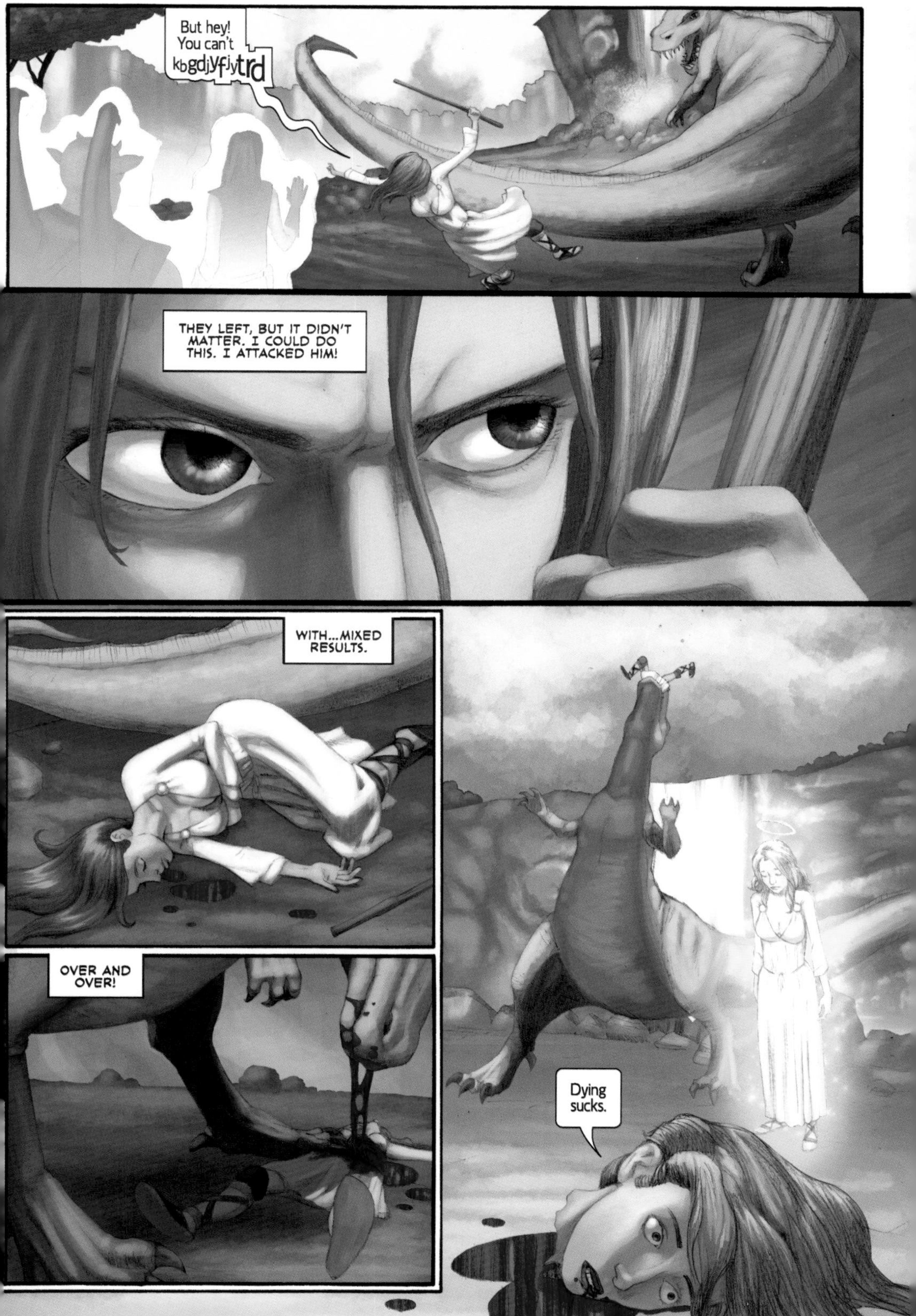
But hey! You can't kbgdjyfjytrd
THEY LEFT, BUT IT DIDN'T MATTER. I COULD DO THIS. I ATTACKED HIM!
WITH...MIXED RESULTS.
OVER AND OVER!
Dying sucks.

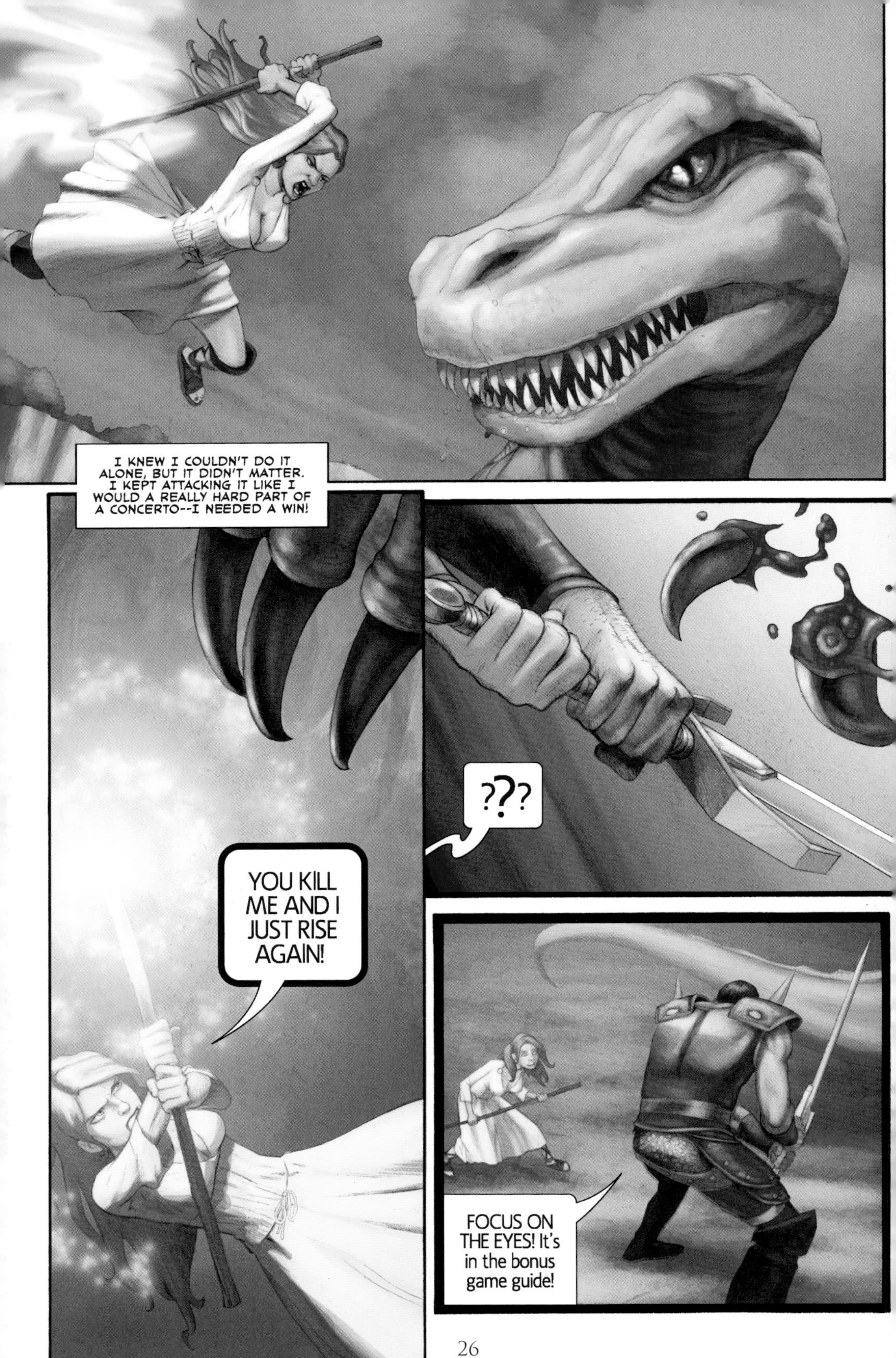
I KNEW I COULDN'T DO IT ALONE, BUT IT DIDN'T MATTER. I KEPT ATTACKING IT LIKE I WOULD A REALLY HARD PART OF A CONCERTO--I NEEDED A WIN!
???
YOU KILL ME AND I JUST RISE AGAIN!
FOCUS ON THE EYES! It's in the bonus game guide!

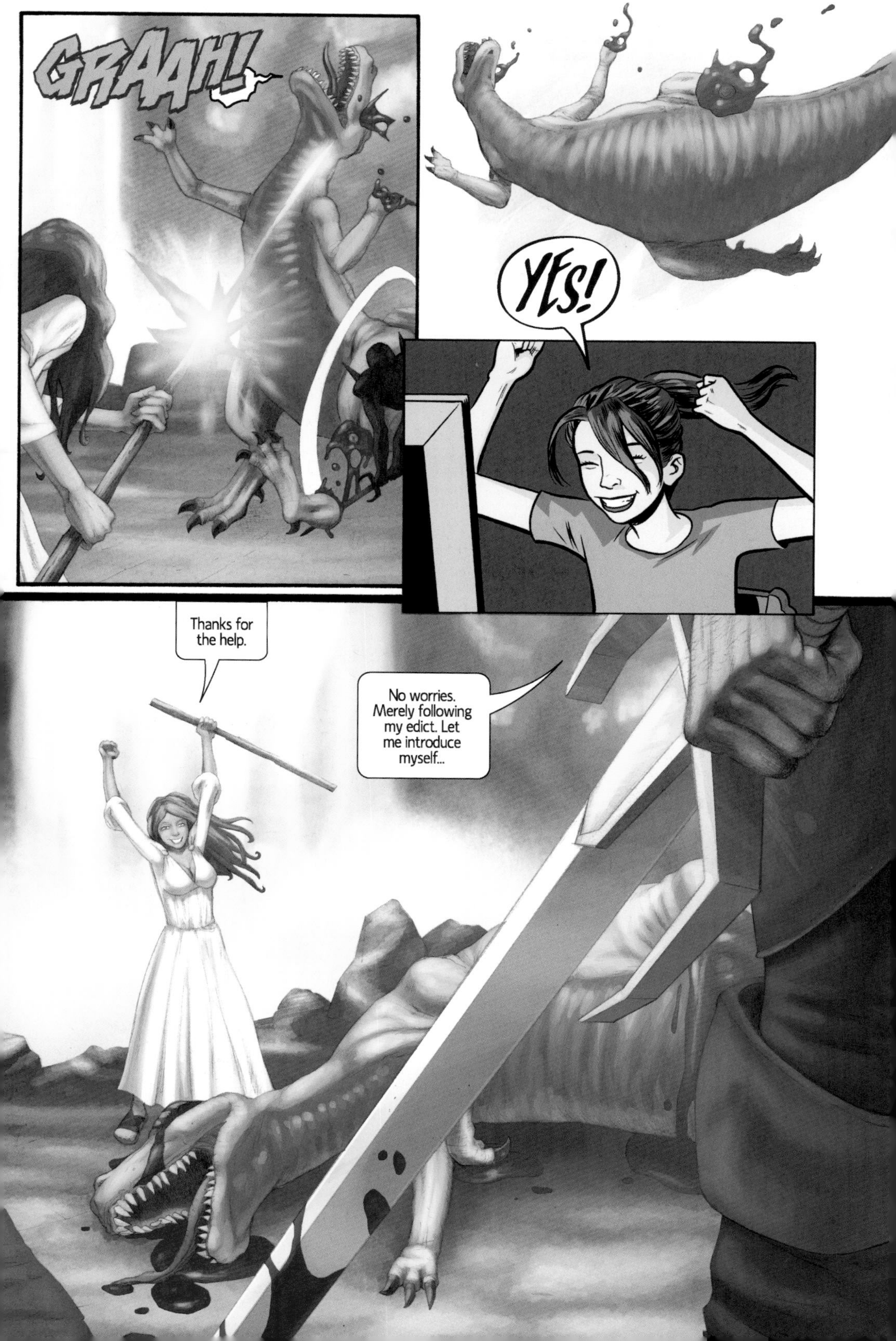
GRAAH!
YES!
Thanks for the help.
No worries. Merely following my edict. Let me introduce myself...

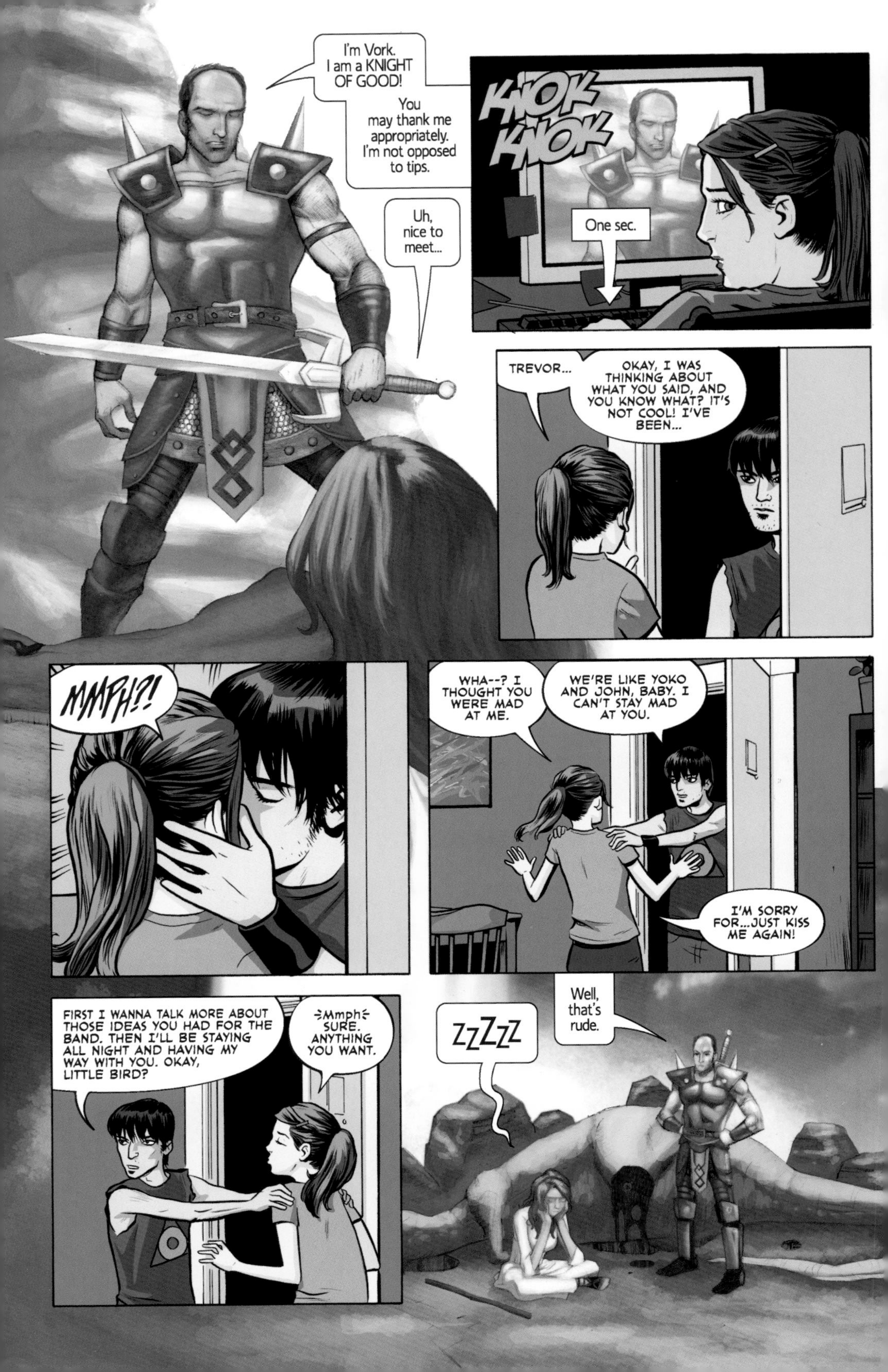
I'm Vork. I am a KNIGHT OF GOOD!
You may thank me appropriately. I'm not opposed to tips.
KNOK KNOK
Uh, nice to meet...
One sec.
TREVOR...
OKAY, I WAS THINKING ABOUT WHAT YOU SAID, AND YOU KNOW WHAT? IT'S NOT COOL! I'VE BEEN...
MMPH?!
WHA--? I THOUGHT YOU WERE MAD AT ME.
WE'RE LIKE YOKO AND JOHN, BABY. I CAN'T STAY MAD AT YOU.
I'M SORRY FOR...JUST KISS ME AGAIN!
FIRST I WANNA TALK MORE ABOUT THOSE IDEAS YOU HAD FOR THE BAND. THEN I'LL BE STAYING ALL NIGHT AND HAVING MY WAY WITH YOU. OKAY, LITTLE BIRD?
Mmph SURE. ANYTHING YOU WANT.
ZZZZZ
Well, that's rude.

CHAPTER 2

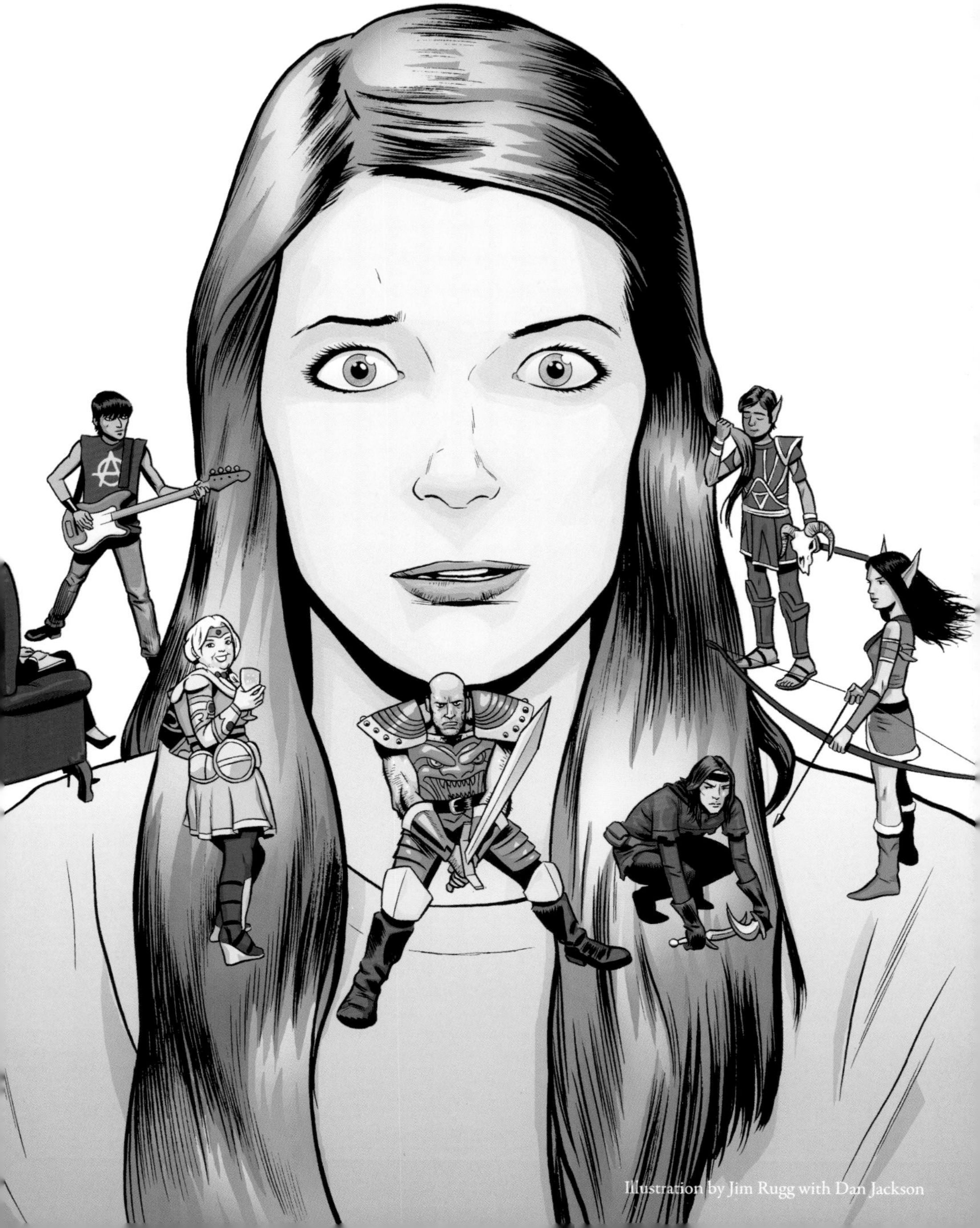

Illustration by Jim Rugg with Dan Jackson

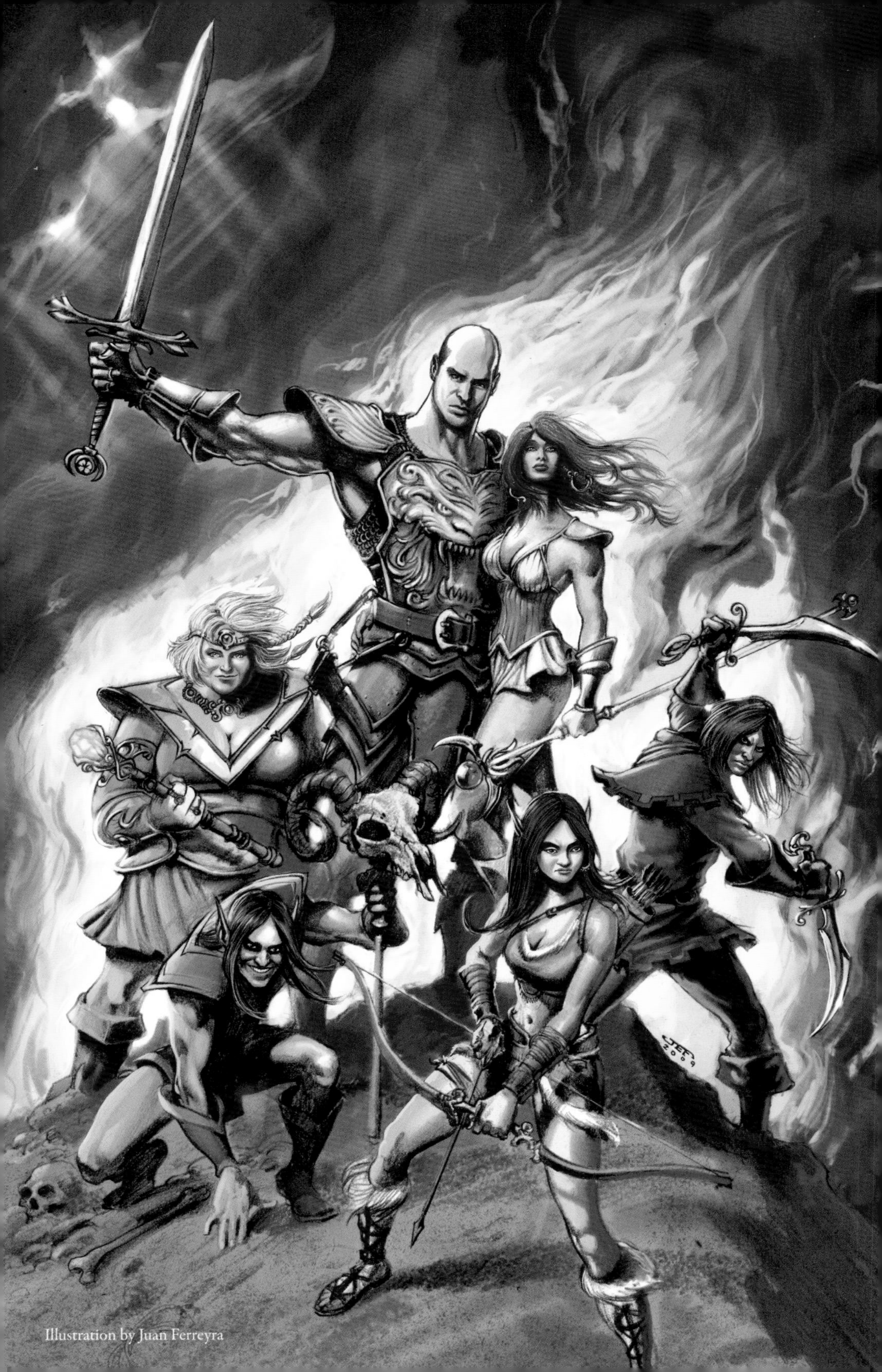
JEFF
2009
Illustration by Juan Ferreyra

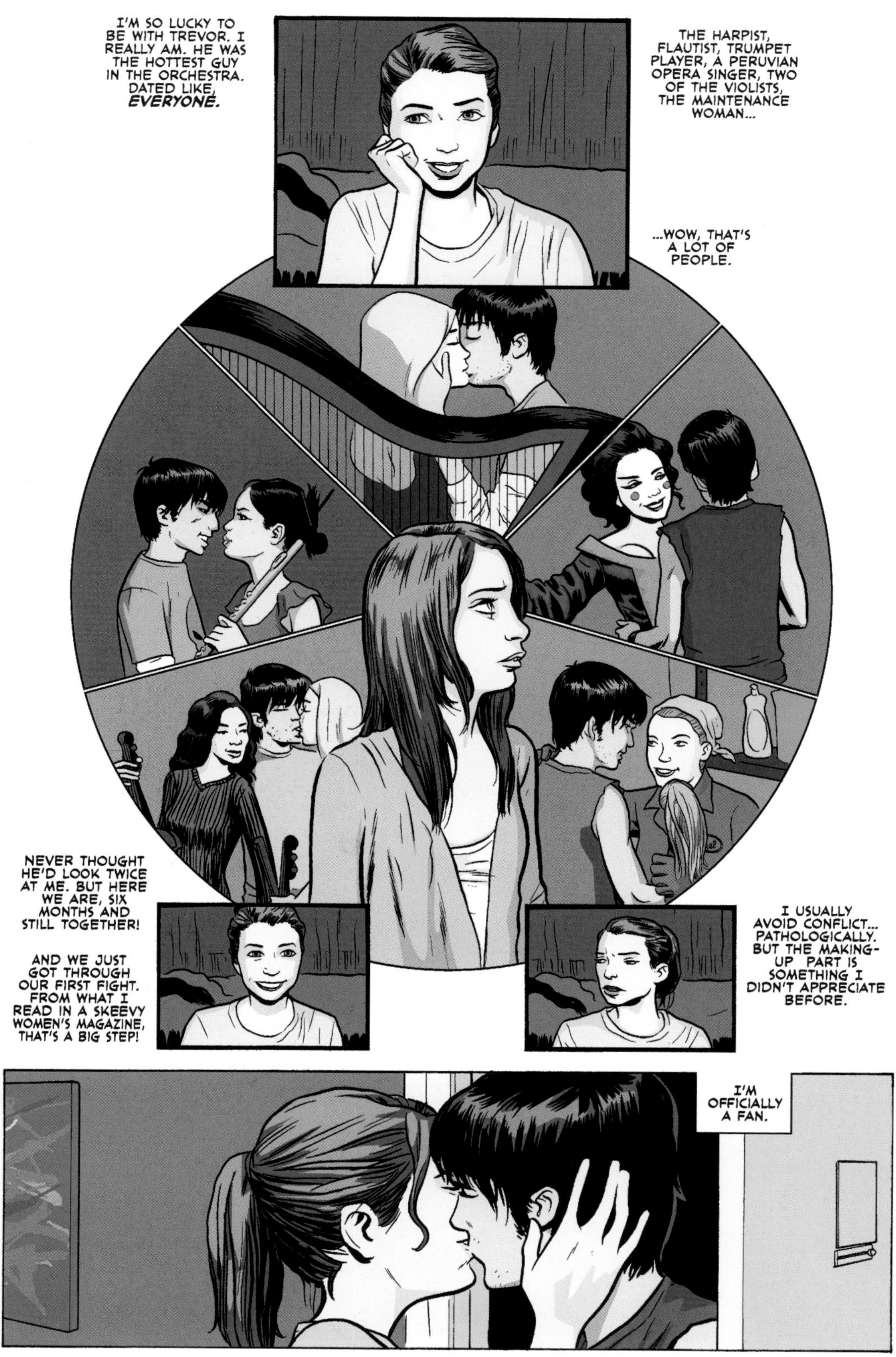
I'M SO LUCKY TO BE WITH TREVOR. I REALLY AM. HE WAS THE HOTTEST GUY IN THE ORCHESTRA. DATED LIKE, *EVERYONE.*
THE HARPIST, FLAUTIST, TRUMPET PLAYER, A PERUVIAN OPERA SINGER, TWO OF THE VIOLISTS, THE MAINTENANCE WOMAN...
...WOW, THAT'S A LOT OF PEOPLE.
NEVER THOUGHT HE'D LOOK TWICE AT ME. BUT HERE WE ARE, SIX MONTHS AND STILL TOGETHER!
AND WE JUST GOT THROUGH OUR FIRST FIGHT. FROM WHAT I READ IN A SKEEVY WOMEN'S MAGAZINE, THAT'S A BIG STEP!
I USUALLY AVOID CONFLICT... PATHOLOGICALLY. BUT THE MAKING-UP PART IS SOMETHING I DIDN'T APPRECIATE BEFORE.
I'M OFFICIALLY A FAN.

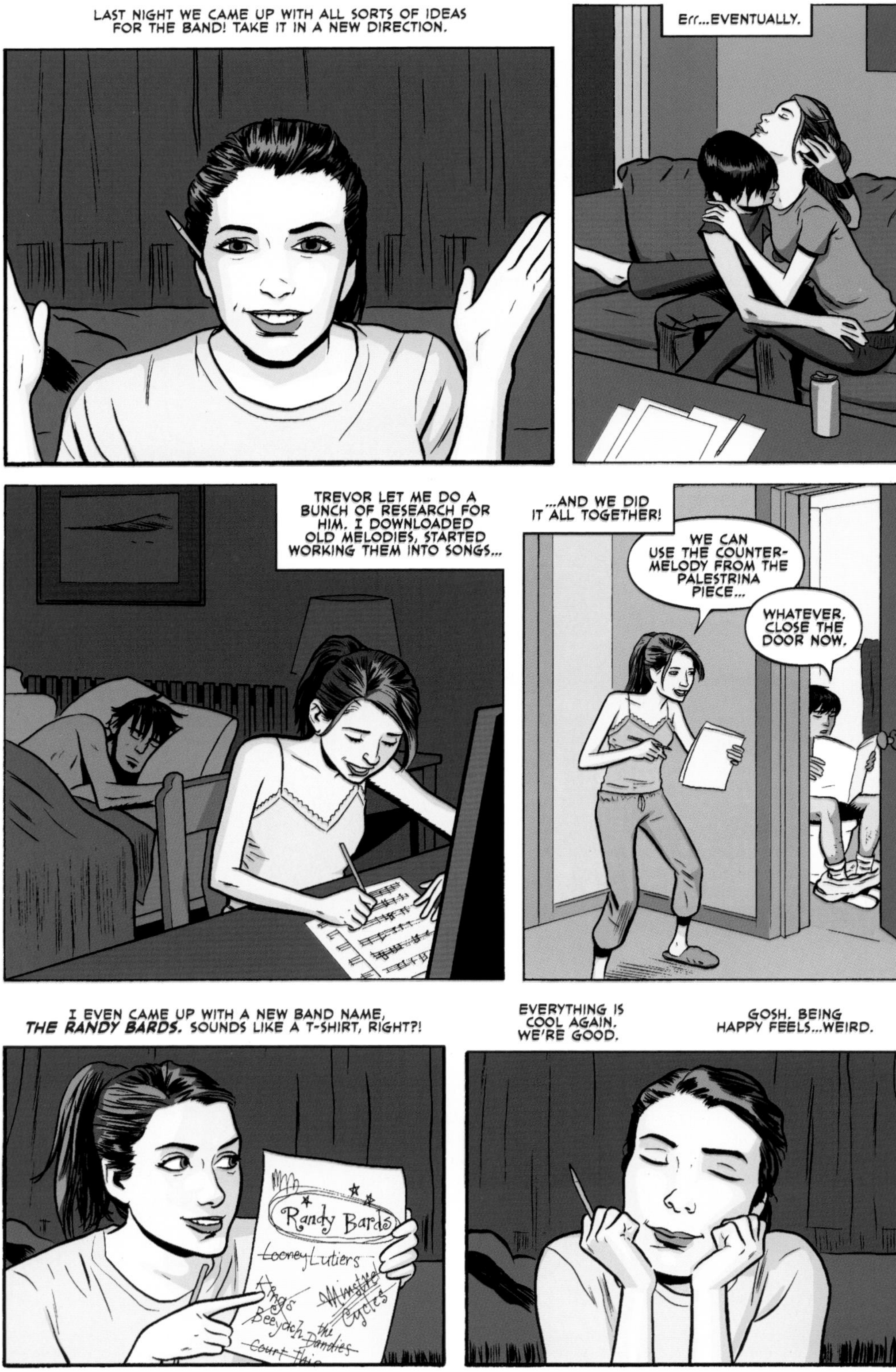
LAST NIGHT WE CAME UP WITH ALL SORTS OF IDEAS FOR THE BAND! TAKE IT IN A NEW DIRECTION.
Err...EVENTUALLY.
TREVOR LET ME DO A BUNCH OF RESEARCH FOR HIM. I DOWNLOADED OLD MELODIES, STARTED WORKING THEM INTO SONGS...
...AND WE DID IT ALL TOGETHER!
WE CAN USE THE COUNTER-MELODY FROM THE PALESTRINA PIECE...
WHATEVER. CLOSE THE DOOR NOW.
I EVEN CAME UP WITH A NEW BAND NAME, *THE RANDY BARDS.* SOUNDS LIKE A T-SHIRT, RIGHT?!
Randy Bards
Looney Lutiers
Kings
Cycles
Beeyach
the Dandies
EVERYTHING IS COOL AGAIN. WE'RE GOOD.
GOSH. BEING HAPPY FEELS...WEIRD.

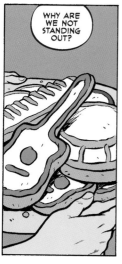

WHY ARE WE NOT STANDING OUT?

ANSWER IS, WE NEED TO MAKE OUR SOUND MORE *UNIQUE.*

QUESTION-- YOU'RE ORDERING PIZZA FOR THIS MEETING, RIGHT?

SURE. CYD, CALL IT IN?

OKAY!

WE'RE GOING SUPER RETRO, LIKE *RENAISSANCE.* BUT ADD A PUNK VIBE. USE OUR CLASSICAL CHOPS TO MAKE A FRESH COMBO!

THANKS-- --I CAME UP WITH IT ALL LAST NIGHT.

Hmm, DOESN'T SUCK.

I'LL GO BACK ON CELLO. FADE WILL MIX UP THE BEATS-- TABLAS, TAMBOURINE... JERRY, CAN YOU PLAY THE LUTE?

≈BURP≈ WHO CAN'T?

I CAN PLAY VIOLIN?

WE NEED TO KEEP THE BAND SMALL, BABE. AND REMEMBER--I'M ALLERGIC TO MUSHROOMS.

I CAME UP WITH A NEW NAME TOO-- *THE RANDY BARDS.*

Uh, HI. I'D LIKE TO PLACE AN ORDER...

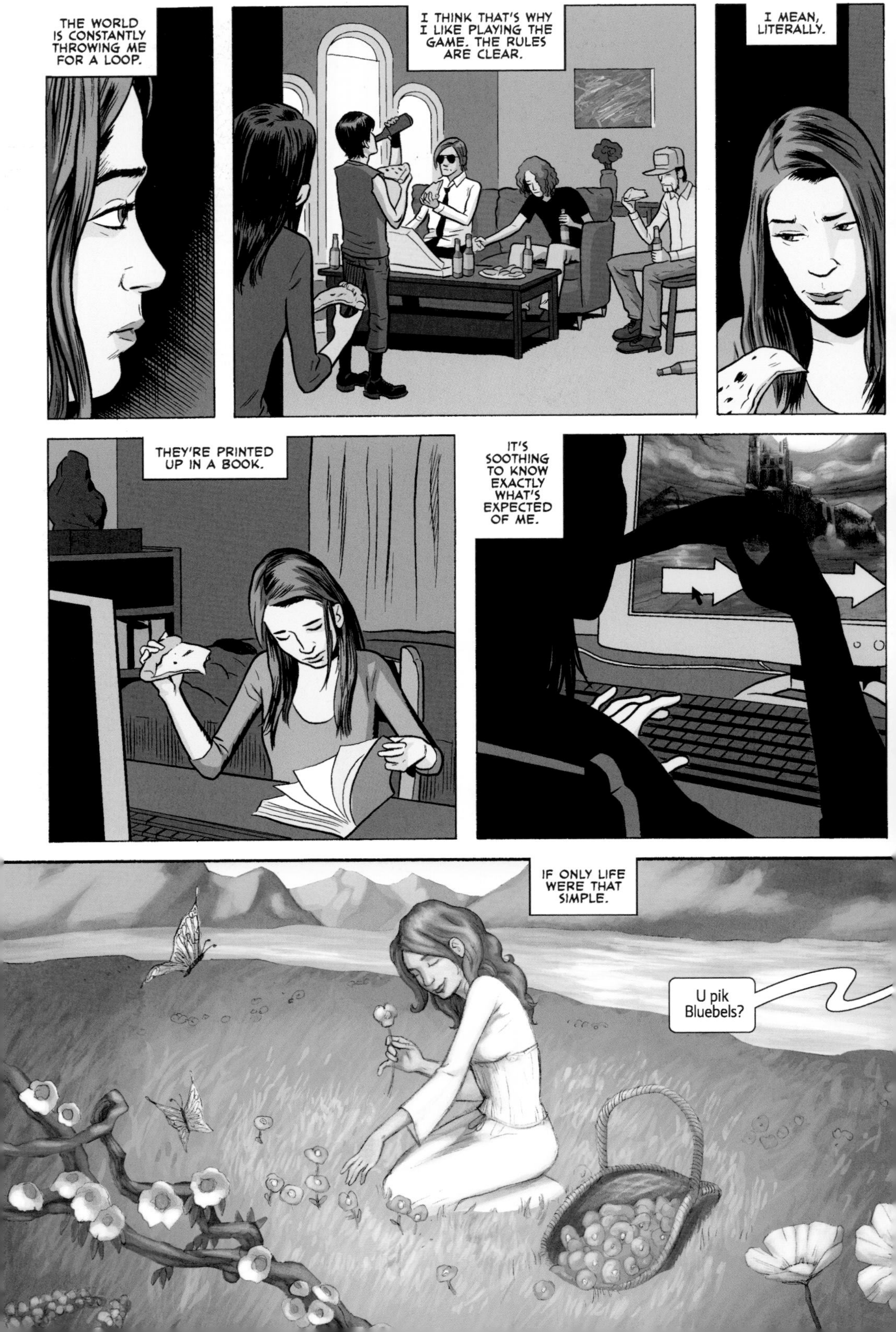
THE WORLD IS CONSTANTLY THROWING ME FOR A LOOP.
I THINK THAT'S WHY I LIKE PLAYING THE GAME. THE RULES ARE CLEAR.
I MEAN, LITERALLY.
THEY'RE PRINTED UP IN A BOOK.
IT'S SOOTHING TO KNOW EXACTLY WHAT'S EXPECTED OF ME.
IF ONLY LIFE WERE THAT SIMPLE.
U pik Bluebels?

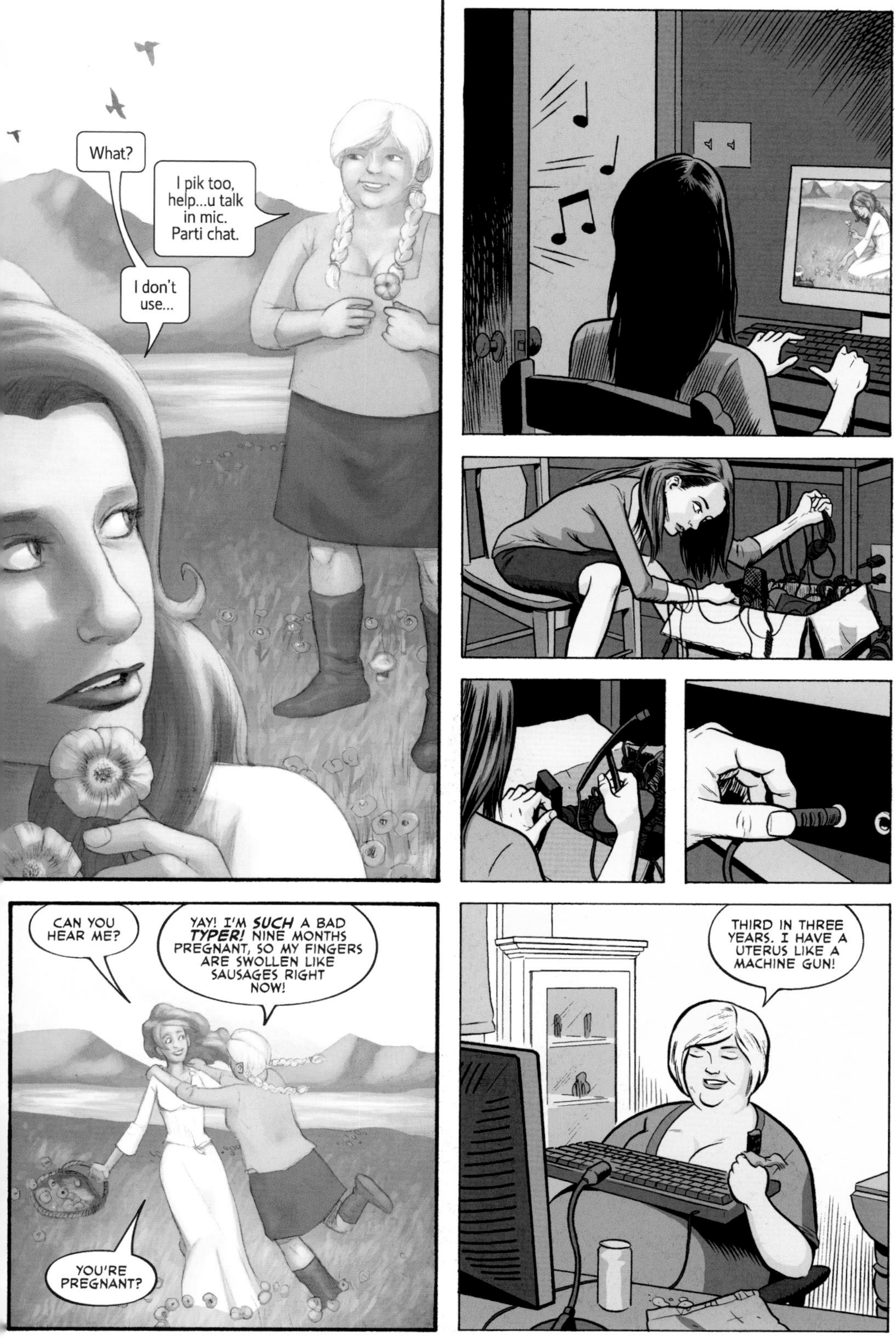
What?
I pik too, help...u talk in mic. Parti chat.
I don't use...
CAN YOU HEAR ME?
YAY! I'M SUCH A BAD TYPER! NINE MONTHS PREGNANT, SO MY FINGERS ARE SWOLLEN LIKE SAUSAGES RIGHT NOW!
YOU'RE PREGNANT?
THIRD IN THREE YEARS. I HAVE A UTERUS LIKE A MACHINE GUN!

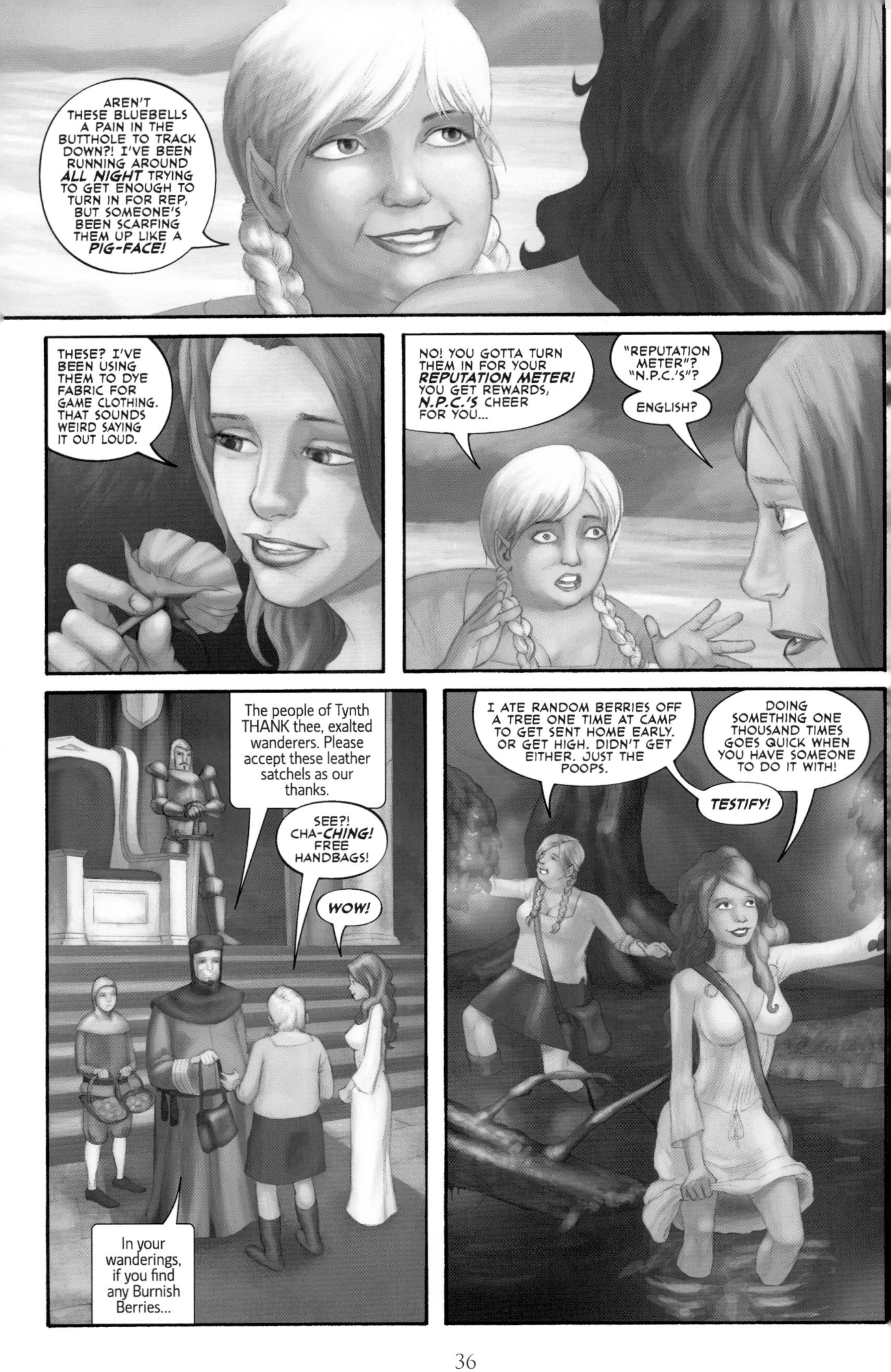
AREN'T THESE BLUEBELLS A PAIN IN THE BUTTHOLE TO TRACK DOWN?! I'VE BEEN RUNNING AROUND ALL NIGHT TRYING TO GET ENOUGH TO TURN IN FOR REP, BUT SOMEONE'S BEEN SCARFING THEM UP LIKE A PIG-FACE!
THESE? I'VE BEEN USING THEM TO DYE FABRIC FOR GAME CLOTHING. THAT SOUNDS WEIRD SAYING IT OUT LOUD.
NO! YOU GOTTA TURN THEM IN FOR YOUR REPUTATION METER! YOU GET REWARDS, N.P.C.'S CHEER FOR YOU...
"REPUTATION METER"? "N.P.C.'S"?
ENGLISH?
The people of Tynth THANK thee, exalted wanderers. Please accept these leather satchels as our thanks.
SEE?! CHA-CHING! FREE HANDBAGS!
WOW!
In your wanderings, if you find any Burnish Berries...
I ATE RANDOM BERRIES OFF A TREE ONE TIME AT CAMP TO GET SENT HOME EARLY. OR GET HIGH. DIDN'T GET EITHER. JUST THE POOPS.
TESTIFY!
DOING SOMETHING ONE THOUSAND TIMES GOES QUICK WHEN YOU HAVE SOMEONE TO DO IT WITH!

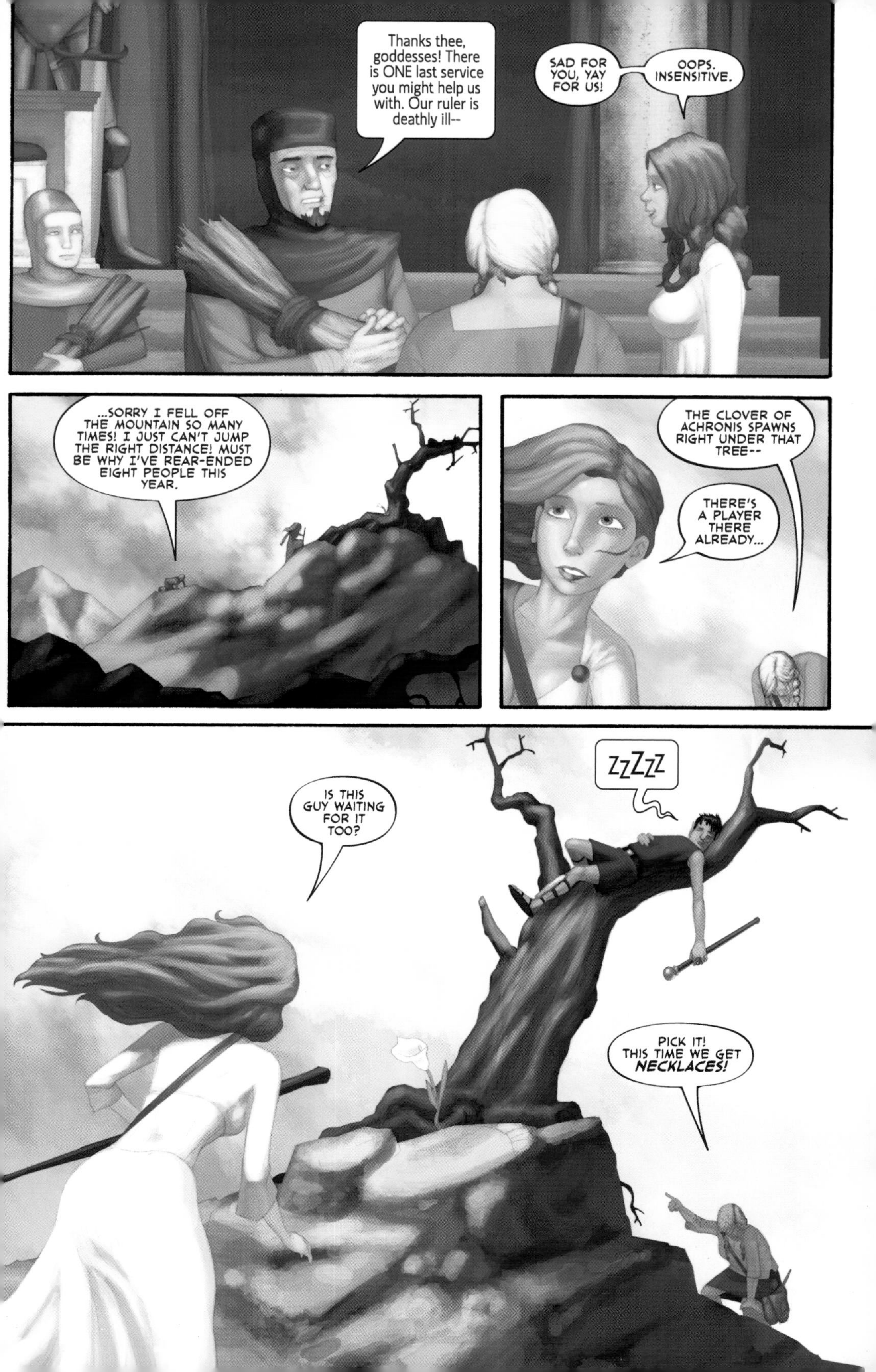
Thanks thee, goddesses! There is ONE last service you might help us with. Our ruler is deathly ill--
SAD FOR YOU, YAY FOR US!
OOPS. INSENSITIVE.
...SORRY I FELL OFF THE MOUNTAIN SO MANY TIMES! I JUST CAN'T JUMP THE RIGHT DISTANCE! MUST BE WHY I'VE REAR-ENDED EIGHT PEOPLE THIS YEAR.
THE CLOVER OF ACHRONIS SPAWNS RIGHT UNDER THAT TREE--
THERE'S A PLAYER THERE ALREADY...
IS THIS GUY WAITING FOR IT TOO?
ZZZZZ
PICK IT! THIS TIME WE GET *NECKLACES!*

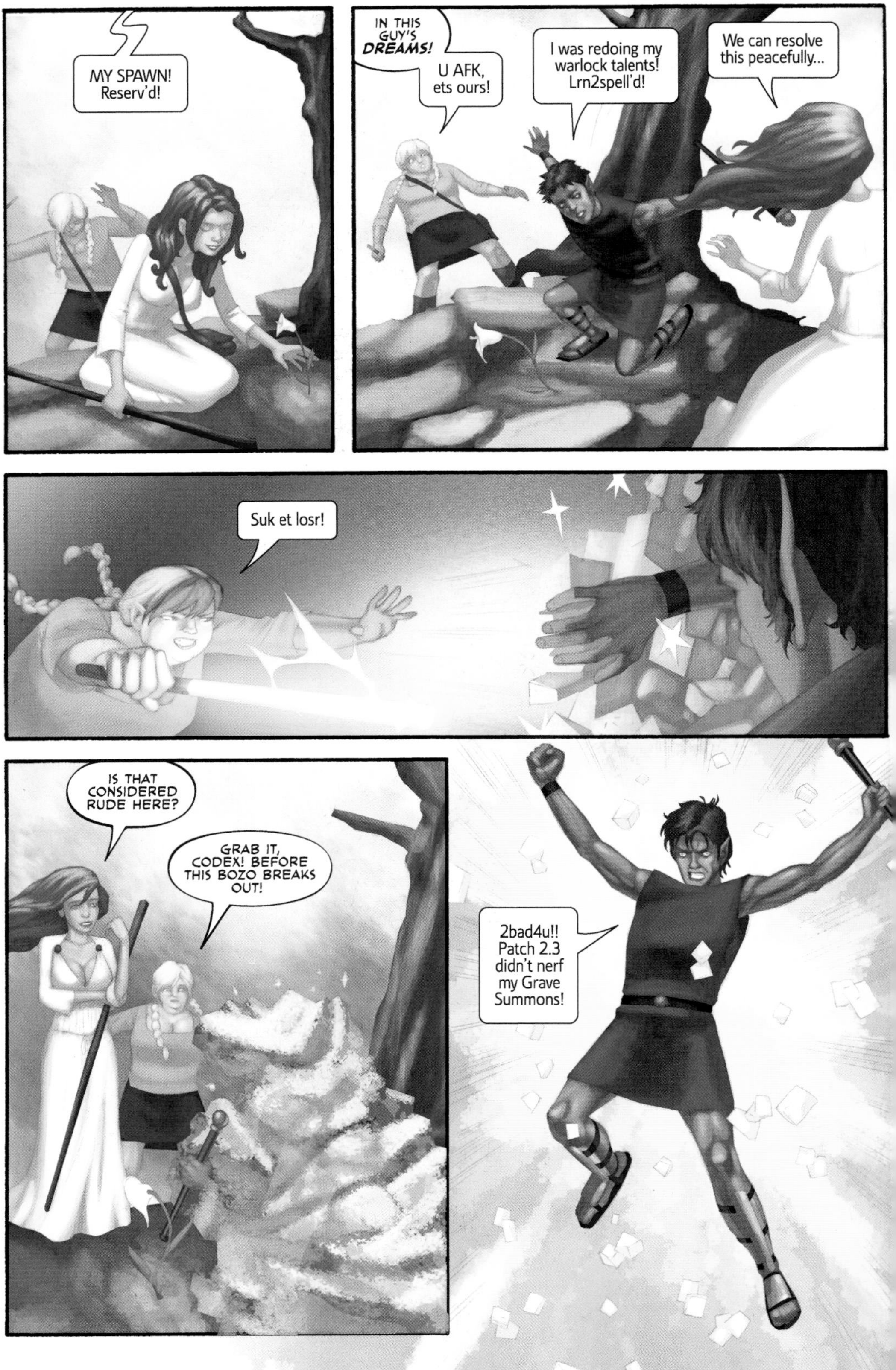
MY SPAWN! Reserv'd!
IN THIS GUY'S DREAMS!
U AFK, ets ours!
I was redoing my warlock talents! Lrn2spell'd!
We can resolve this peacefully...
Suk et losr!
IS THAT CONSIDERED RUDE HERE?
GRAB IT, CODEX! BEFORE THIS BOZO BREAKS OUT!
2bad4u!! Patch 2.3 didn't nerf my Grave Summons!

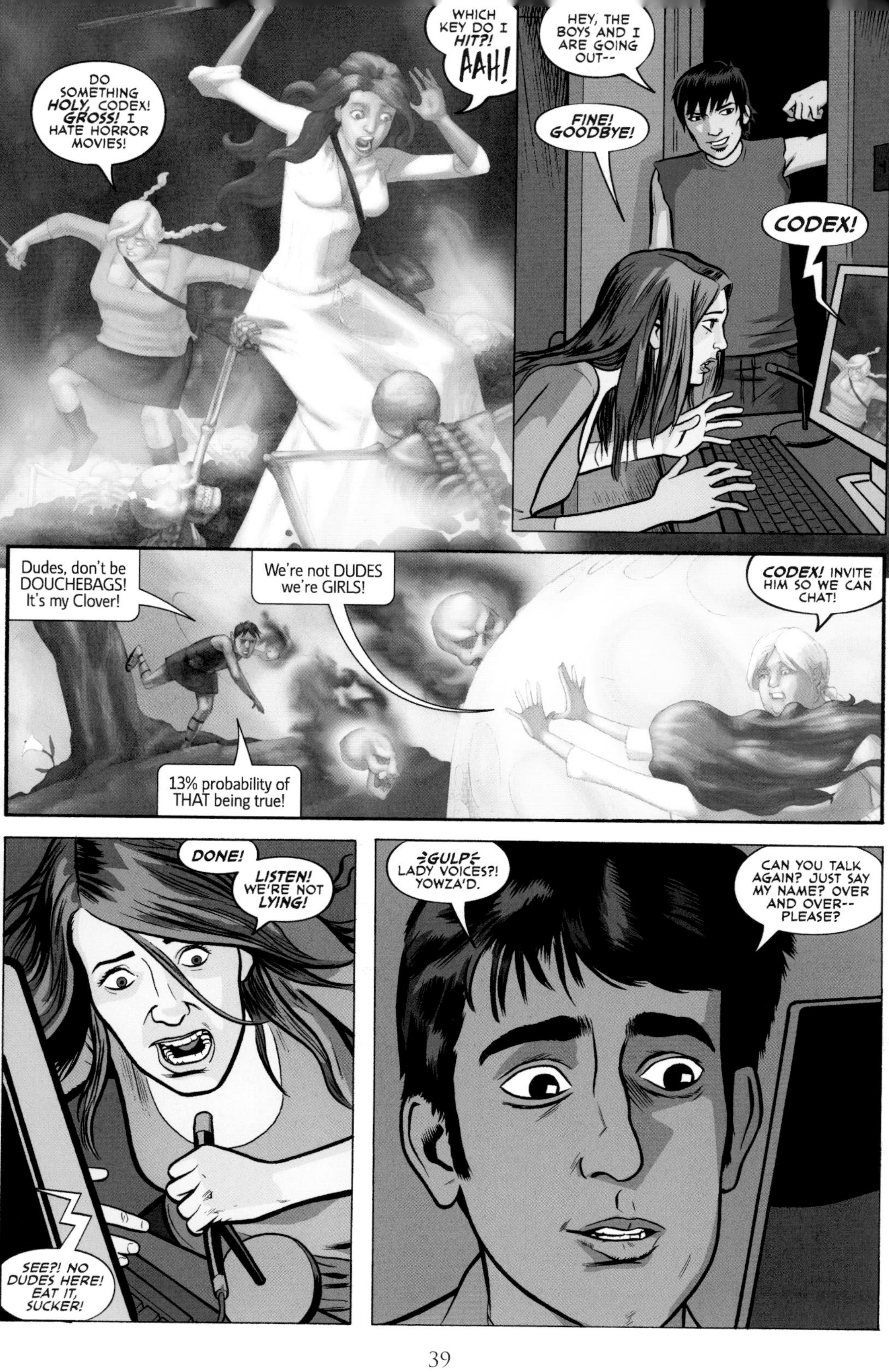
DO SOMETHING HOLY, CODEX! GROSS! I HATE HORROR MOVIES!
WHICH KEY DO I HIT?! AAH!
HEY, THE BOYS AND I ARE GOING OUT--
FINE! GOODBYE!
CODEX!
Dudes, don't be DOUCHEBAGS! It's my Clover!
We're not DUDES we're GIRLS!
13% probability of THAT being true!
CODEX! INVITE HIM SO WE CAN CHAT!
DONE!
LISTEN! WE'RE NOT LYING!
SEE?! NO DUDES HERE! EAT IT, SUCKER!
GULP
LADY VOICES?! YOWZA'D.
CAN YOU TALK AGAIN? JUST SAY MY NAME? OVER AND OVER-- PLEASE?

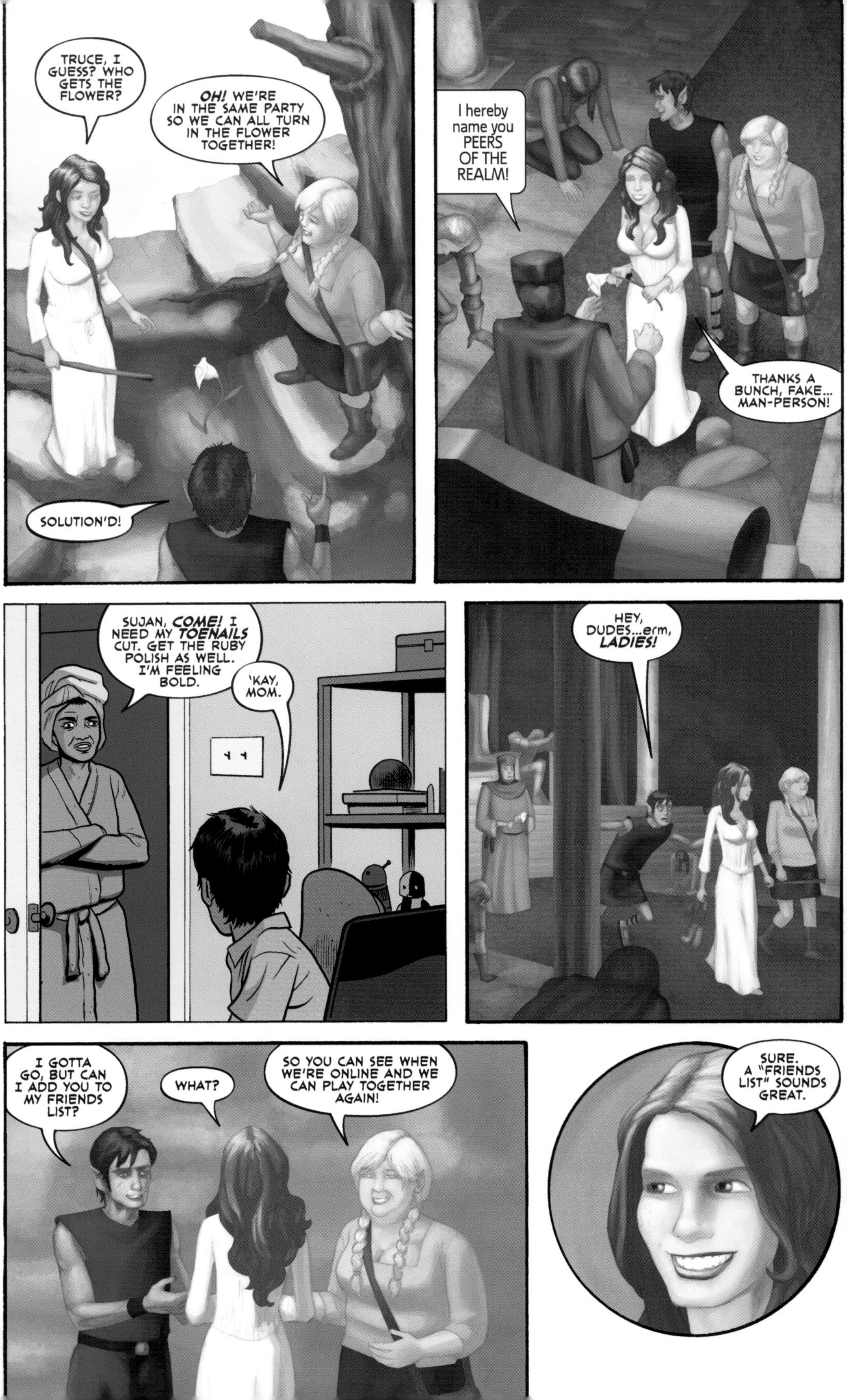
TRUCE, I GUESS? WHO GETS THE FLOWER?
OH! WE'RE IN THE SAME PARTY SO WE CAN ALL TURN IN THE FLOWER TOGETHER!
SOLUTION'D!
I hereby name you PEERS OF THE REALM!
THANKS A BUNCH, FAKE... MAN-PERSON!
SUJAN, COME! I NEED MY TOENAILS CUT. GET THE RUBY POLISH AS WELL. I'M FEELING BOLD.
'KAY, MOM.
HEY, DUDES...erm, LADIES!
I GOTTA GO, BUT CAN I ADD YOU TO MY FRIENDS LIST?
WHAT?
SO YOU CAN SEE WHEN WE'RE ONLINE AND WE CAN PLAY TOGETHER AGAIN!
SURE. A "FRIENDS LIST" SOUNDS GREAT.

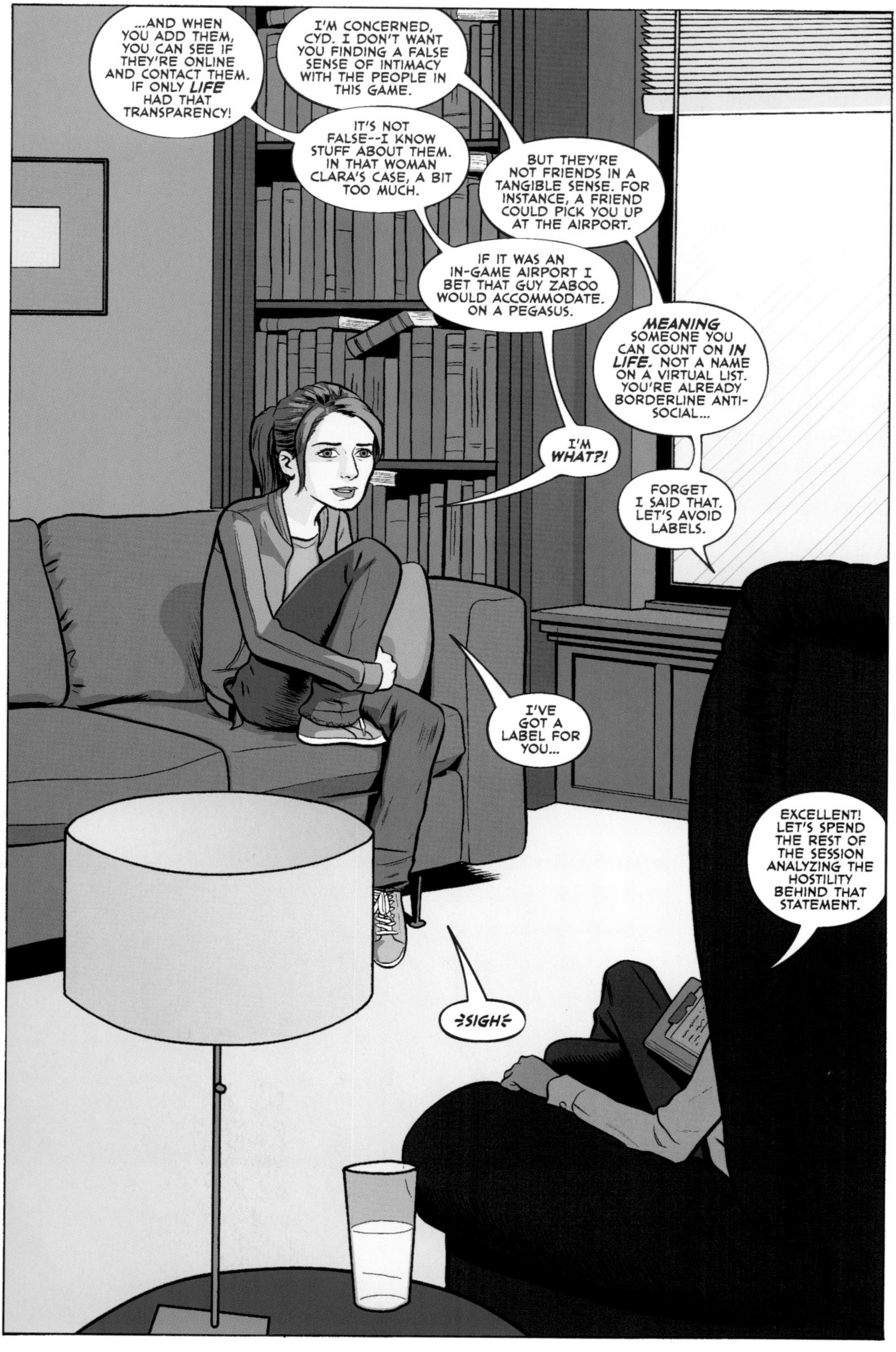
...AND WHEN YOU ADD THEM, YOU CAN SEE IF THEY'RE ONLINE AND CONTACT THEM. IF ONLY LIFE HAD THAT TRANSPARENCY!
I'M CONCERNED, CYD. I DON'T WANT YOU FINDING A FALSE SENSE OF INTIMACY WITH THE PEOPLE IN THIS GAME.
IT'S NOT FALSE--I KNOW STUFF ABOUT THEM. IN THAT WOMAN CLARA'S CASE, A BIT TOO MUCH.
BUT THEY'RE NOT FRIENDS IN A TANGIBLE SENSE. FOR INSTANCE, A FRIEND COULD PICK YOU UP AT THE AIRPORT.
IF IT WAS AN IN-GAME AIRPORT I BET THAT GUY ZABOO WOULD ACCOMMODATE. ON A PEGASUS.
MEANING SOMEONE YOU CAN COUNT ON IN LIFE. NOT A NAME ON A VIRTUAL LIST. YOU'RE ALREADY BORDERLINE ANTI-SOCIAL...
I'M WHAT?!
FORGET I SAID THAT. LET'S AVOID LABELS.
I'VE GOT A LABEL FOR YOU...
EXCELLENT! LET'S SPEND THE REST OF THE SESSION ANALYZING THE HOSTILITY BEHIND THAT STATEMENT.
SIGH

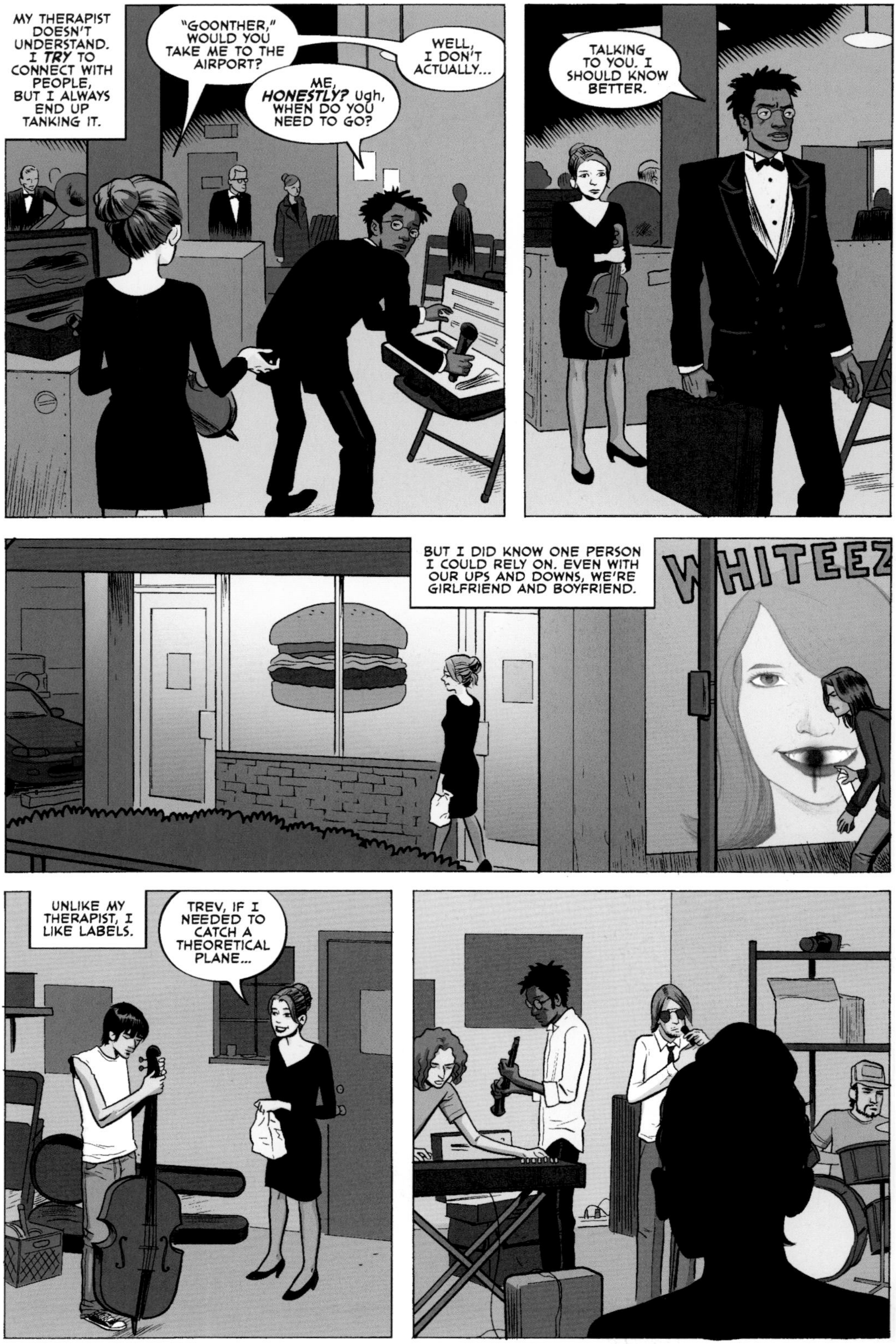
MY THERAPIST DOESN'T UNDERSTAND. I TRY TO CONNECT WITH PEOPLE, BUT I ALWAYS END UP TANKING IT.
"GOONTHER," WOULD YOU TAKE ME TO THE AIRPORT?
WELL, I DON'T ACTUALLY...
ME, HONESTLY? Ugh, WHEN DO YOU NEED TO GO?
TALKING TO YOU. I SHOULD KNOW BETTER.
BUT I DID KNOW ONE PERSON I COULD RELY ON. EVEN WITH OUR UPS AND DOWNS, WE'RE GIRLFRIEND AND BOYFRIEND.
WHITEEZ
UNLIKE MY THERAPIST, I LIKE LABELS.
TREV, IF I NEEDED TO CATCH A THEORETICAL PLANE...

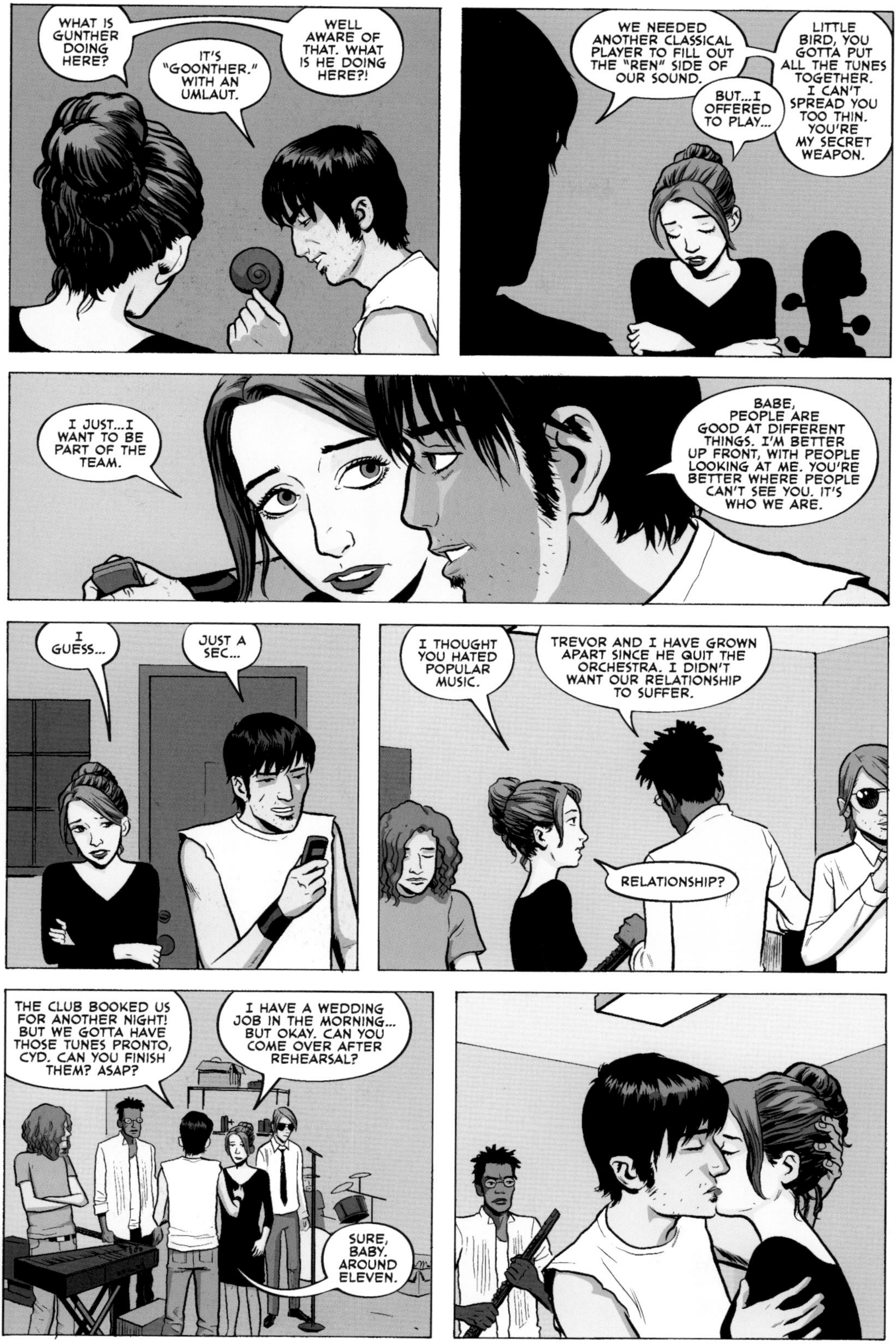
WHAT IS GUNTHER DOING HERE?
IT'S "GOONTHER." WITH AN UMLAUT.
WELL AWARE OF THAT. WHAT IS HE DOING HERE?!
WE NEEDED ANOTHER CLASSICAL PLAYER TO FILL OUT THE "REN" SIDE OF OUR SOUND.
BUT...I OFFERED TO PLAY...
LITTLE BIRD, YOU GOTTA PUT ALL THE TUNES TOGETHER. I CAN'T SPREAD YOU TOO THIN. YOU'RE MY SECRET WEAPON.
I JUST...I WANT TO BE PART OF THE TEAM.
BABE, PEOPLE ARE GOOD AT DIFFERENT THINGS. I'M BETTER UP FRONT, WITH PEOPLE LOOKING AT ME. YOU'RE BETTER WHERE PEOPLE CAN'T SEE YOU. IT'S WHO WE ARE.
I GUESS...
JUST A SEC...
I THOUGHT YOU HATED POPULAR MUSIC.
TREVOR AND I HAVE GROWN APART SINCE HE QUIT THE ORCHESTRA. I DIDN'T WANT OUR RELATIONSHIP TO SUFFER.
RELATIONSHIP?
THE CLUB BOOKED US FOR ANOTHER NIGHT! BUT WE GOTTA HAVE THOSE TUNES PRONTO, CYD. CAN YOU FINISH THEM? ASAP?
I HAVE A WEDDING JOB IN THE MORNING... BUT OKAY. CAN YOU COME OVER AFTER REHEARSAL?
SURE, BABY. AROUND ELEVEN.

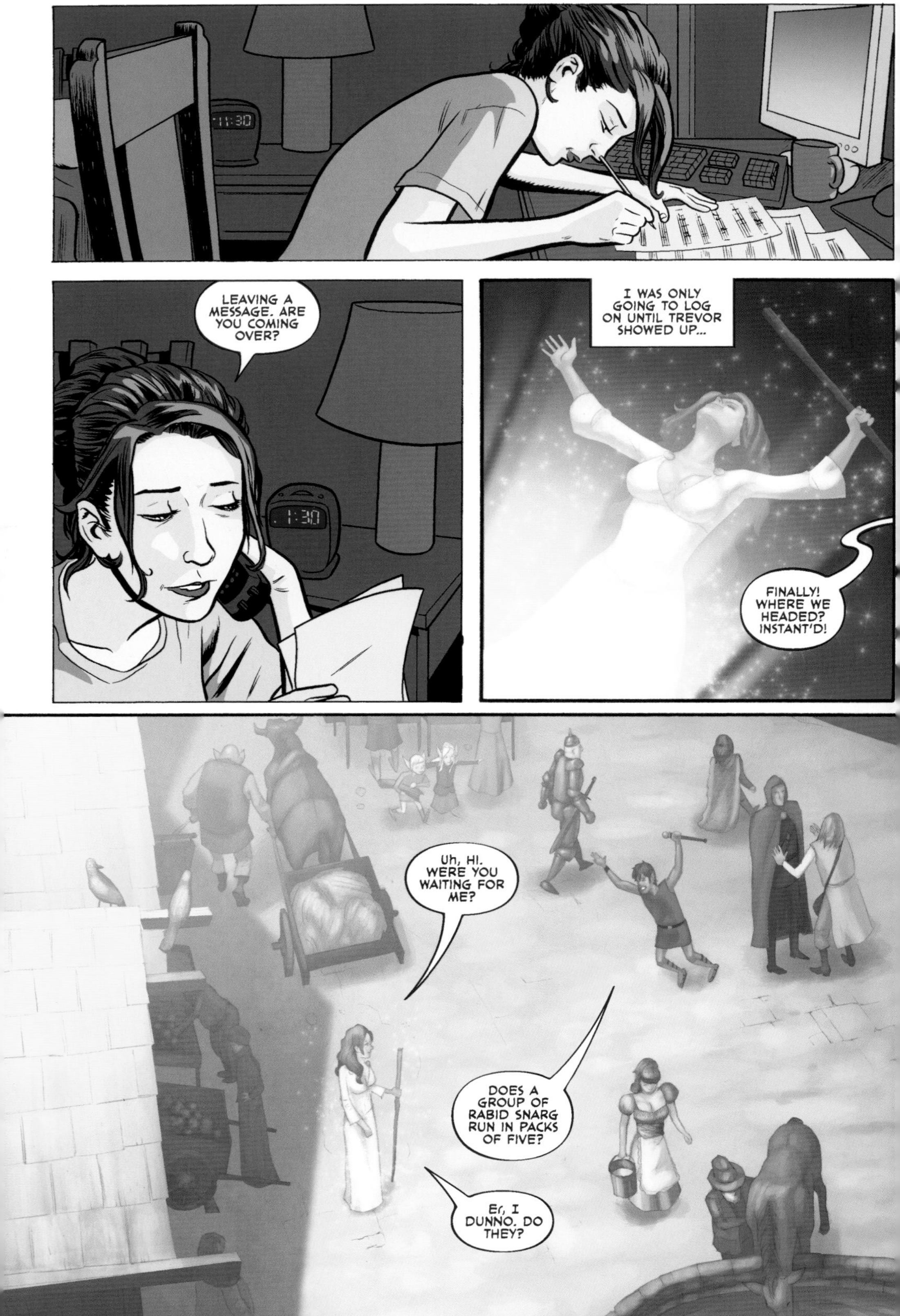

11:30
LEAVING A MESSAGE. ARE YOU COMING OVER?
1:30
I WAS ONLY GOING TO LOG ON UNTIL TREVOR SHOWED UP...
FINALLY! WHERE WE HEADED? INSTANT'D!
Uh, HI. WERE YOU WAITING FOR ME?
DOES A GROUP OF RABID SNARG RUN IN PACKS OF FIVE?
Er, I DUNNO. DO THEY?

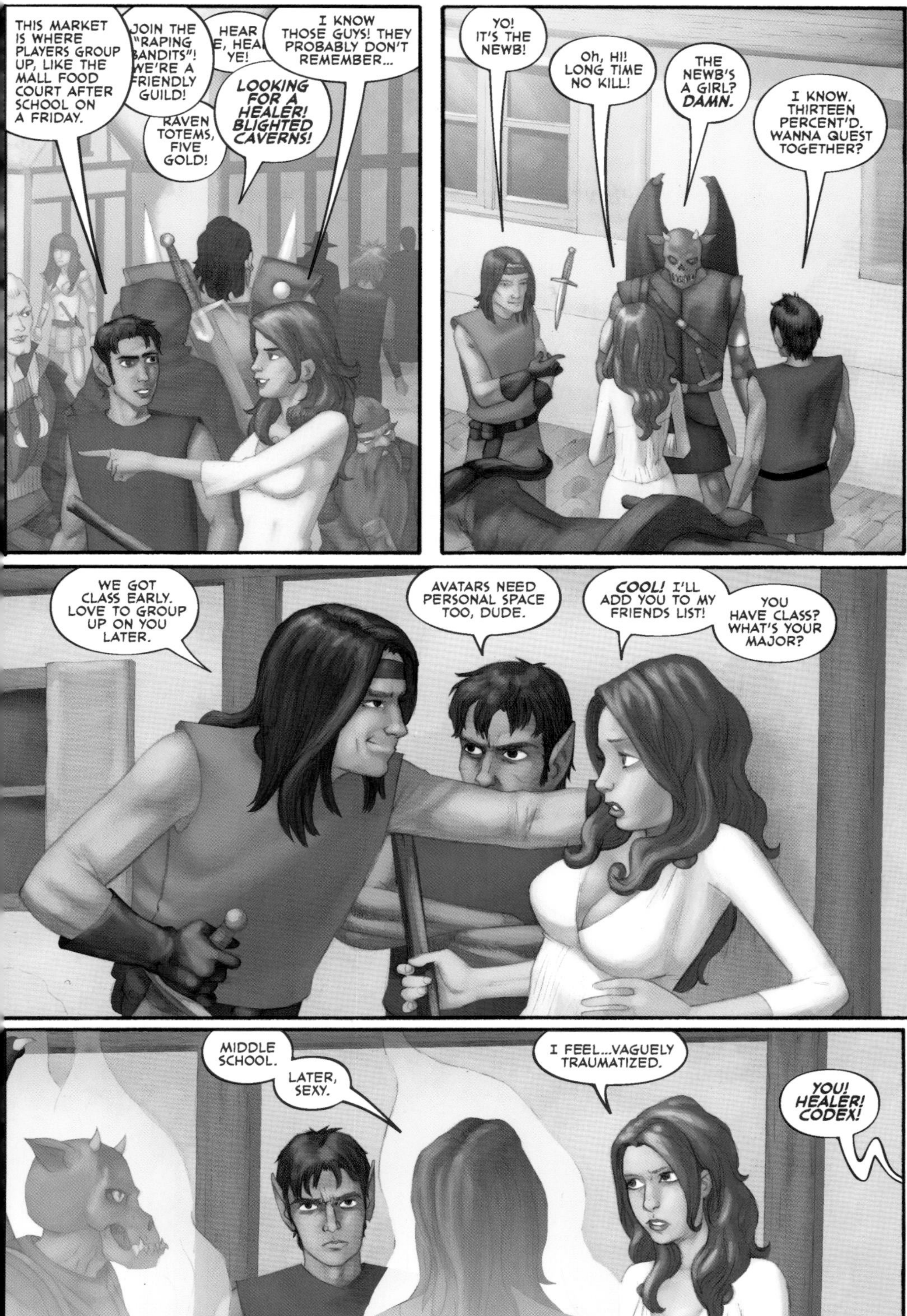
THIS MARKET IS WHERE PLAYERS GROUP UP, LIKE THE MALL FOOD COURT AFTER SCHOOL ON A FRIDAY.
JOIN THE "RAPING BANDITS"! WE'RE A FRIENDLY GUILD!
HEAR E, HEA YE!
RAVEN TOTEMS, FIVE GOLD!
LOOKING FOR A HEALER! BLIGHTED CAVERNS!
I KNOW THOSE GUYS! THEY PROBABLY DON'T REMEMBER...
YO! IT'S THE NEWB!
Oh, HI! LONG TIME NO KILL!
THE NEWB'S A GIRL? DAMN.
I KNOW. THIRTEEN PERCENT'D. WANNA QUEST TOGETHER?
WE GOT CLASS EARLY. LOVE TO GROUP UP ON YOU LATER.
AVATARS NEED PERSONAL SPACE TOO, DUDE.
COOL! I'LL ADD YOU TO MY FRIENDS LIST!
YOU HAVE CLASS? WHAT'S YOUR MAJOR?
MIDDLE SCHOOL.
LATER, SEXY.
I FEEL...VAGUELY TRAUMATIZED.
YOU! HEALER! CODEX!

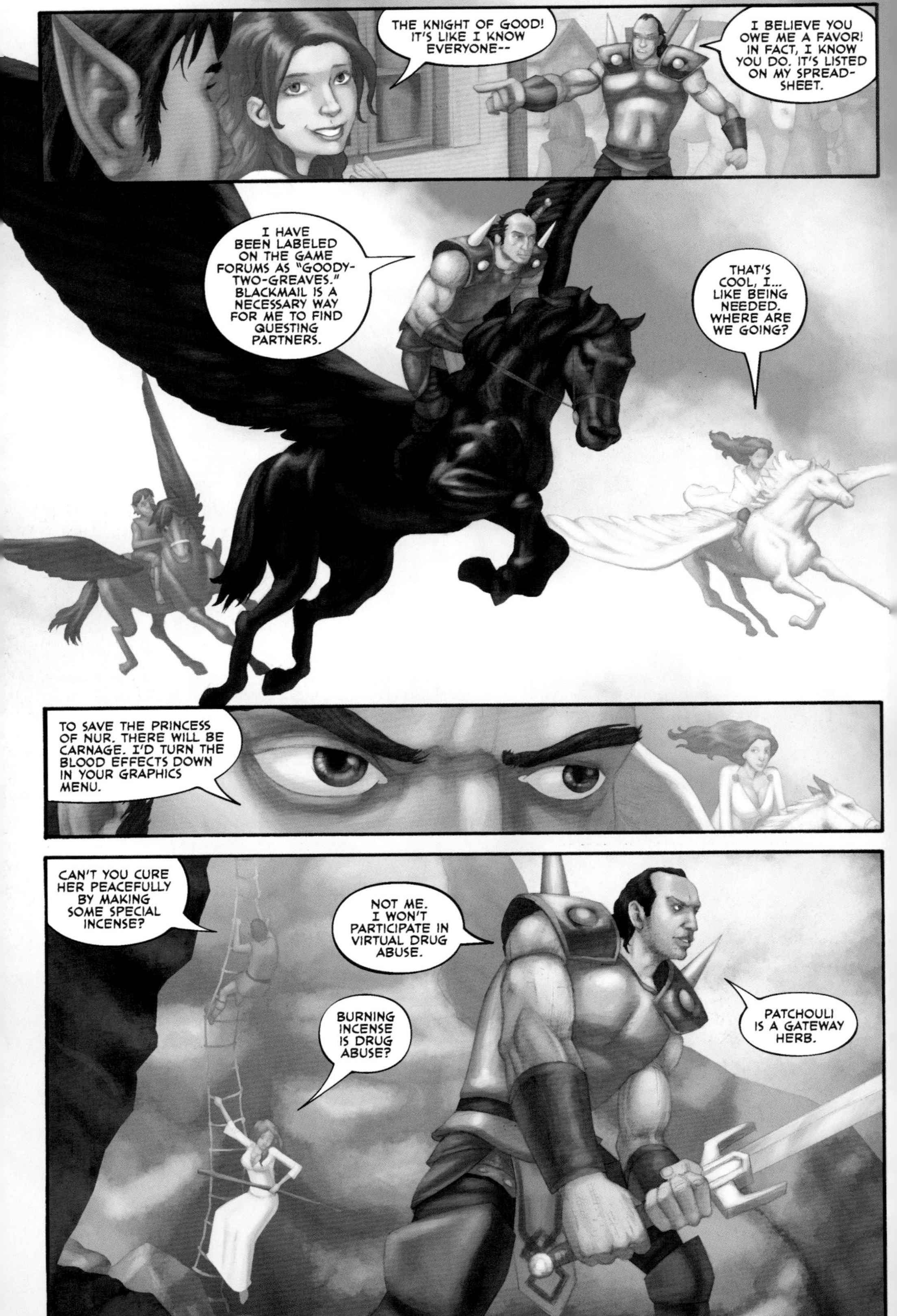
THE KNIGHT OF GOOD! IT'S LIKE I KNOW EVERYONE--
I BELIEVE YOU OWE ME A FAVOR! IN FACT, I KNOW YOU DO. IT'S LISTED ON MY SPREAD-SHEET.
I HAVE BEEN LABELED ON THE GAME FORUMS AS "GOODY-TWO-GREAVES." BLACKMAIL IS A NECESSARY WAY FOR ME TO FIND QUESTING PARTNERS.
THAT'S COOL, I... LIKE BEING NEEDED. WHERE ARE WE GOING?
TO SAVE THE PRINCESS OF NUR. THERE WILL BE CARNAGE. I'D TURN THE BLOOD EFFECTS DOWN IN YOUR GRAPHICS MENU.
CAN'T YOU CURE HER PEACEFULLY BY MAKING SOME SPECIAL INCENSE?
NOT ME. I WON'T PARTICIPATE IN VIRTUAL DRUG ABUSE.
BURNING INCENSE IS DRUG ABUSE?
PATCHOULI IS A GATEWAY HERB.

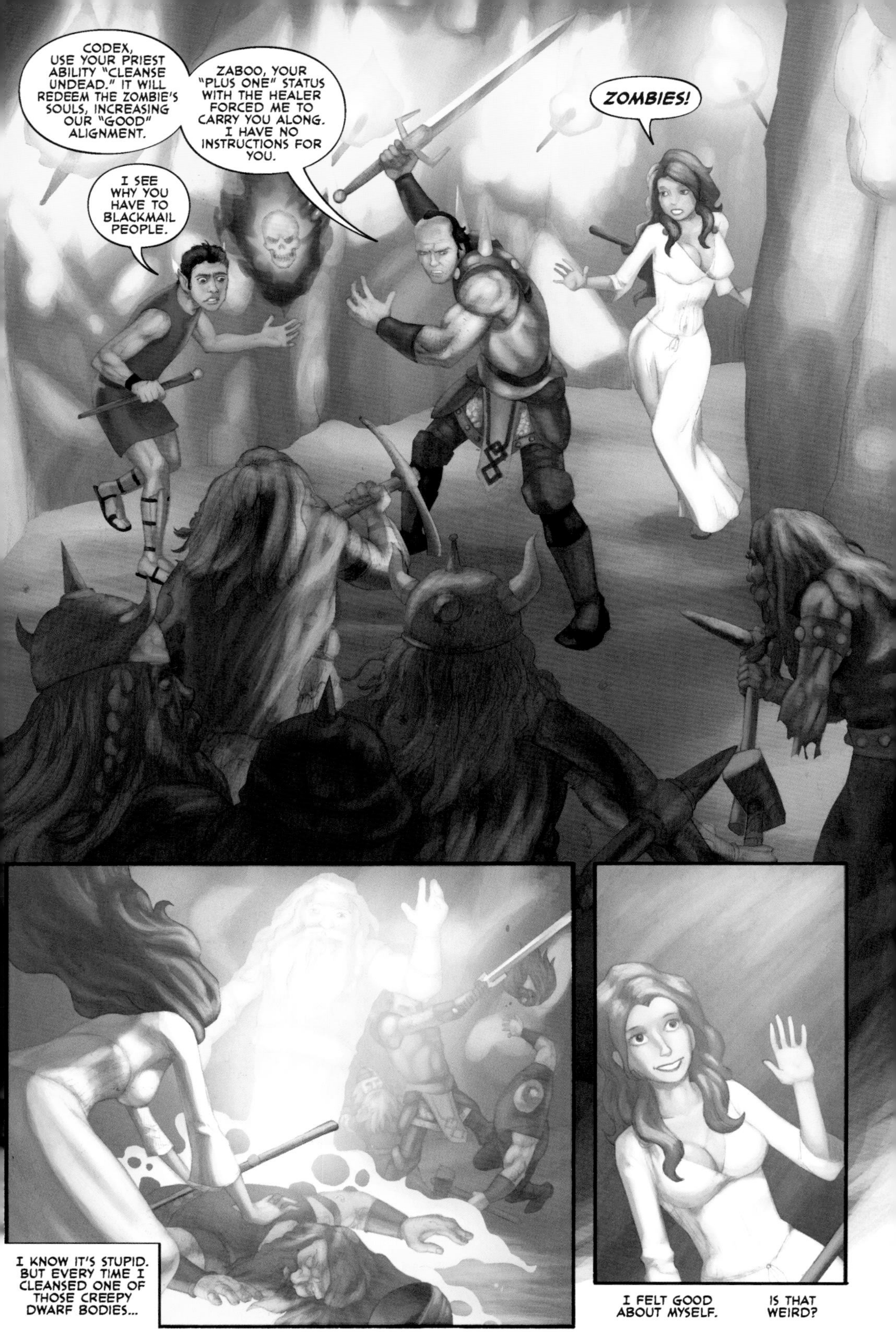
CODEX, USE YOUR PRIEST ABILITY "CLEANSE UNDEAD." IT WILL REDEEM THE ZOMBIE'S SOULS, INCREASING OUR "GOOD" ALIGNMENT.
ZABOO, YOUR "PLUS ONE" STATUS WITH THE HEALER FORCED ME TO CARRY YOU ALONG. I HAVE NO INSTRUCTIONS FOR YOU.
ZOMBIES!
I SEE WHY YOU HAVE TO BLACKMAIL PEOPLE.
I KNOW IT'S STUPID. BUT EVERY TIME I CLEANSED ONE OF THOSE CREEPY DWARF BODIES...
I FELT GOOD ABOUT MYSELF.
IS THAT WEIRD?

AND WHEN WE FACED THE BOSS...

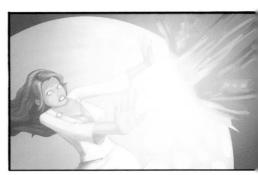

...AND KILLED THE EVIL LICHE...

...AND HIS WEREWOLF SERVANT, LORD BANSHEE...

MY *WRAITH* IS TOTALLY *FRENCHING* THIS GUY!

...AND FREED THE PRINCESS...

YOU'RE TOTALLY PRETTIER THAN HER.

...AND GOT REWARDED...

LIVE LONG AND PROSPER.

WRONG... EVERYTHING, DUDE.

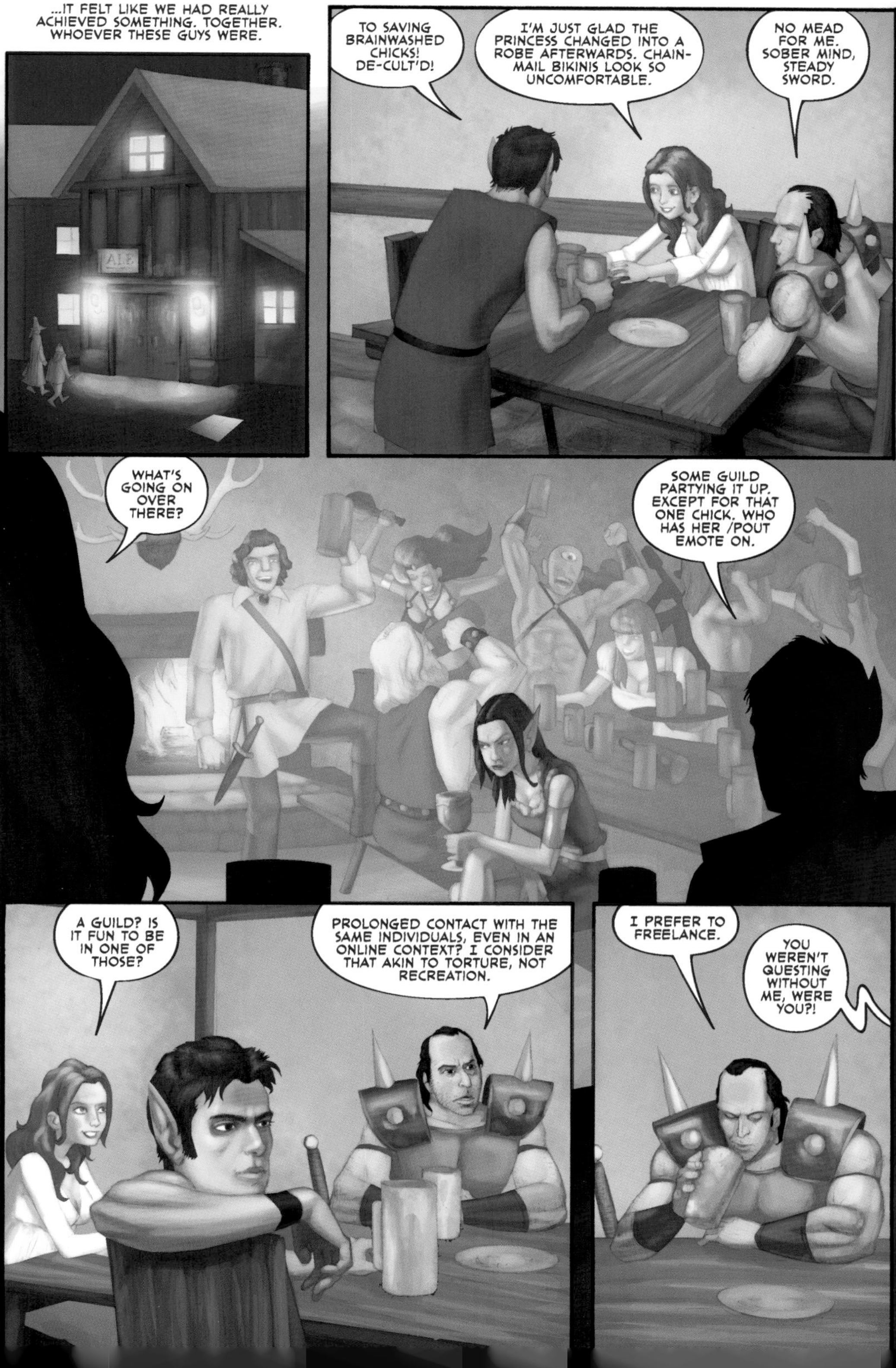
...IT FELT LIKE WE HAD REALLY ACHIEVED SOMETHING. TOGETHER. WHOEVER THESE GUYS WERE.
ALE
TO SAVING BRAINWASHED CHICKS! DE-CULT'D!
I'M JUST GLAD THE PRINCESS CHANGED INTO A ROBE AFTERWARDS. CHAIN-MAIL BIKINIS LOOK SO UNCOMFORTABLE.
NO MEAD FOR ME. SOBER MIND, STEADY SWORD.
WHAT'S GOING ON OVER THERE?
SOME GUILD PARTYING IT UP. EXCEPT FOR THAT ONE CHICK. WHO HAS HER /POUT EMOTE ON.
A GUILD? IS IT FUN TO BE IN ONE OF THOSE?
PROLONGED CONTACT WITH THE SAME INDIVIDUALS, EVEN IN AN ONLINE CONTEXT? I CONSIDER THAT AKIN TO TORTURE, NOT RECREATION.
I PREFER TO FREELANCE.
YOU WEREN'T QUESTING WITHOUT ME, WERE YOU?!

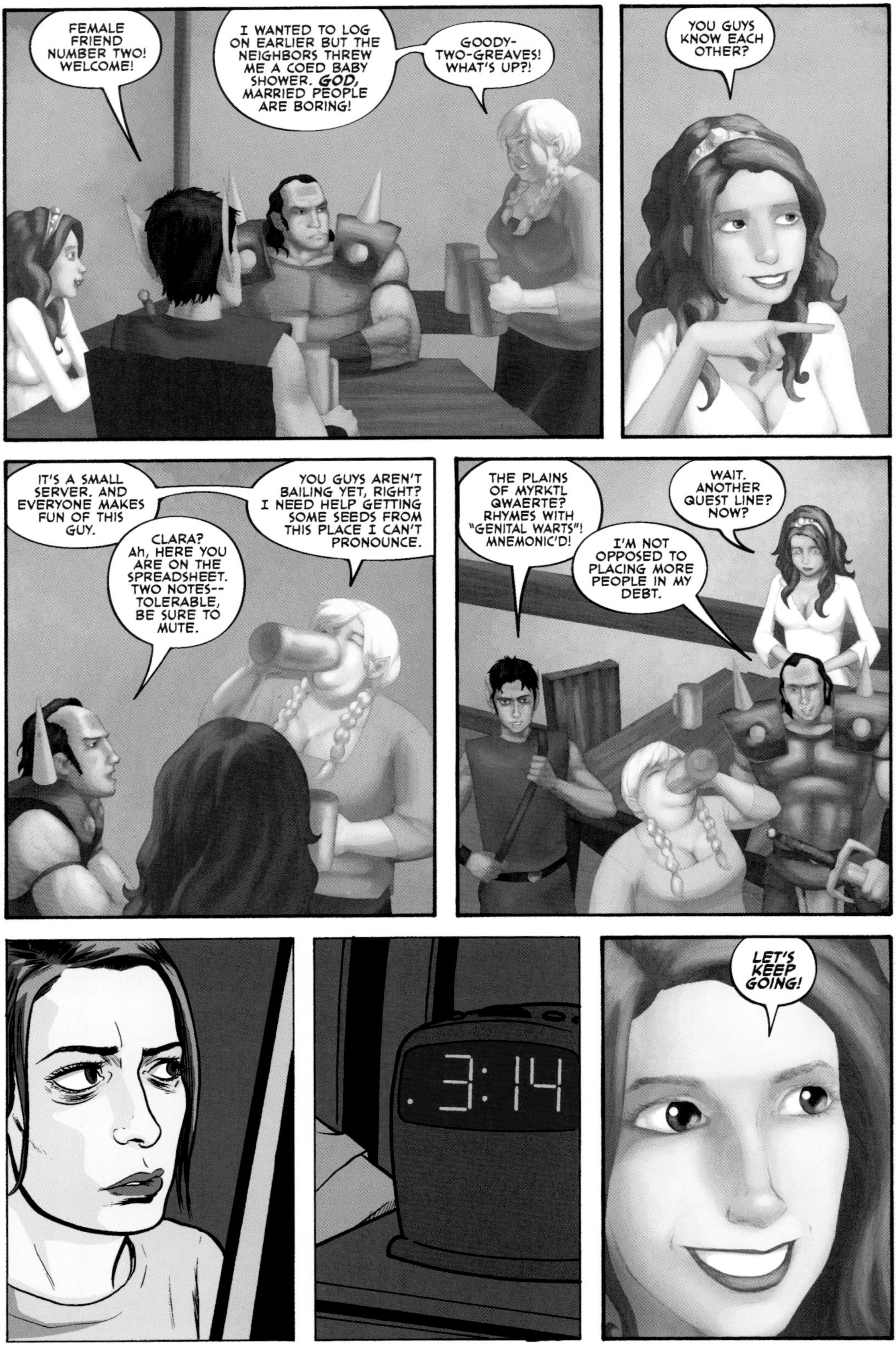
FEMALE FRIEND NUMBER TWO! WELCOME!
I WANTED TO LOG ON EARLIER BUT THE NEIGHBORS THREW ME A COED BABY SHOWER. GOD, MARRIED PEOPLE ARE BORING!
GOODY-TWO-GREAVES! WHAT'S UP?!
YOU GUYS KNOW EACH OTHER?
IT'S A SMALL SERVER. AND EVERYONE MAKES FUN OF THIS GUY.
CLARA? Ah, HERE YOU ARE ON THE SPREADSHEET. TWO NOTES-- TOLERABLE, BE SURE TO MUTE.
YOU GUYS AREN'T BAILING YET, RIGHT? I NEED HELP GETTING SOME SEEDS FROM THIS PLACE I CAN'T PRONOUNCE.
THE PLAINS OF MYRKTL QWAERTE? RHYMES WITH "GENITAL WARTS"! MNEMONIC'D!
I'M NOT OPPOSED TO PLACING MORE PEOPLE IN MY DEBT.
WAIT. ANOTHER QUEST LINE? NOW?
3:14
LET'S KEEP GOING!

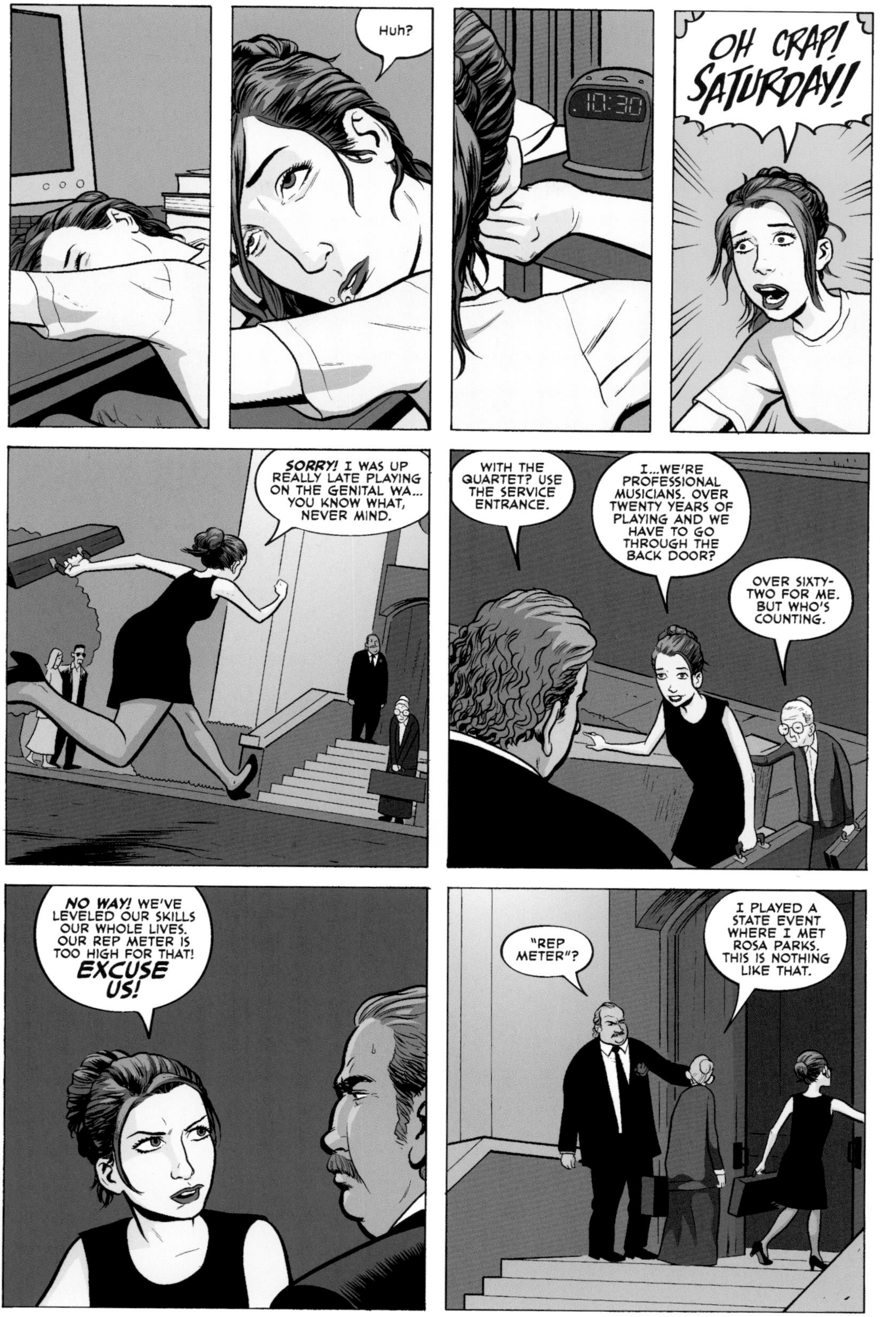
Huh?
OH CRAP! SATURDAY!
SORRY! I WAS UP REALLY LATE PLAYING ON THE GENITAL WA... YOU KNOW WHAT, NEVER MIND.
WITH THE QUARTET? USE THE SERVICE ENTRANCE.
I...WE'RE PROFESSIONAL MUSICIANS. OVER TWENTY YEARS OF PLAYING AND WE HAVE TO GO THROUGH THE BACK DOOR?
OVER SIXTY-TWO FOR ME. BUT WHO'S COUNTING.
NO WAY! WE'VE LEVELED OUR SKILLS OUR WHOLE LIVES. OUR REP METER IS TOO HIGH FOR THAT! EXCUSE US!
"REP METER"?
I PLAYED A STATE EVENT WHERE I MET ROSA PARKS. THIS IS NOTHING LIKE THAT.

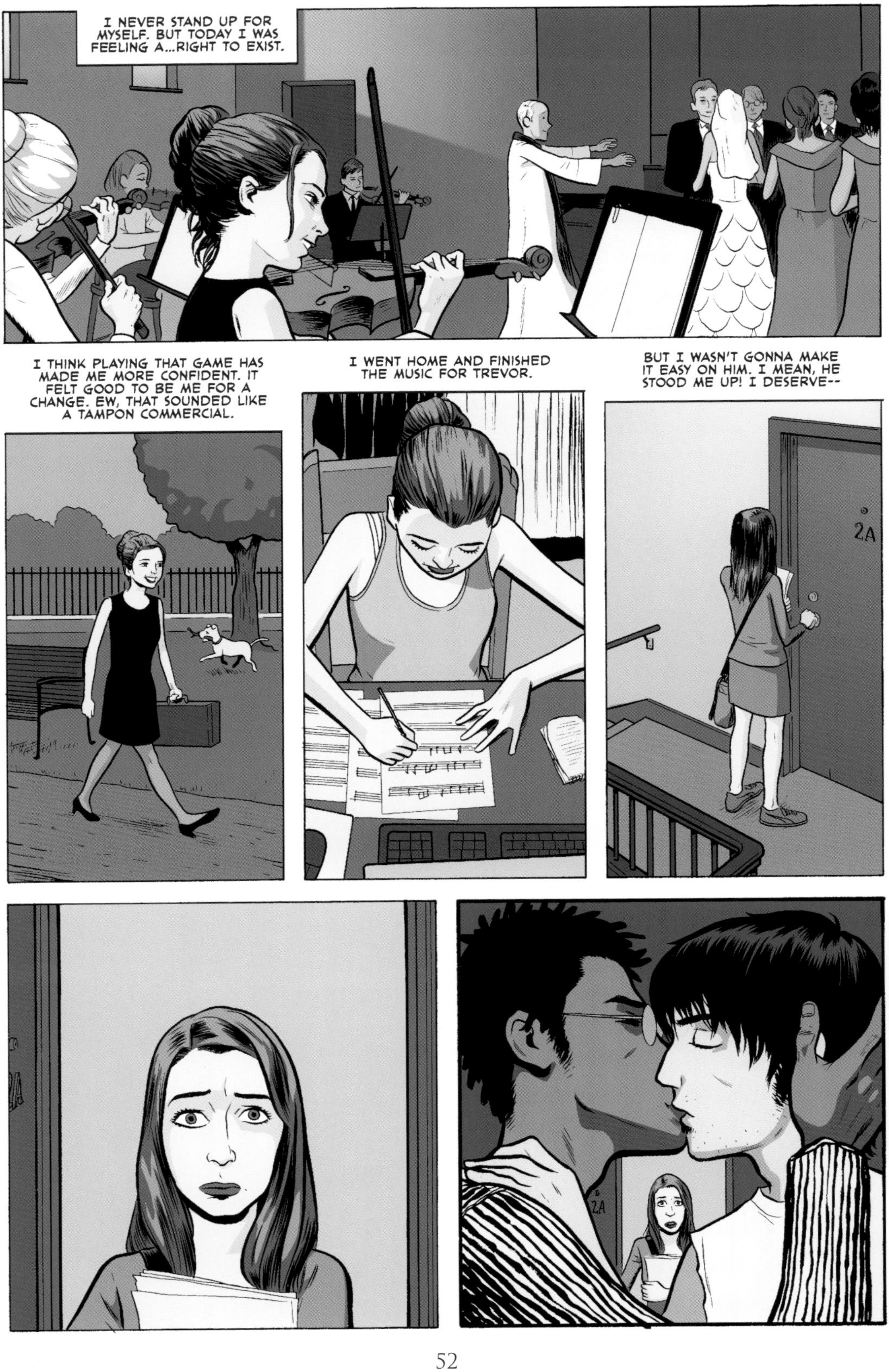

I NEVER STAND UP FOR MYSELF. BUT TODAY I WAS FEELING A...RIGHT TO EXIST.
I THINK PLAYING THAT GAME HAS MADE ME MORE CONFIDENT. IT FELT GOOD TO BE ME FOR A CHANGE. EW, THAT SOUNDED LIKE A TAMPON COMMERCIAL.
I WENT HOME AND FINISHED THE MUSIC FOR TREVOR.
BUT I WASN'T GONNA MAKE IT EASY ON HIM. I MEAN, HE STOOD ME UP! I DESERVE--
2A
2A

CHAPTER 3

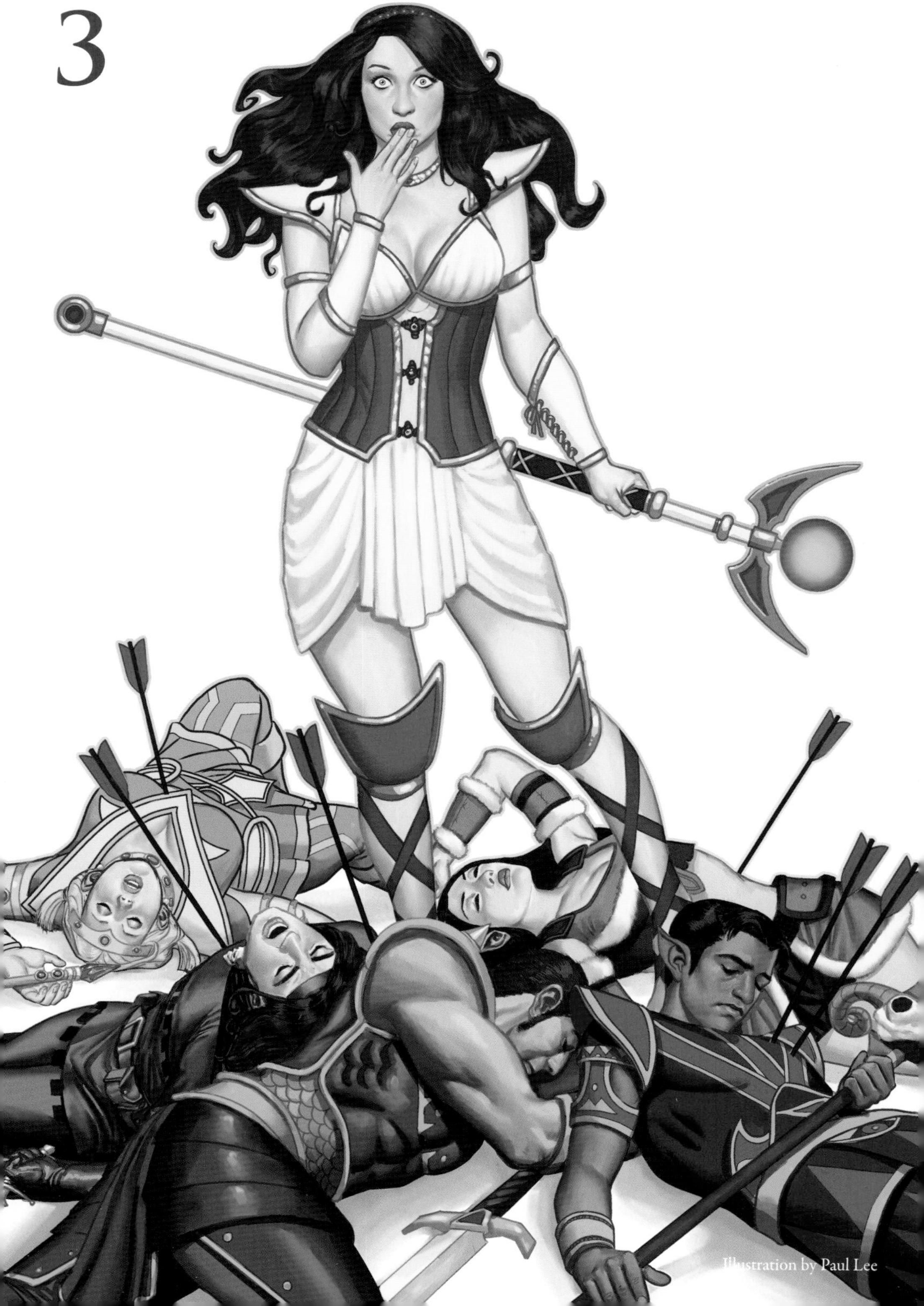

Illustration by Paul Lee

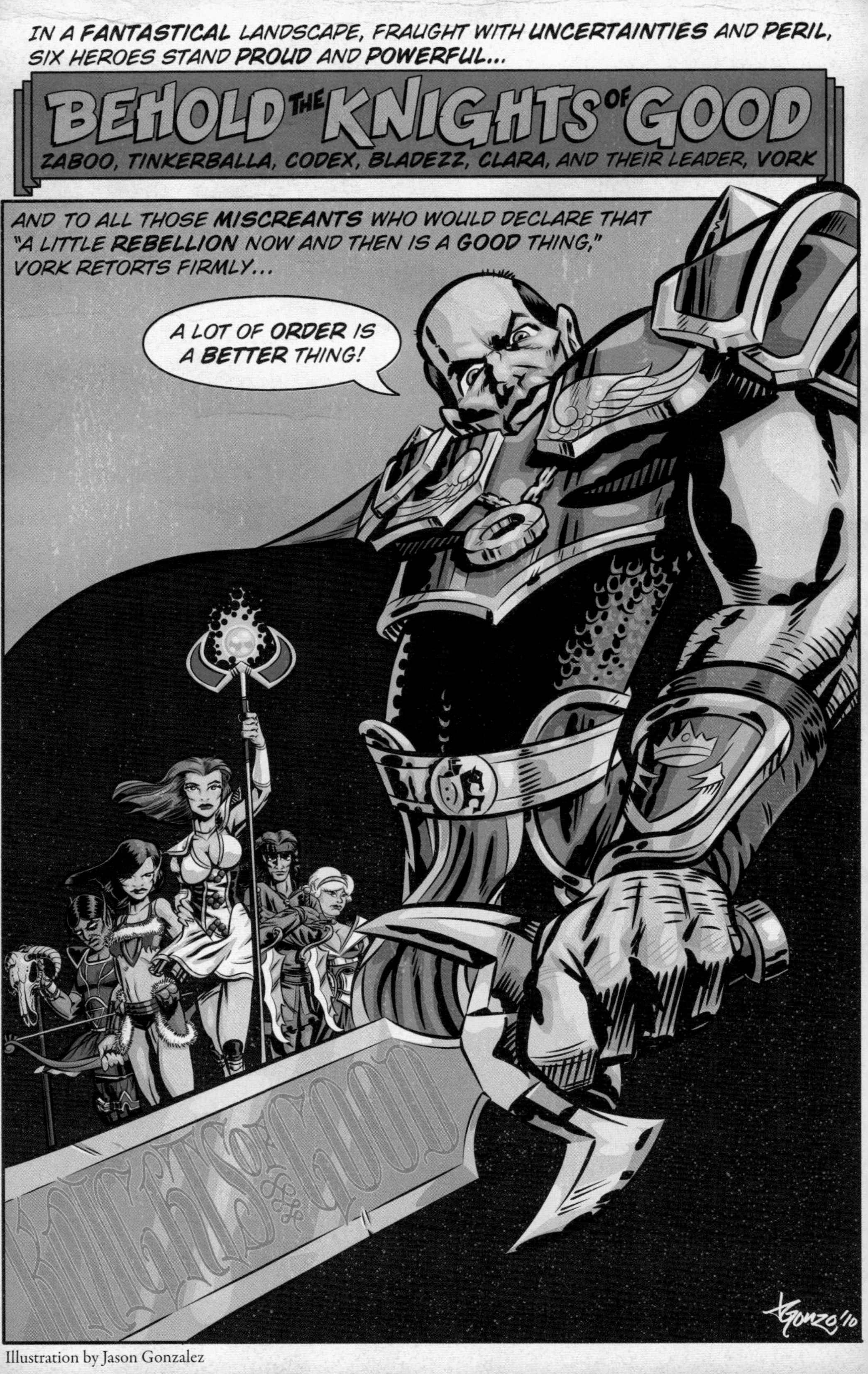
IN A FANTASTICAL LANDSCAPE, FRAUGHT WITH UNCERTAINTIES AND PERIL, SIX HEROES STAND PROUD AND POWERFUL...
BEHOLD THE KNIGHTS OF GOOD
ZABOO, TINKERBALLA, CODEX, BLADEZZ, CLARA, AND THEIR LEADER, VORK
AND TO ALL THOSE MISCREANTS WHO WOULD DECLARE THAT "A LITTLE REBELLION NOW AND THEN IS A GOOD THING," VORK RETORTS FIRMLY...
A LOT OF ORDER IS A BETTER THING!
KNIGHTS OF GOOD
Gonzo '10
Illustration by Jason Gonzalez

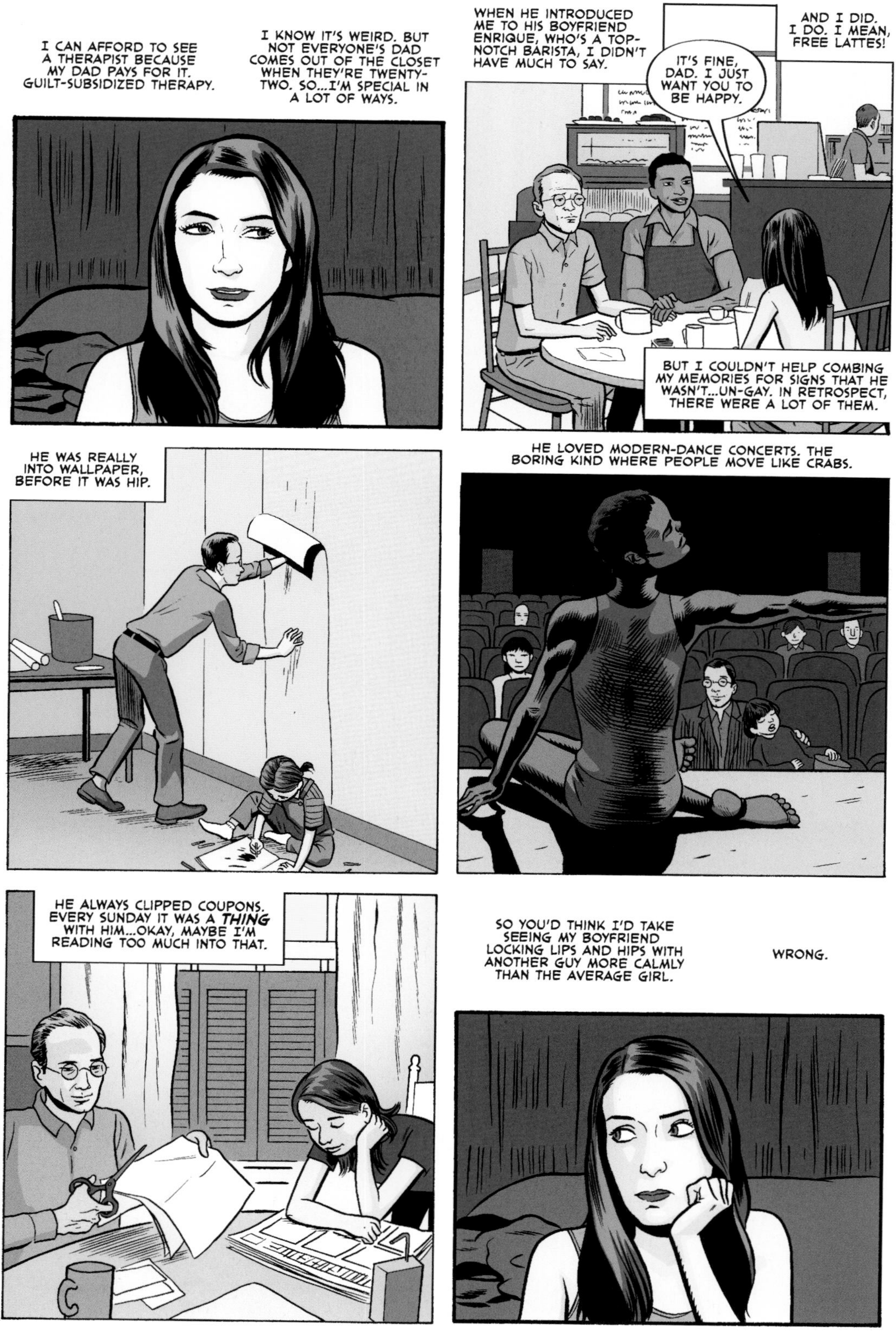
I CAN AFFORD TO SEE A THERAPIST BECAUSE MY DAD PAYS FOR IT. GUILT-SUBSIDIZED THERAPY.
I KNOW IT'S WEIRD. BUT NOT EVERYONE'S DAD COMES OUT OF THE CLOSET WHEN THEY'RE TWENTY-TWO. SO...I'M SPECIAL IN A LOT OF WAYS.
WHEN HE INTRODUCED ME TO HIS BOYFRIEND ENRIQUE, WHO'S A TOP-NOTCH BARISTA, I DIDN'T HAVE MUCH TO SAY.
IT'S FINE, DAD. I JUST WANT YOU TO BE HAPPY.
AND I DID. I DO. I MEAN, FREE LATTES!
BUT I COULDN'T HELP COMBING MY MEMORIES FOR SIGNS THAT HE WASN'T...UN-GAY. IN RETROSPECT, THERE WERE A LOT OF THEM.
HE WAS REALLY INTO WALLPAPER, BEFORE IT WAS HIP.
HE LOVED MODERN-DANCE CONCERTS. THE BORING KIND WHERE PEOPLE MOVE LIKE CRABS.
HE ALWAYS CLIPPED COUPONS. EVERY SUNDAY IT WAS A *THING* WITH HIM...OKAY, MAYBE I'M READING TOO MUCH INTO THAT.
SO YOU'D THINK I'D TAKE SEEING MY BOYFRIEND LOCKING LIPS AND HIPS WITH ANOTHER GUY MORE CALMLY THAN THE AVERAGE GIRL.
WRONG.

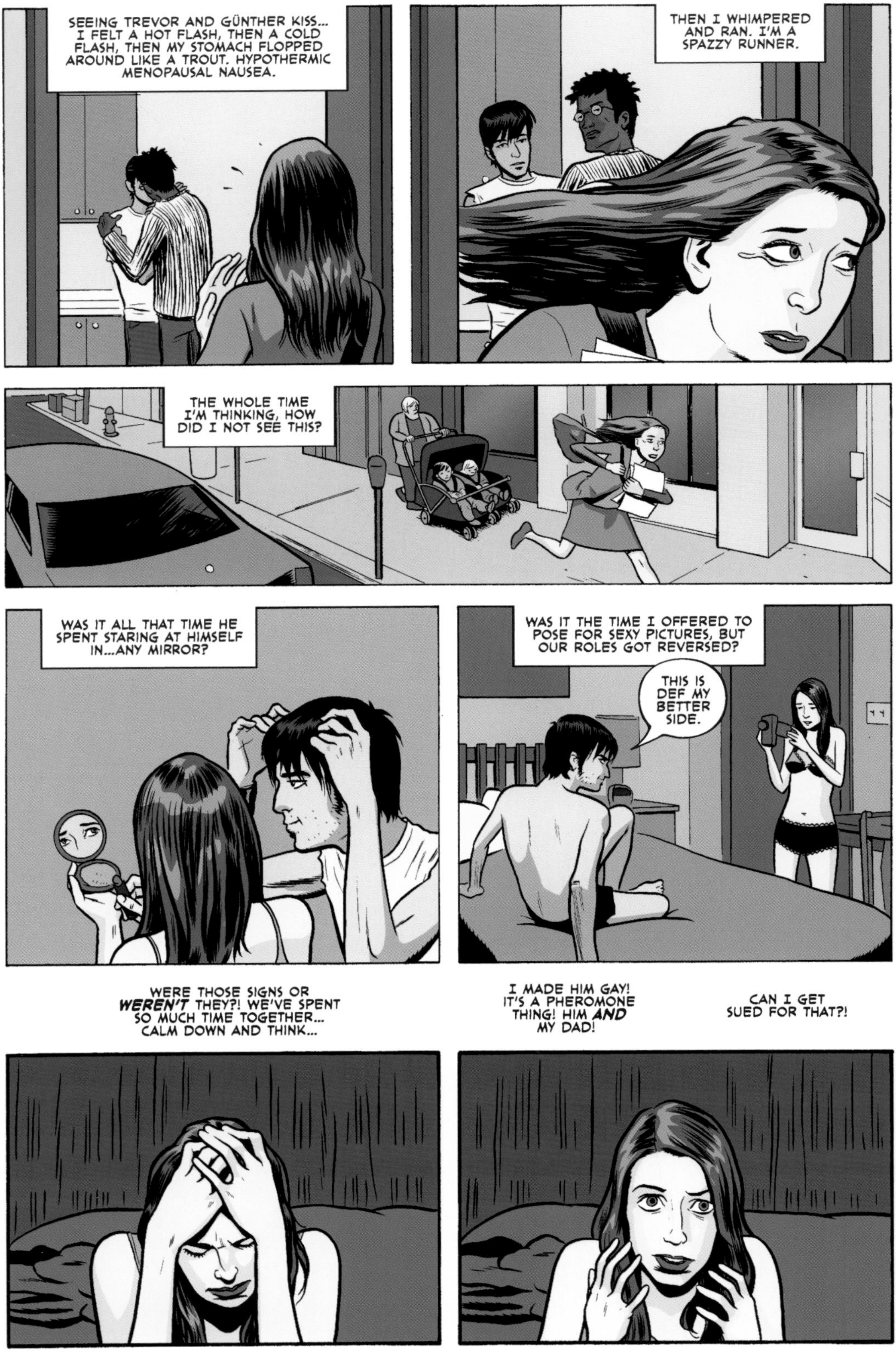
SEEING TREVOR AND GÜNTHER KISS... I FELT A HOT FLASH, THEN A COLD FLASH, THEN MY STOMACH FLOPPED AROUND LIKE A TROUT. HYPOTHERMIC MENOPAUSAL NAUSEA.
THEN I WHIMPERED AND RAN. I'M A SPAZZY RUNNER.
THE WHOLE TIME I'M THINKING, HOW DID I NOT SEE THIS?
WAS IT ALL THAT TIME HE SPENT STARING AT HIMSELF IN...ANY MIRROR?
WAS IT THE TIME I OFFERED TO POSE FOR SEXY PICTURES, BUT OUR ROLES GOT REVERSED?
THIS IS DEF MY BETTER SIDE.
WERE THOSE SIGNS OR WEREN'T THEY?! WE'VE SPENT SO MUCH TIME TOGETHER... CALM DOWN AND THINK...
I MADE HIM GAY! IT'S A PHEROMONE THING! HIM AND MY DAD!
CAN I GET SUED FOR THAT?!

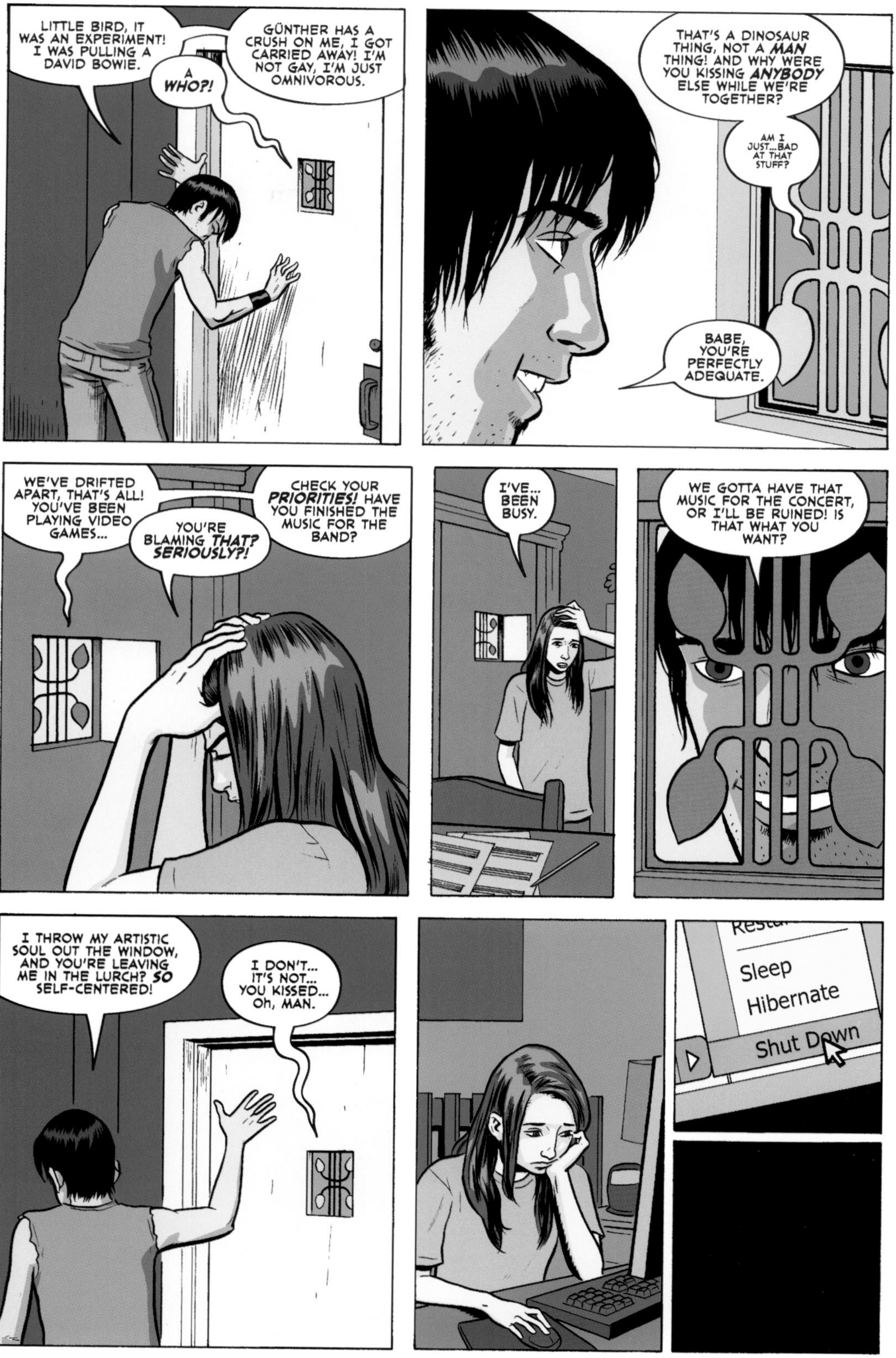

LITTLE BIRD, IT WAS AN EXPERIMENT! I WAS PULLING A DAVID BOWIE.
A WHO?!
GÜNTHER HAS A CRUSH ON ME, I GOT CARRIED AWAY! I'M NOT GAY, I'M JUST OMNIVOROUS.
THAT'S A DINOSAUR THING, NOT A MAN THING! AND WHY WERE YOU KISSING ANYBODY ELSE WHILE WE'RE TOGETHER?
AM I JUST...BAD AT THAT STUFF?
BABE, YOU'RE PERFECTLY ADEQUATE.
WE'VE DRIFTED APART, THAT'S ALL! YOU'VE BEEN PLAYING VIDEO GAMES...
YOU'RE BLAMING THAT? SERIOUSLY?!
CHECK YOUR PRIORITIES! HAVE YOU FINISHED THE MUSIC FOR THE BAND?
I'VE... BEEN BUSY.
WE GOTTA HAVE THAT MUSIC FOR THE CONCERT, OR I'LL BE RUINED! IS THAT WHAT YOU WANT?
I THROW MY ARTISTIC SOUL OUT THE WINDOW, AND YOU'RE LEAVING ME IN THE LURCH? SO SELF-CENTERED!
I DON'T... IT'S NOT... YOU KISSED... Oh, MAN.
Sleep
Hibernate
Shut Down

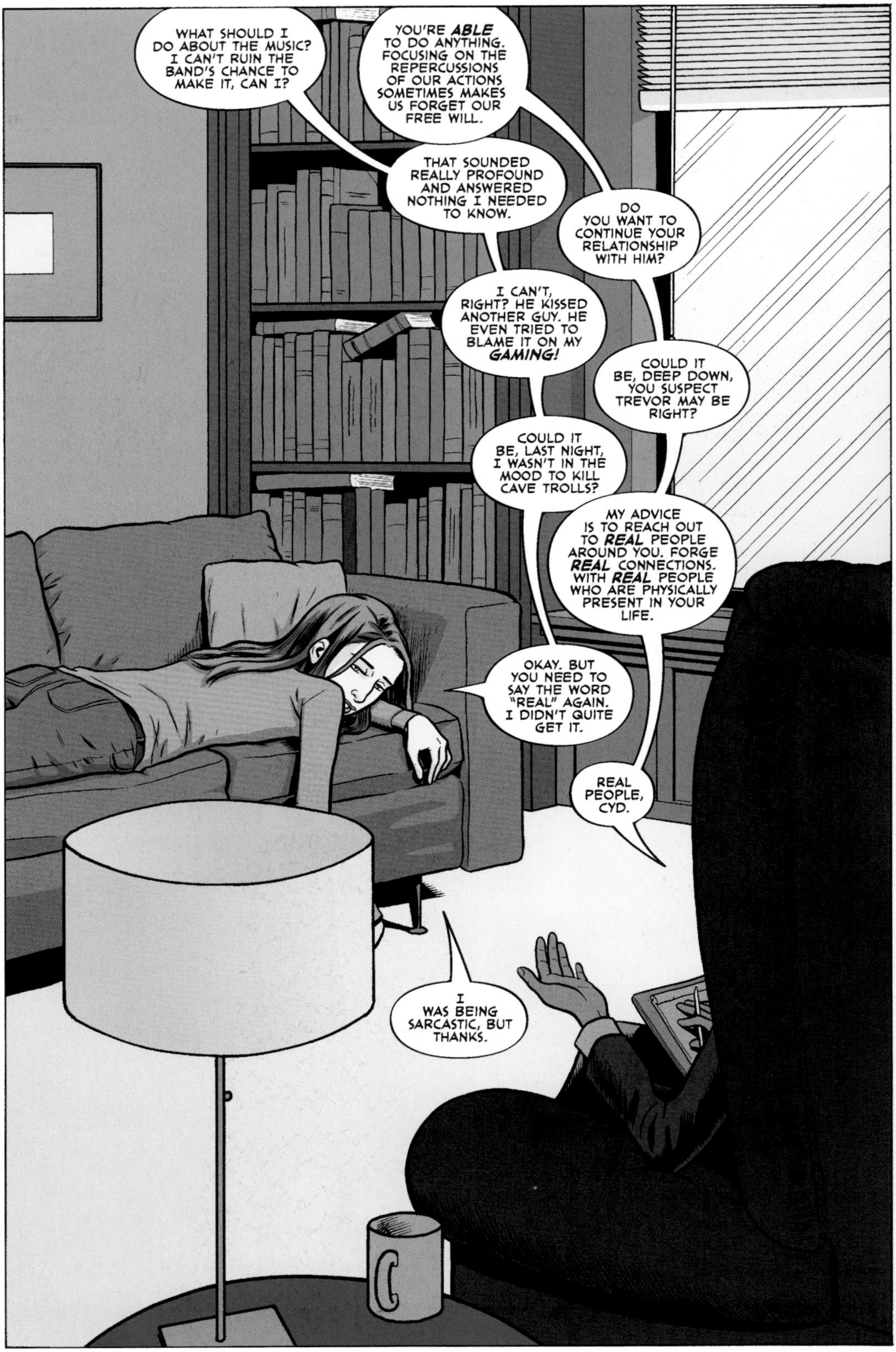
WHAT SHOULD I DO ABOUT THE MUSIC? I CAN'T RUIN THE BAND'S CHANCE TO MAKE IT, CAN I?
YOU'RE *ABLE* TO DO ANYTHING. FOCUSING ON THE REPERCUSSIONS OF OUR ACTIONS SOMETIMES MAKES US FORGET OUR FREE WILL.
THAT SOUNDED REALLY PROFOUND AND ANSWERED NOTHING I NEEDED TO KNOW.
DO YOU WANT TO CONTINUE YOUR RELATIONSHIP WITH HIM?
I CAN'T, RIGHT? HE KISSED ANOTHER GUY. HE EVEN TRIED TO BLAME IT ON MY *GAMING!*
COULD IT BE, DEEP DOWN, YOU SUSPECT TREVOR MAY BE RIGHT?
COULD IT BE, LAST NIGHT, I WASN'T IN THE MOOD TO KILL CAVE TROLLS?
MY ADVICE IS TO REACH OUT TO *REAL* PEOPLE AROUND YOU. FORGE *REAL* CONNECTIONS. WITH *REAL* PEOPLE WHO ARE PHYSICALLY PRESENT IN YOUR LIFE.
OKAY. BUT YOU NEED TO SAY THE WORD "REAL" AGAIN. I DIDN'T QUITE GET IT.
REAL PEOPLE, CYD.
I WAS BEING SARCASTIC, BUT THANKS.

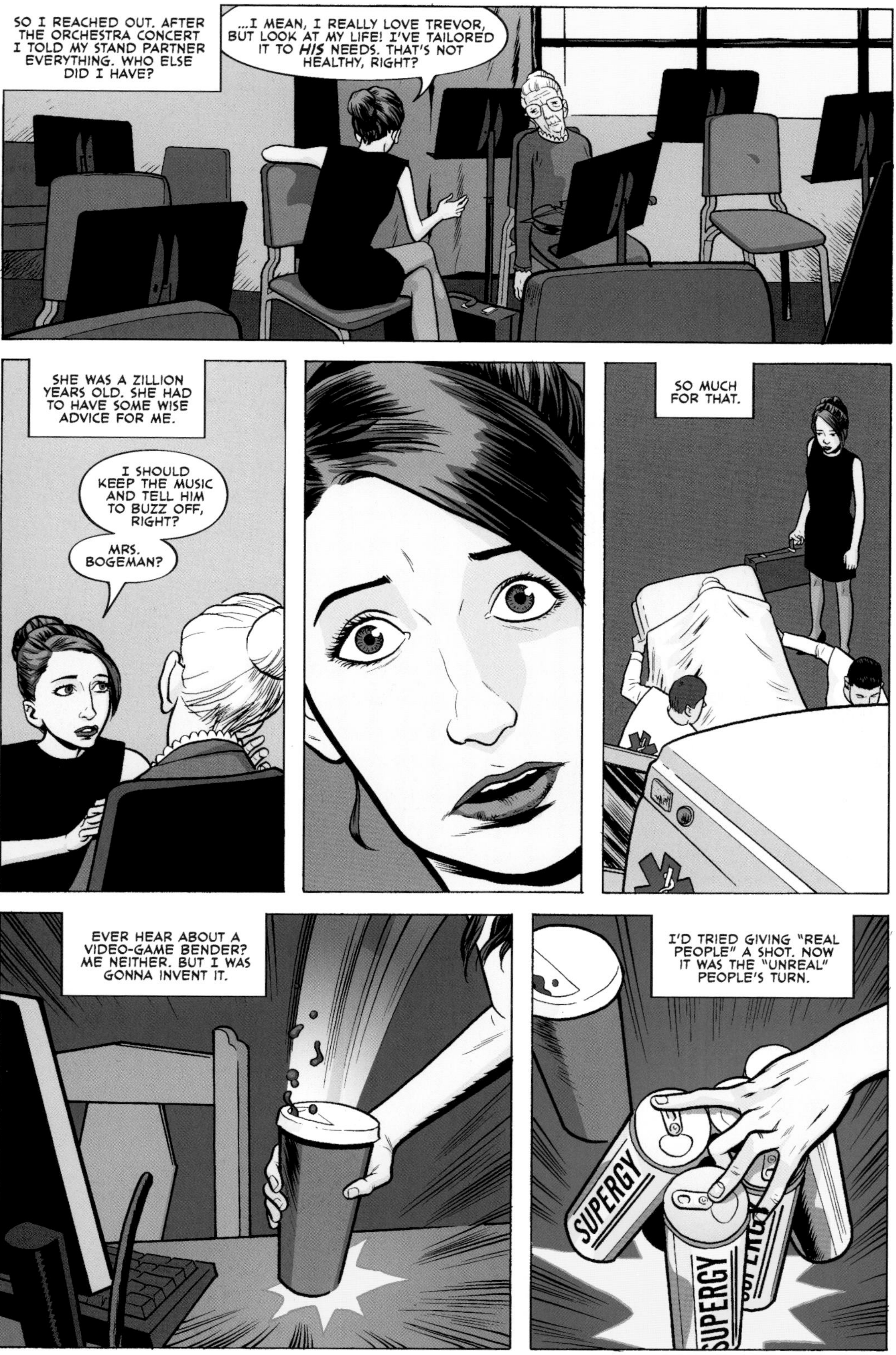

SO I REACHED OUT. AFTER THE ORCHESTRA CONCERT I TOLD MY STAND PARTNER EVERYTHING. WHO ELSE DID I HAVE?
...I MEAN, I REALLY LOVE TREVOR, BUT LOOK AT MY LIFE! I'VE TAILORED IT TO HIS NEEDS. THAT'S NOT HEALTHY, RIGHT?
SHE WAS A ZILLION YEARS OLD. SHE HAD TO HAVE SOME WISE ADVICE FOR ME.
I SHOULD KEEP THE MUSIC AND TELL HIM TO BUZZ OFF, RIGHT?
MRS. BOGEMAN?
SO MUCH FOR THAT.
EVER HEAR ABOUT A VIDEO-GAME BENDER? ME NEITHER. BUT I WAS GONNA INVENT IT.
I'D TRIED GIVING "REAL PEOPLE" A SHOT. NOW IT WAS THE "UNREAL" PEOPLE'S TURN.
SUPERGY
SUPERGY
SUPERGY

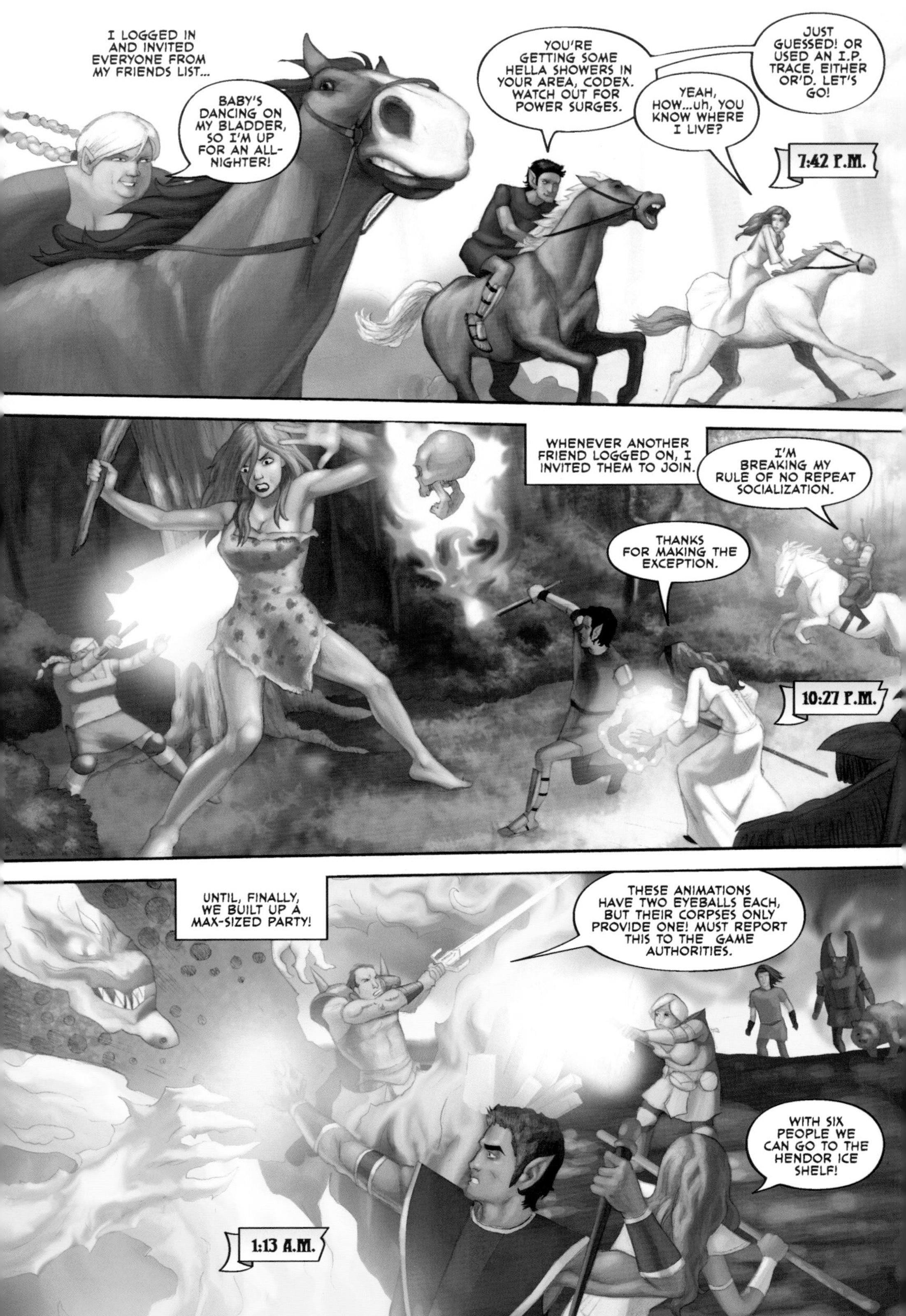
I LOGGED IN AND INVITED EVERYONE FROM MY FRIENDS LIST...
BABY'S DANCING ON MY BLADDER, SO I'M UP FOR AN ALL-NIGHTER!
YOU'RE GETTING SOME HELLA SHOWERS IN YOUR AREA, CODEX. WATCH OUT FOR POWER SURGES.
YEAH, HOW...uh, YOU KNOW WHERE I LIVE?
JUST GUESSED! OR USED AN I.P. TRACE, EITHER OR'D. LET'S GO!
7:42 P.M.
WHENEVER ANOTHER FRIEND LOGGED ON, I INVITED THEM TO JOIN.
I'M BREAKING MY RULE OF NO REPEAT SOCIALIZATION.
THANKS FOR MAKING THE EXCEPTION.
10:27 P.M.
UNTIL, FINALLY, WE BUILT UP A MAX-SIZED PARTY!
THESE ANIMATIONS HAVE TWO EYEBALLS EACH, BUT THEIR CORPSES ONLY PROVIDE ONE! MUST REPORT THIS TO THE GAME AUTHORITIES.
WITH SIX PEOPLE WE CAN GO TO THE HENDOR ICE SHELF!
1:13 A.M.

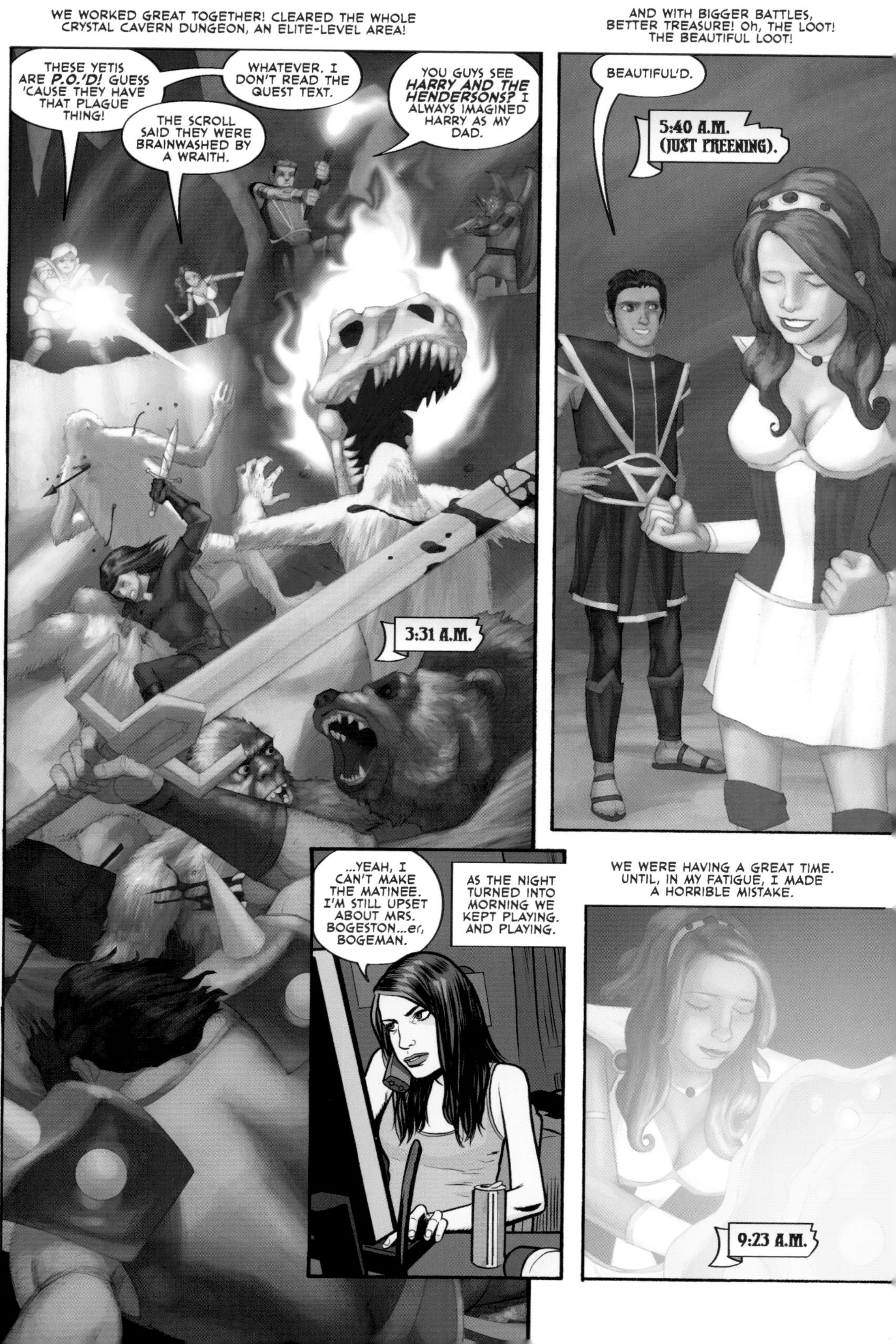
WE WORKED GREAT TOGETHER! CLEARED THE WHOLE CRYSTAL CAVERN DUNGEON, AN ELITE-LEVEL AREA!
THESE YETIS ARE P.O.'D! GUESS 'CAUSE THEY HAVE THAT PLAGUE THING!
THE SCROLL SAID THEY WERE BRAINWASHED BY A WRAITH.
WHATEVER. I DON'T READ THE QUEST TEXT.
YOU GUYS SEE HARRY AND THE HENDERSONS? I ALWAYS IMAGINED HARRY AS MY DAD.
3:31 A.M.
AND WITH BIGGER BATTLES, BETTER TREASURE! Oh, THE LOOT! THE BEAUTIFUL LOOT!
BEAUTIFUL'D.
5:40 A.M. (JUST PREENING).
...YEAH, I CAN'T MAKE THE MATINEE. I'M STILL UPSET ABOUT MRS. BOGESTON...er, BOGEMAN.
AS THE NIGHT TURNED INTO MORNING WE KEPT PLAYING. AND PLAYING.
WE WERE HAVING A GREAT TIME. UNTIL, IN MY FATIGUE, I MADE A HORRIBLE MISTAKE.
9:23 A.M.

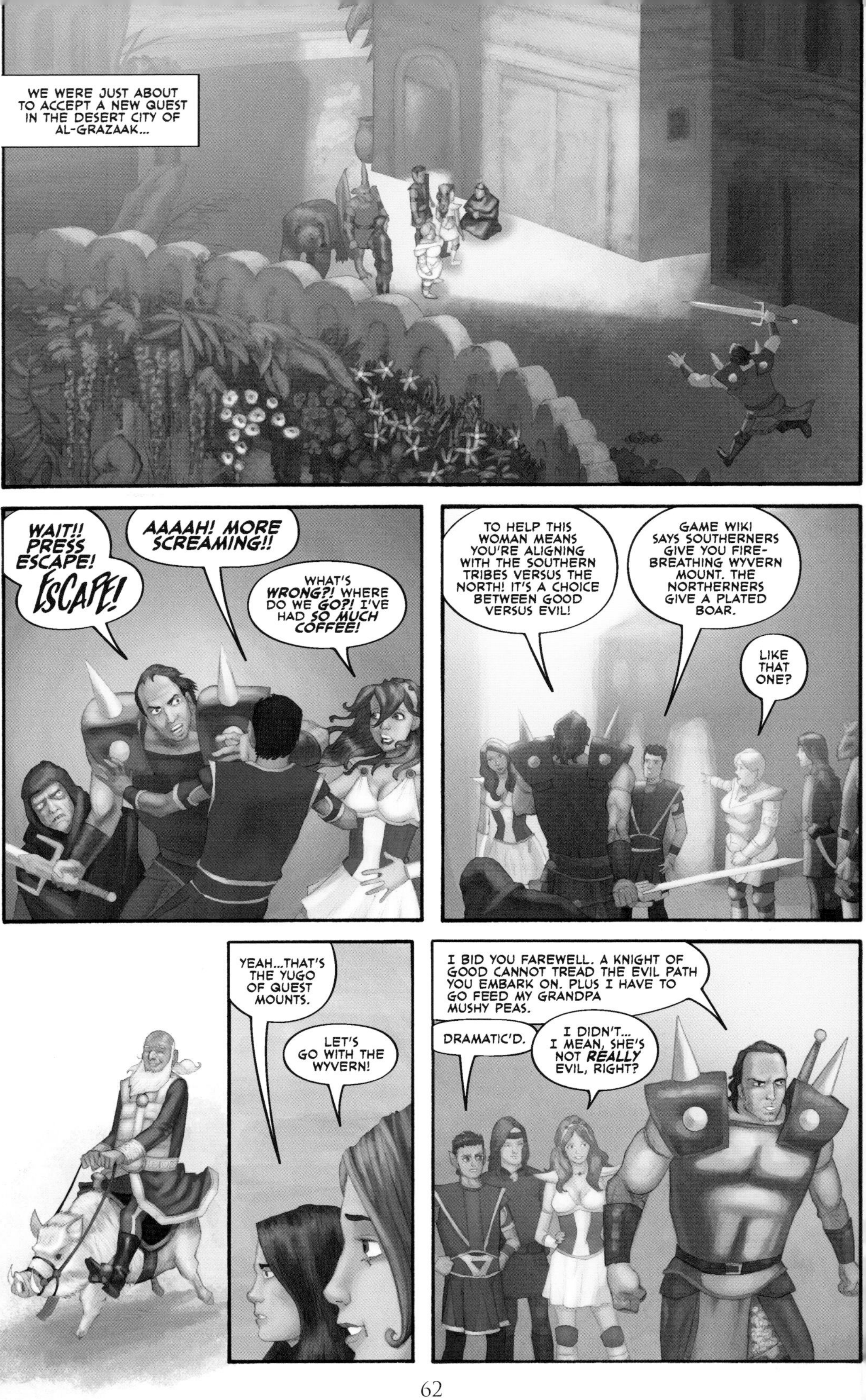
WE WERE JUST ABOUT TO ACCEPT A NEW QUEST IN THE DESERT CITY OF AL-GRAZAAK...
WAIT!! PRESS ESCAPE! ESCAPE!
AAAAH! MORE SCREAMING!!
WHAT'S WRONG?! WHERE DO WE GO?! I'VE HAD SO MUCH COFFEE!
TO HELP THIS WOMAN MEANS YOU'RE ALIGNING WITH THE SOUTHERN TRIBES VERSUS THE NORTH! IT'S A CHOICE BETWEEN GOOD VERSUS EVIL!
GAME WIKI SAYS SOUTHERNERS GIVE YOU FIRE-BREATHING WYVERN MOUNT. THE NORTHERNERS GIVE A PLATED BOAR.
LIKE THAT ONE?
YEAH...THAT'S THE YUGO OF QUEST MOUNTS.
LET'S GO WITH THE WYVERN!
I BID YOU FAREWELL. A KNIGHT OF GOOD CANNOT TREAD THE EVIL PATH YOU EMBARK ON. PLUS I HAVE TO GO FEED MY GRANDPA MUSHY PEAS.
DRAMATIC'D.
I DIDN'T... I MEAN, SHE'S NOT REALLY EVIL, RIGHT?

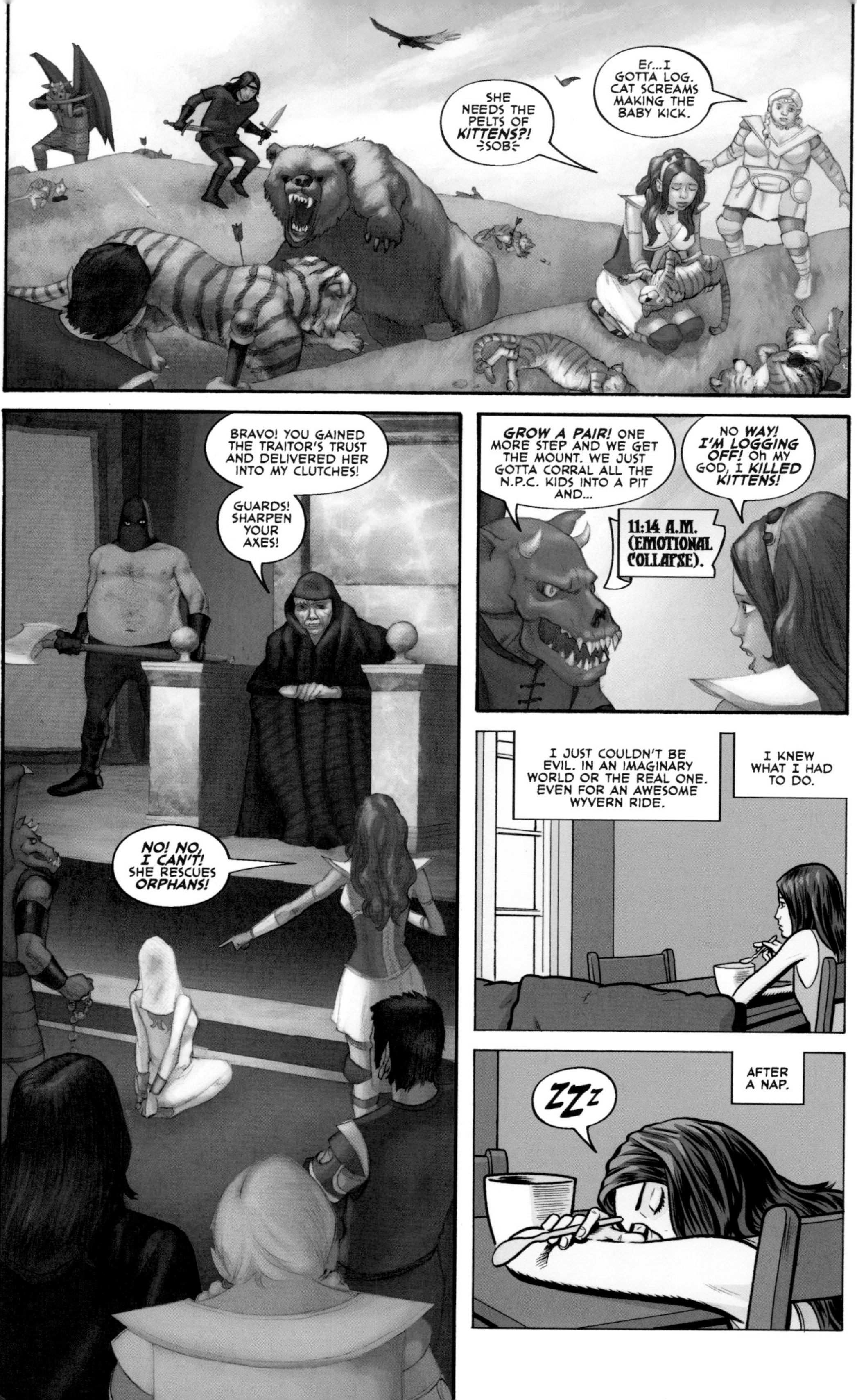
SHE NEEDS THE PELTS OF KITTENS?! SOB
Er...I GOTTA LOG. CAT SCREAMS MAKING THE BABY KICK.
BRAVO! YOU GAINED THE TRAITOR'S TRUST AND DELIVERED HER INTO MY CLUTCHES!
GUARDS! SHARPEN YOUR AXES!
NO! NO, I CAN'T! SHE RESCUES ORPHANS!
GROW A PAIR! ONE MORE STEP AND WE GET THE MOUNT. WE JUST GOTTA CORRAL ALL THE N.P.C. KIDS INTO A PIT AND...
NO WAY! I'M LOGGING OFF! Oh MY GOD, I KILLED KITTENS!
11:14 A.M. (EMOTIONAL COLLAPSE).
I JUST COULDN'T BE EVIL. IN AN IMAGINARY WORLD OR THE REAL ONE. EVEN FOR AN AWESOME WYVERN RIDE.
I KNEW WHAT I HAD TO DO.
ZZz
AFTER A NAP.

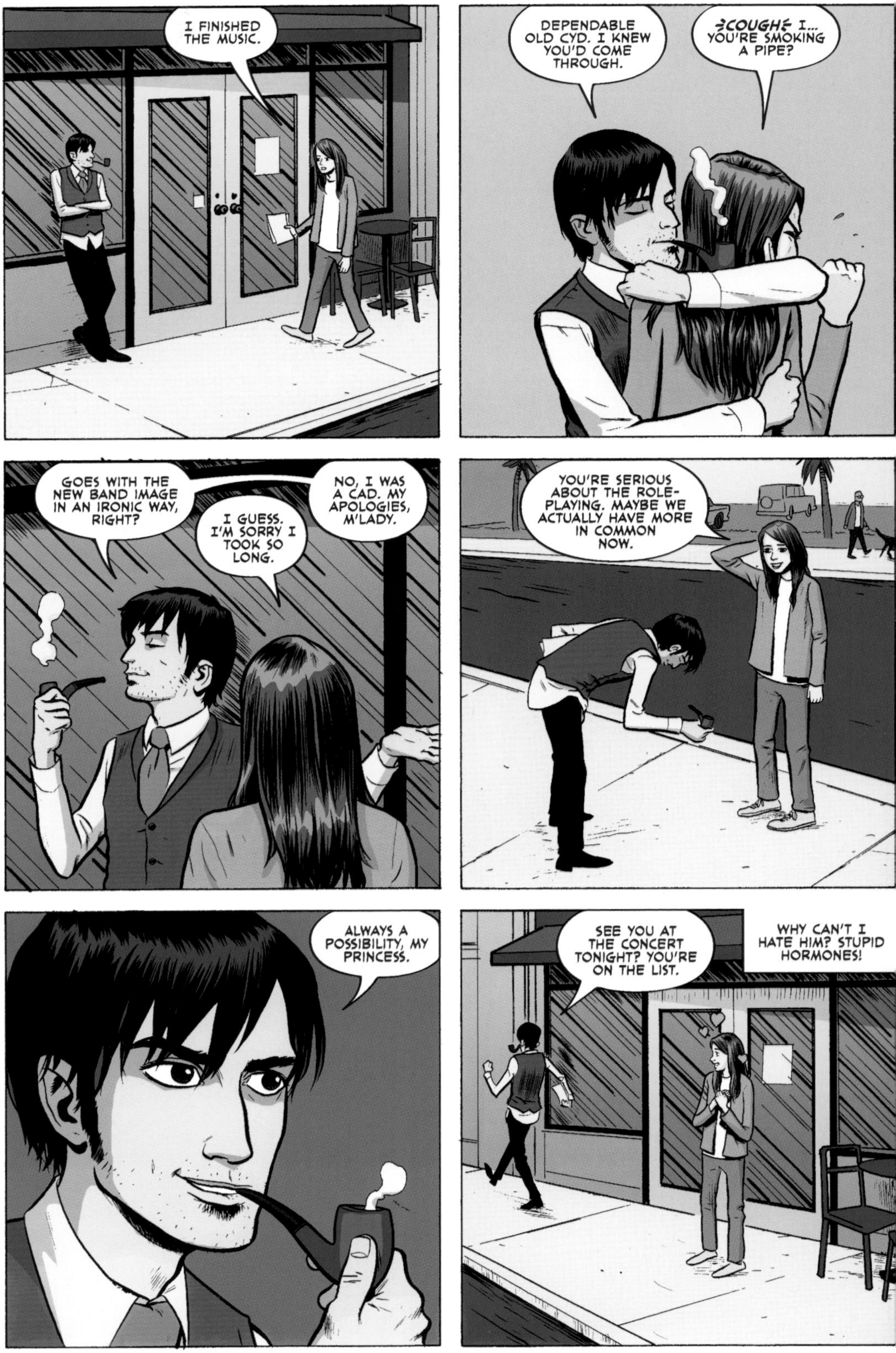
I FINISHED THE MUSIC.
DEPENDABLE OLD CYD. I KNEW YOU'D COME THROUGH.
COUGH I... YOU'RE SMOKING A PIPE?
GOES WITH THE NEW BAND IMAGE IN AN IRONIC WAY, RIGHT?
I GUESS. I'M SORRY I TOOK SO LONG.
NO, I WAS A CAD. MY APOLOGIES, M'LADY.
YOU'RE SERIOUS ABOUT THE ROLE-PLAYING. MAYBE WE ACTUALLY HAVE MORE IN COMMON NOW.
ALWAYS A POSSIBILITY, MY PRINCESS.
SEE YOU AT THE CONCERT TONIGHT? YOU'RE ON THE LIST.
WHY CAN'T I HATE HIM? STUPID HORMONES!

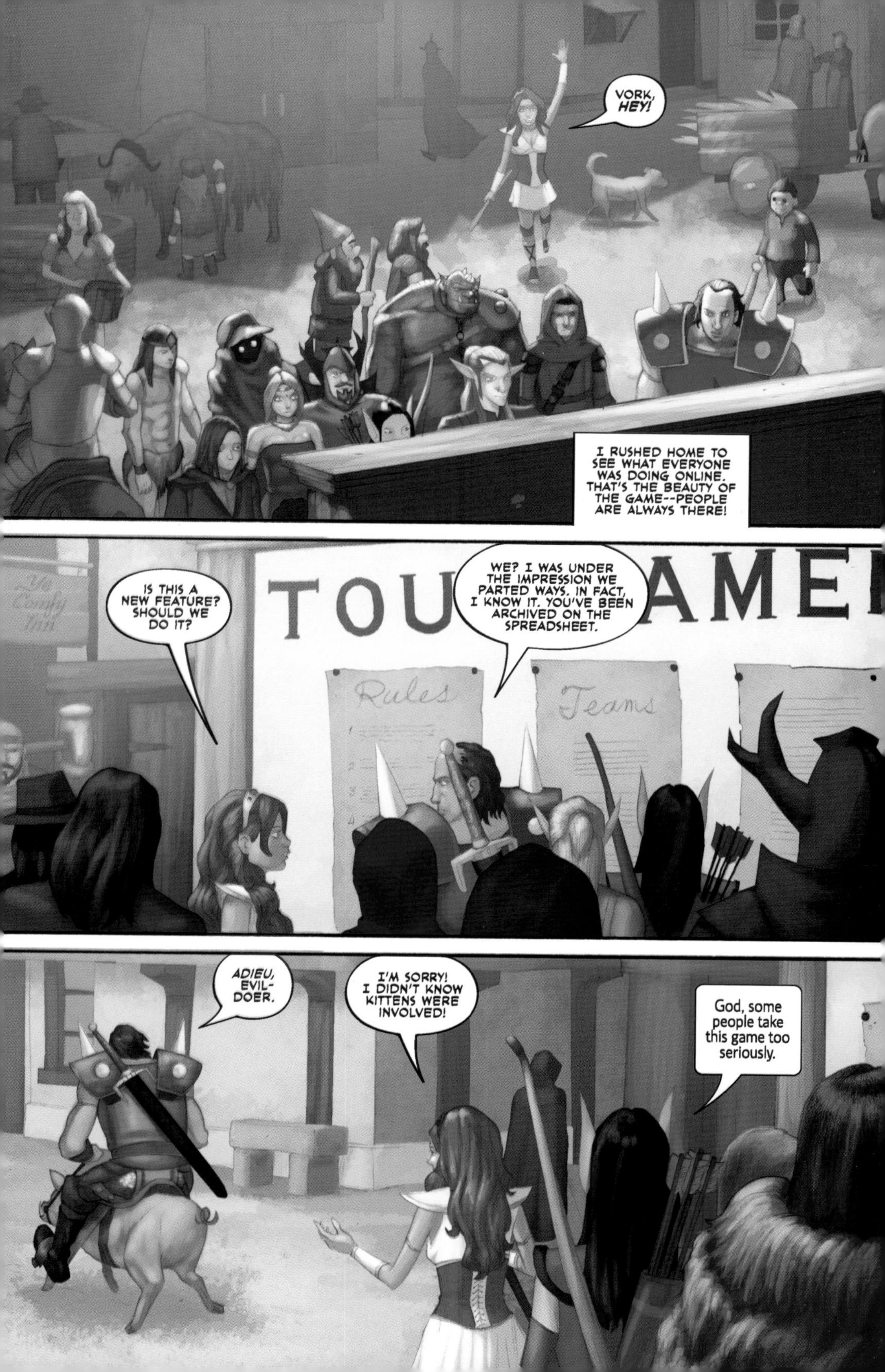

VORK, HEY!
I RUSHED HOME TO SEE WHAT EVERYONE WAS DOING ONLINE. THAT'S THE BEAUTY OF THE GAME--PEOPLE ARE ALWAYS THERE!
Ye Comfy Inn
TOU AME
Rules
Teams
IS THIS A NEW FEATURE? SHOULD WE DO IT?
WE? I WAS UNDER THE IMPRESSION WE PARTED WAYS. IN FACT, I KNOW IT. YOU'VE BEEN ARCHIVED ON THE SPREADSHEET.
ADIEU, EVIL-DOER.
I'M SORRY! I DIDN'T KNOW KITTENS WERE INVOLVED!
God, some people take this game too seriously.

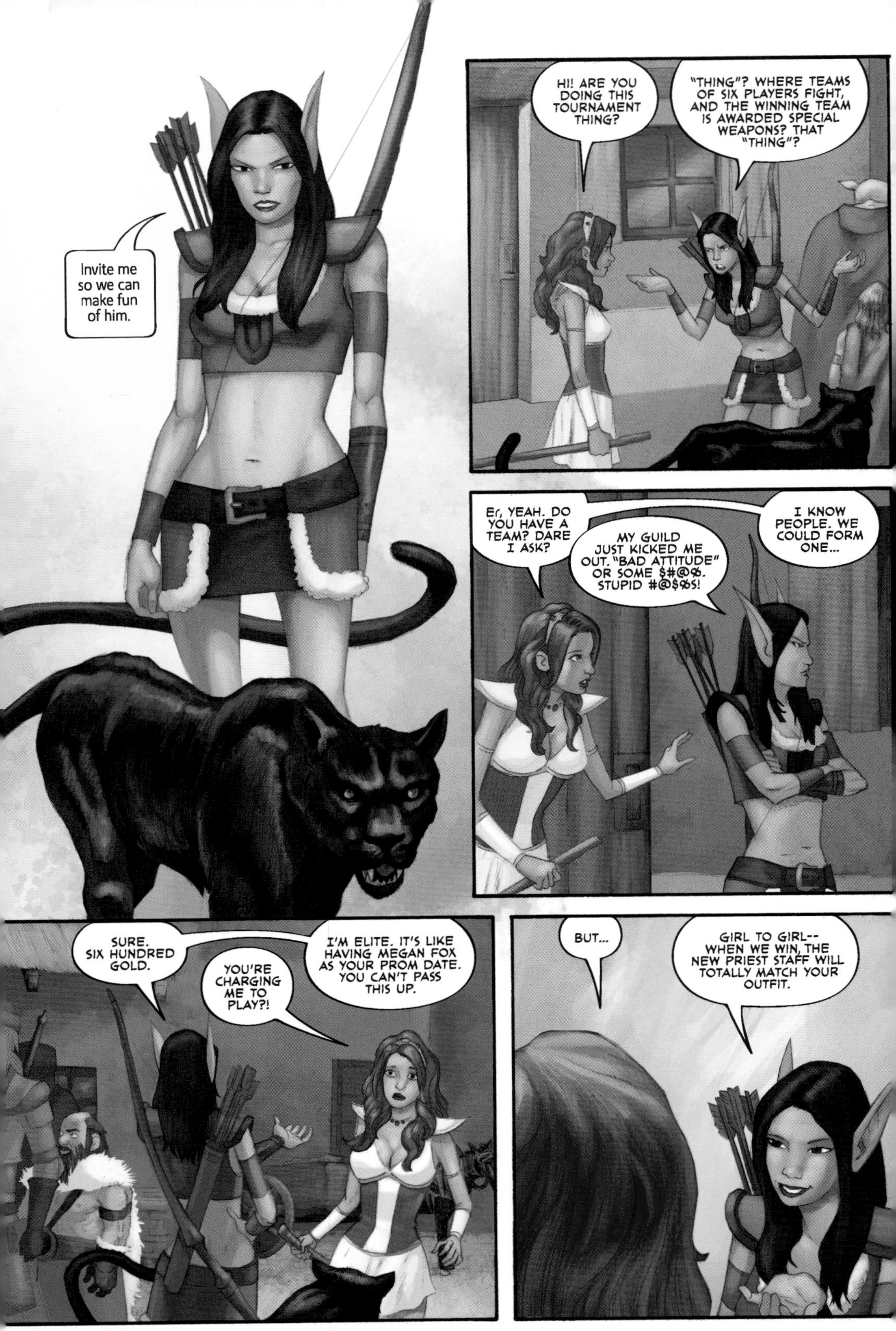
Invite me so we can make fun of him.
HI! ARE YOU DOING THIS TOURNAMENT THING?
"THING"? WHERE TEAMS OF SIX PLAYERS FIGHT, AND THE WINNING TEAM IS AWARDED SPECIAL WEAPONS? THAT "THING"?
Er, YEAH. DO YOU HAVE A TEAM? DARE I ASK?
MY GUILD JUST KICKED ME OUT. "BAD ATTITUDE" OR SOME $#@%. STUPID #@$%S!
I KNOW PEOPLE. WE COULD FORM ONE...
SURE. SIX HUNDRED GOLD.
YOU'RE CHARGING ME TO PLAY?!
I'M ELITE. IT'S LIKE HAVING MEGAN FOX AS YOUR PROM DATE. YOU CAN'T PASS THIS UP.
BUT...
GIRL TO GIRL-- WHEN WE WIN, THE NEW PRIEST STAFF WILL TOTALLY MATCH YOUR OUTFIT.

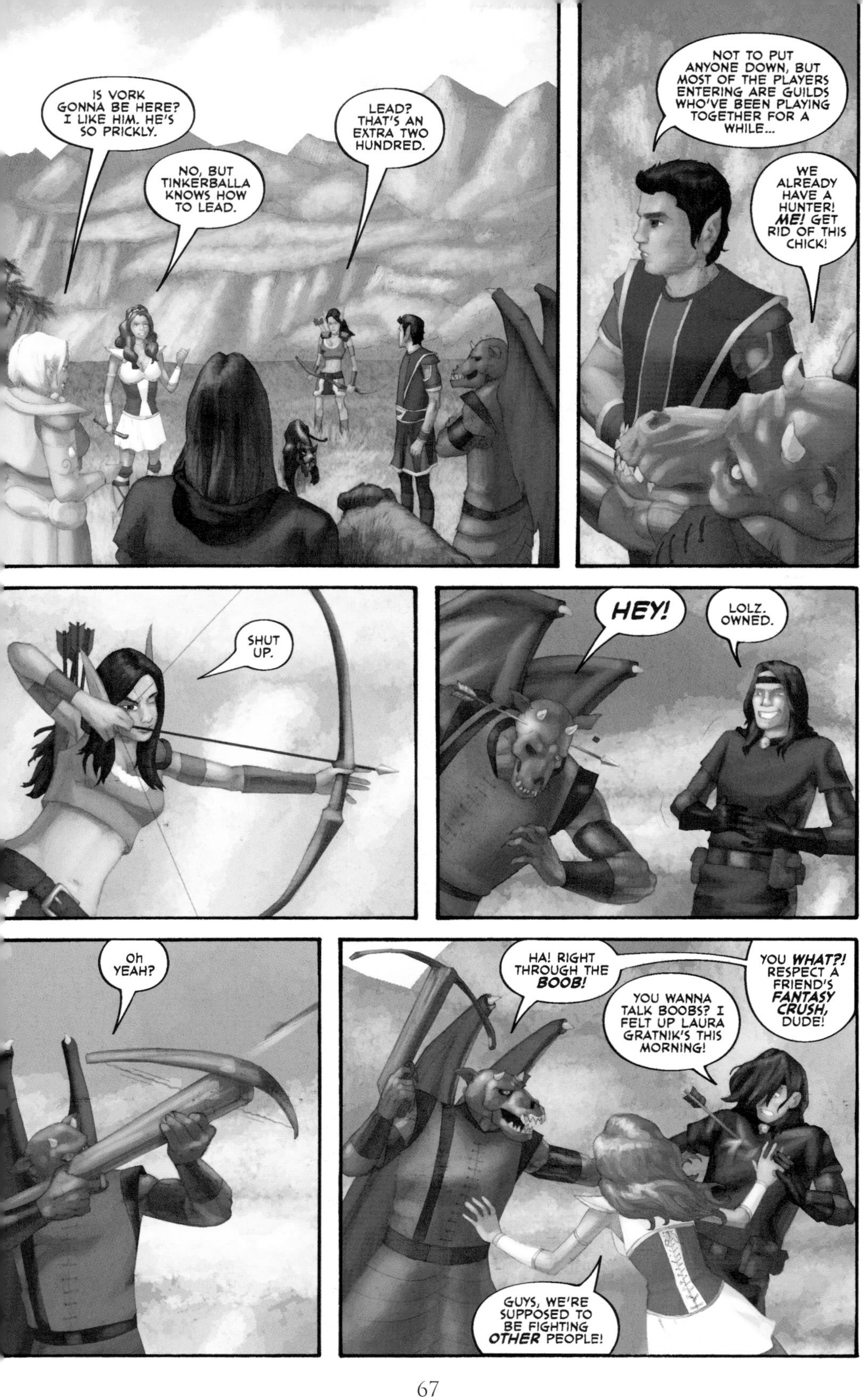
IS VORK GONNA BE HERE? I LIKE HIM. HE'S SO PRICKLY.
NO, BUT TINKERBALLA KNOWS HOW TO LEAD.
LEAD? THAT'S AN EXTRA TWO HUNDRED.
NOT TO PUT ANYONE DOWN, BUT MOST OF THE PLAYERS ENTERING ARE GUILDS WHO'VE BEEN PLAYING TOGETHER FOR A WHILE...
WE ALREADY HAVE A HUNTER! ME! GET RID OF THIS CHICK!
SHUT UP.
HEY!
LOLZ. OWNED.
Oh YEAH?
HA! RIGHT THROUGH THE BOOB!
YOU WANNA TALK BOOBS? I FELT UP LAURA GRATNIK'S THIS MORNING!
YOU WHAT?! RESPECT A FRIEND'S FANTASY CRUSH, DUDE!
GUYS, WE'RE SUPPOSED TO BE FIGHTING OTHER PEOPLE!

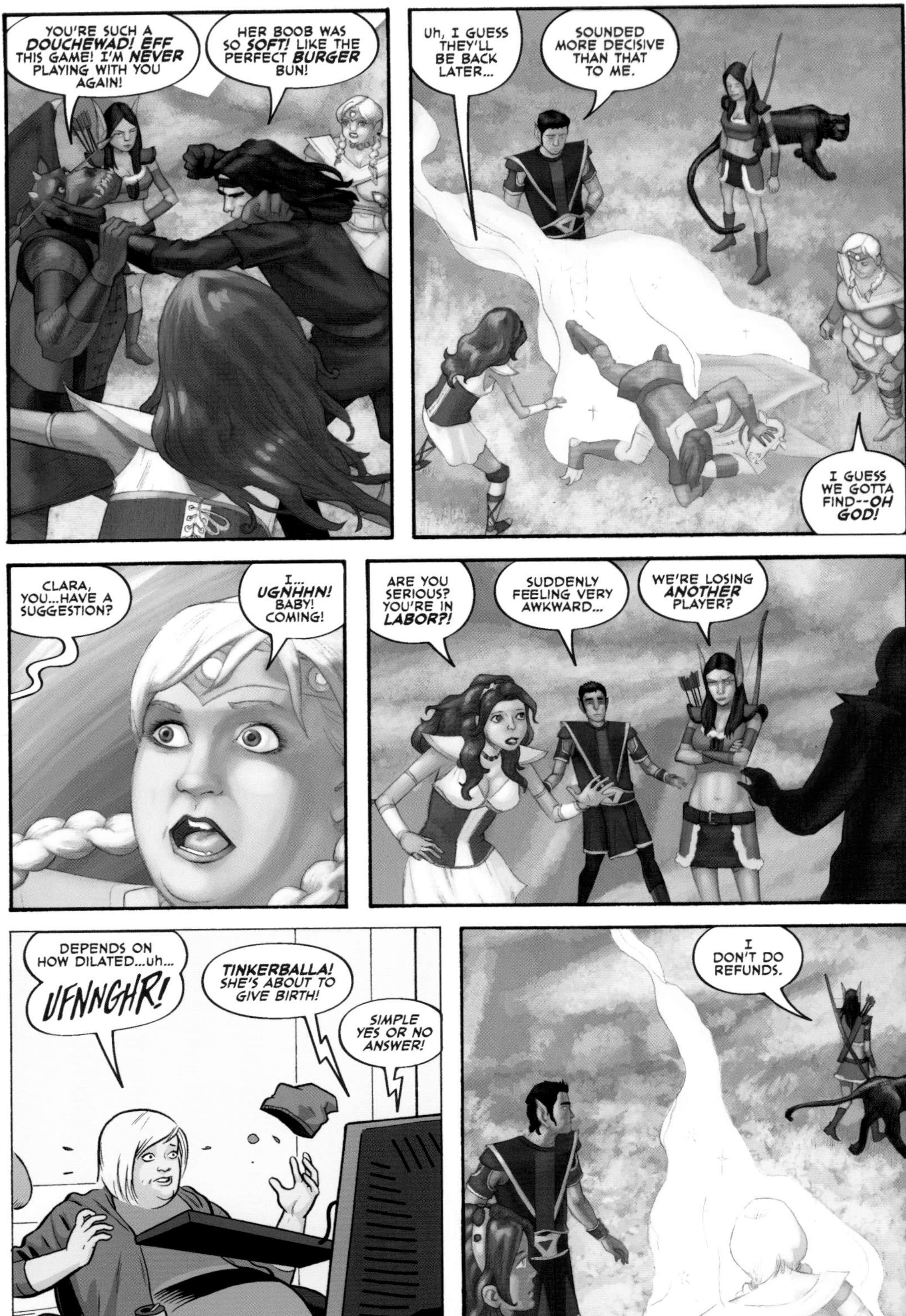
YOU'RE SUCH A DOUCHEWAD! EFF THIS GAME! I'M NEVER PLAYING WITH YOU AGAIN!
HER BOOB WAS SO SOFT! LIKE THE PERFECT BURGER BUN!
Uh, I GUESS THEY'LL BE BACK LATER...
SOUNDED MORE DECISIVE THAN THAT TO ME.
I GUESS WE GOTTA FIND--OH GOD!
CLARA, YOU...HAVE A SUGGESTION?
I... UGNHHN! BABY! COMING!
ARE YOU SERIOUS? YOU'RE IN LABOR?!
SUDDENLY FEELING VERY AWKWARD...
WE'RE LOSING ANOTHER PLAYER?
DEPENDS ON HOW DILATED...uh... UFNNGHR!
TINKERBALLA! SHE'S ABOUT TO GIVE BIRTH!
SIMPLE YES OR NO ANSWER!
I DON'T DO REFUNDS.

GUESS THINGS CAN GO WRONG IN A FANTASY WORLD TOO.

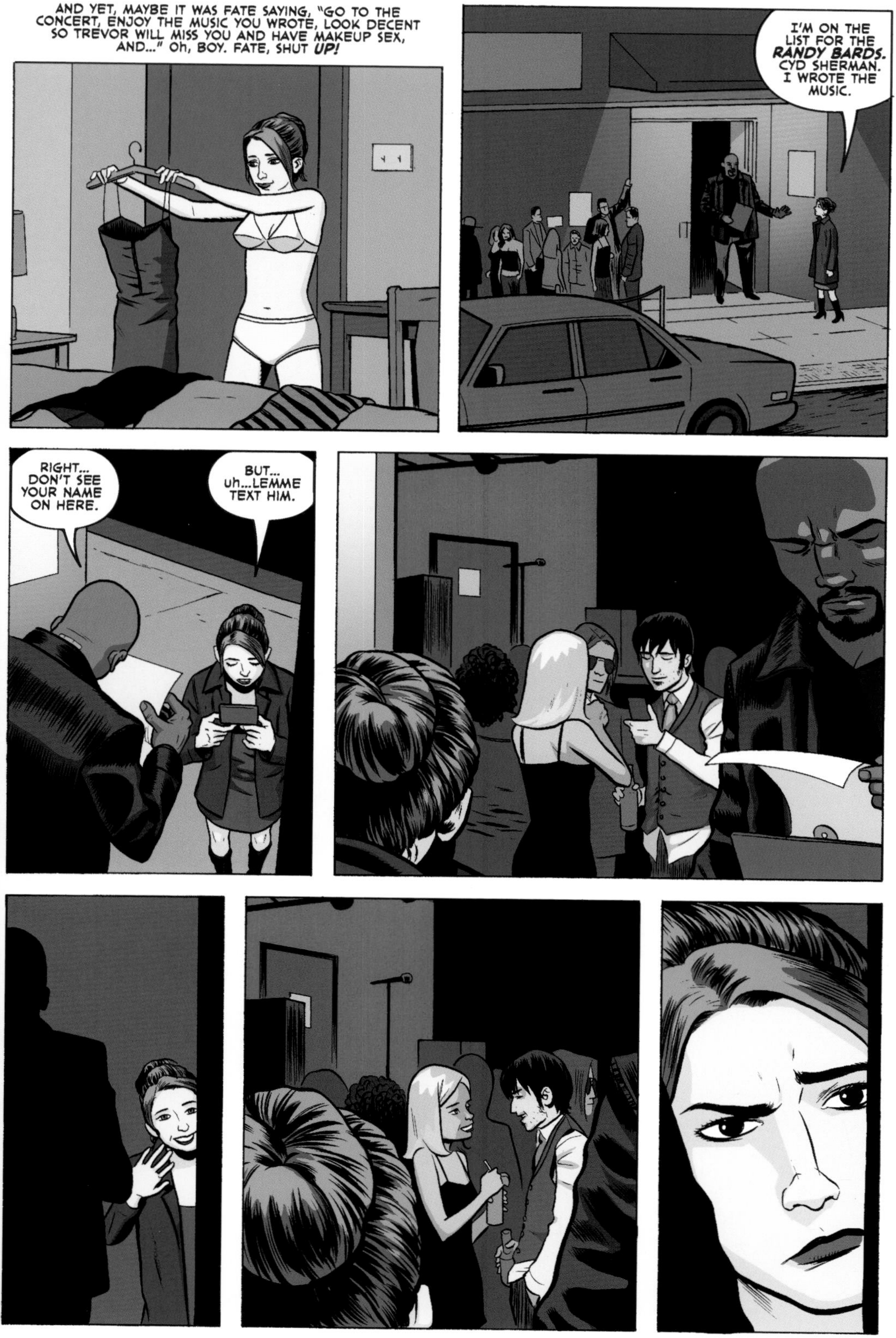
AND YET, MAYBE IT WAS FATE SAYING, "GO TO THE CONCERT, ENJOY THE MUSIC YOU WROTE, LOOK DECENT SO TREVOR WILL MISS YOU AND HAVE MAKEUP SEX, AND..." Oh, BOY. FATE, SHUT *UP!*
I'M ON THE LIST FOR THE *RANDY BARDS.* CYD SHERMAN. I WROTE THE MUSIC.
RIGHT... DON'T SEE YOUR NAME ON HERE.
BUT... uh...LEMME TEXT HIM.

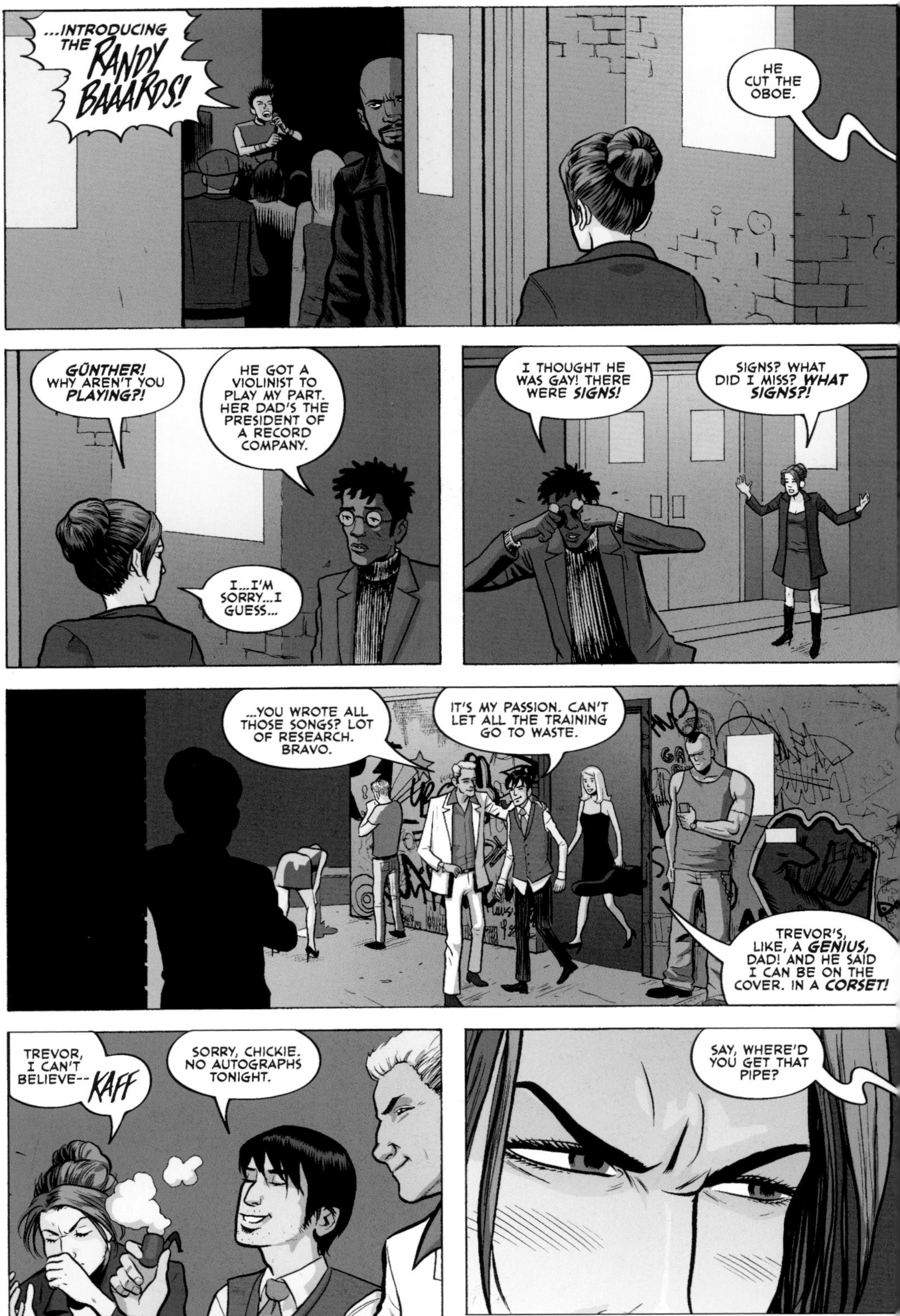
...INTRODUCING THE RANDY BAAARDS!
HE CUT THE OBOE.
GÜNTHER! WHY AREN'T YOU PLAYING?!
HE GOT A VIOLINIST TO PLAY MY PART. HER DAD'S THE PRESIDENT OF A RECORD COMPANY.
I...I'M SORRY...I GUESS...
I THOUGHT HE WAS GAY! THERE WERE SIGNS!
SIGNS? WHAT DID I MISS? WHAT SIGNS?!
...YOU WROTE ALL THOSE SONGS? LOT OF RESEARCH. BRAVO.
IT'S MY PASSION. CAN'T LET ALL THE TRAINING GO TO WASTE.
TREVOR'S, LIKE, A GENIUS, DAD! AND HE SAID I CAN BE ON THE COVER. IN A CORSET!
TREVOR, I CAN'T BELIEVE--KAFF
SORRY, CHICKIE. NO AUTOGRAPHS TONIGHT.
SAY, WHERE'D YOU GET THAT PIPE?
YOU EVER HAVE A MOMENT WHERE EVERYTHING BECOMES CRYSTAL CLEAR?

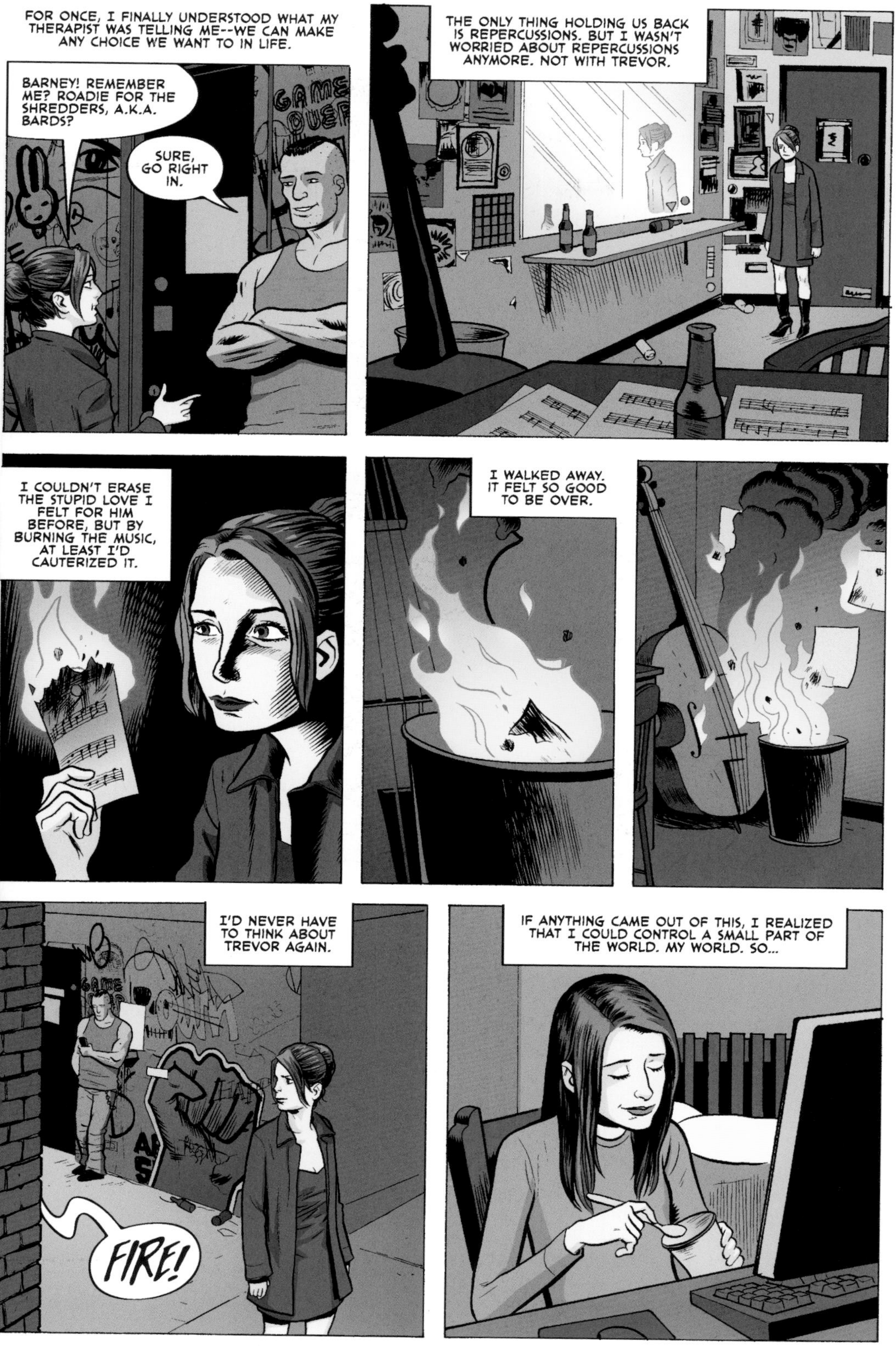
FOR ONCE, I FINALLY UNDERSTOOD WHAT MY THERAPIST WAS TELLING ME--WE CAN MAKE ANY CHOICE WE WANT TO IN LIFE.
BARNEY! REMEMBER ME? ROADIE FOR THE SHREDDERS, A.K.A. BARDS?
SURE, GO RIGHT IN.
GAME OVER
THE ONLY THING HOLDING US BACK IS REPERCUSSIONS. BUT I WASN'T WORRIED ABOUT REPERCUSSIONS ANYMORE. NOT WITH TREVOR.
I COULDN'T ERASE THE STUPID LOVE I FELT FOR HIM BEFORE, BUT BY BURNING THE MUSIC, AT LEAST I'D CAUTERIZED IT.
I WALKED AWAY. IT FELT SO GOOD TO BE OVER.
I'D NEVER HAVE TO THINK ABOUT TREVOR AGAIN.
FIRE!
IF ANYTHING CAME OUT OF THIS, I REALIZED THAT I COULD CONTROL A SMALL PART OF THE WORLD. MY WORLD. SO...

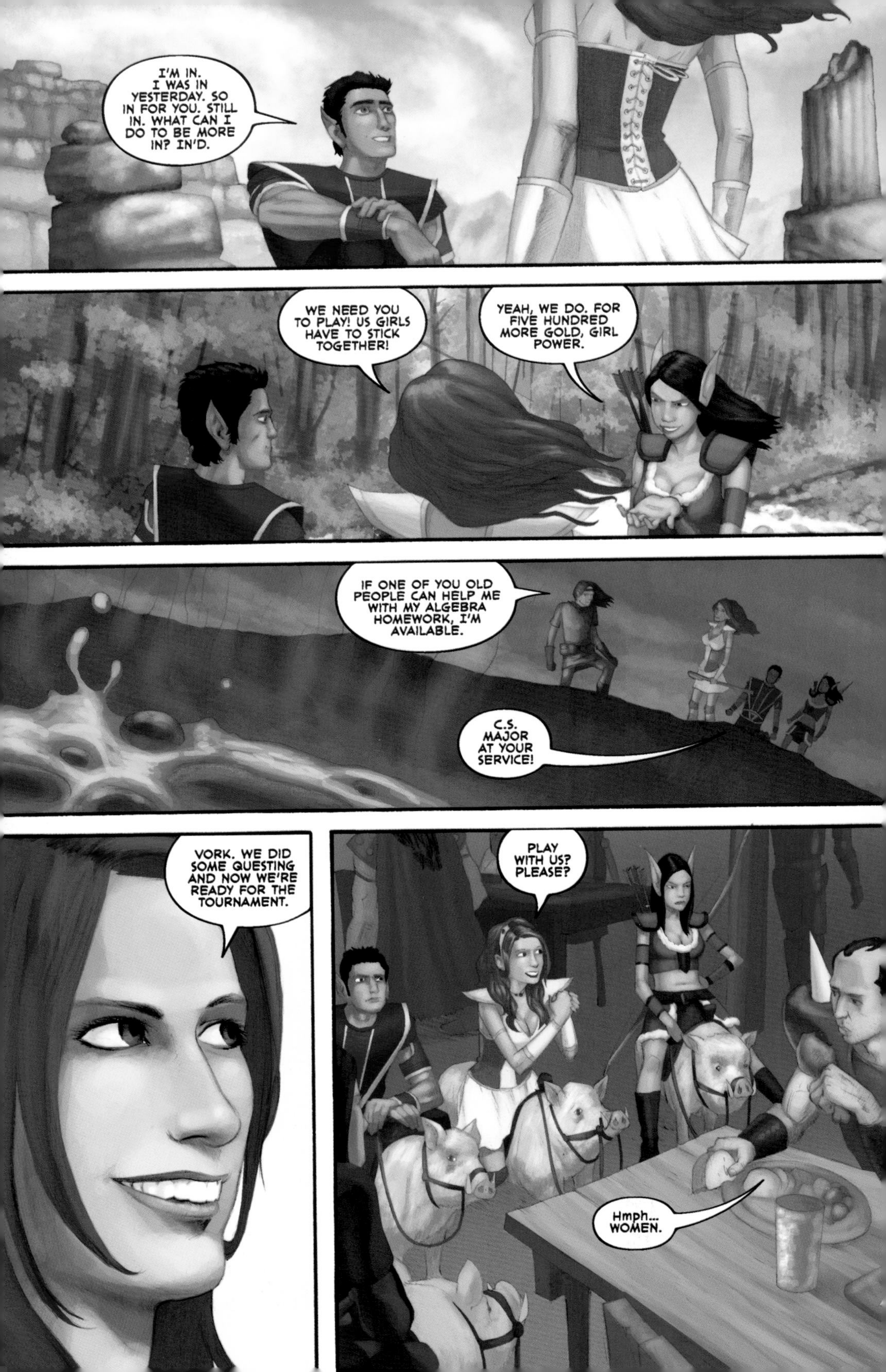
I'M IN. I WAS IN YESTERDAY. SO IN FOR YOU. STILL IN. WHAT CAN I DO TO BE MORE IN? IN'D.
WE NEED YOU TO PLAY! US GIRLS HAVE TO STICK TOGETHER!
YEAH, WE DO. FOR FIVE HUNDRED MORE GOLD, GIRL POWER.
IF ONE OF YOU OLD PEOPLE CAN HELP ME WITH MY ALGEBRA HOMEWORK, I'M AVAILABLE.
C.S. MAJOR AT YOUR SERVICE!
VORK. WE DID SOME QUESTING AND NOW WE'RE READY FOR THE TOURNAMENT.
PLAY WITH US? PLEASE?
Hmph... WOMEN.

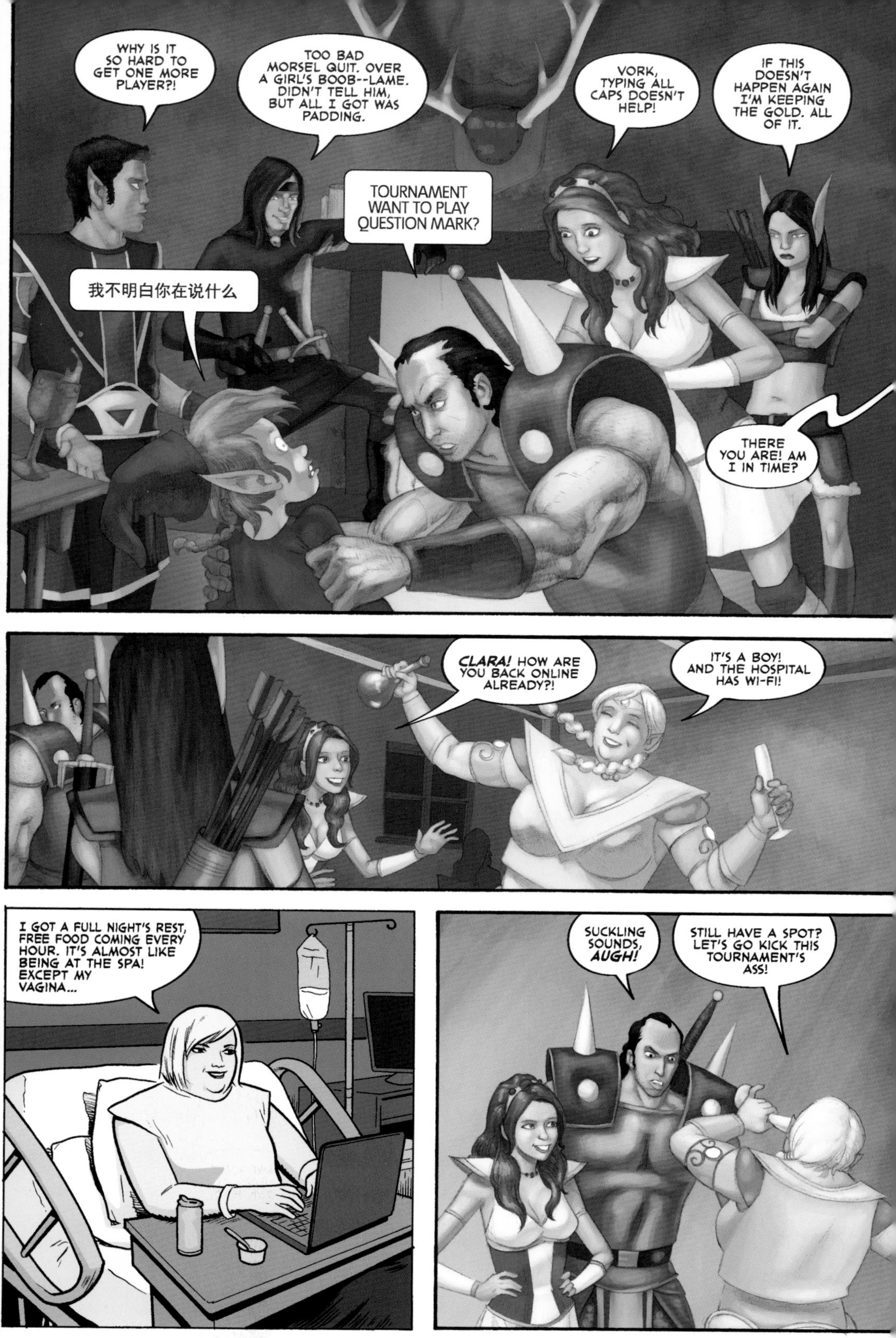
WHY IS IT SO HARD TO GET ONE MORE PLAYER?!
TOO BAD MORSEL QUIT. OVER A GIRL'S BOOB--LAME. DIDN'T TELL HIM, BUT ALL I GOT WAS PADDING.
VORK, TYPING ALL CAPS DOESN'T HELP!
IF THIS DOESN'T HAPPEN AGAIN I'M KEEPING THE GOLD. ALL OF IT.
TOURNAMENT WANT TO PLAY QUESTION MARK?
我不明白你在说什么
THERE YOU ARE! AM I IN TIME?
CLARA! HOW ARE YOU BACK ONLINE ALREADY?!
IT'S A BOY! AND THE HOSPITAL HAS WI-FI!
I GOT A FULL NIGHT'S REST, FREE FOOD COMING EVERY HOUR. IT'S ALMOST LIKE BEING AT THE SPA! EXCEPT MY VAGINA...
SUCKLING SOUNDS, AUGH!
STILL HAVE A SPOT? LET'S GO KICK THIS TOURNAMENT'S ASS!

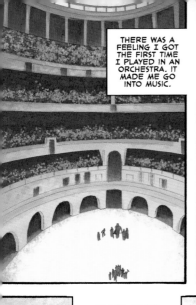

THERE WAS A FEELING I GOT THE FIRST TIME I PLAYED IN AN ORCHESTRA. IT MADE ME GO INTO MUSIC.

IT WAS THE FEELING OF REALLY FITTING MYSELF INTO THE WHOLE, LIKE A PUZZLE PIECE, HELPING TO COMPLETE IT.

PLAYING IN THE TOURNAMENT, I FELT IT AGAIN. US, WORKING AS A TEAM.

ZABOO, MORE D.P.S. ON THEIR HEALER!

HEY! WHAT AM I, GROUND TURKEY?

CHOPPED LIVER.

WATCH WHO YOU'RE CALLING NAMES, BUCKO!

I'D LOVE TO SAY WE BEAT EVERYONE ON THE SERVER AND GOT THE BADASS WEAPONS WITHOUT EVER PRACTICING TOGETHER...BUT THAT WOULD NOT BE REALISTIC.

REALITY IS, WE GOT TAKEN DOWN BY A GROUP OF SATYRS ON STEROIDS.

CREEPY GOAT MEN STOMPING ON MY FACE, EW!

AWESOME. STARING AT MY OWN FOOT.

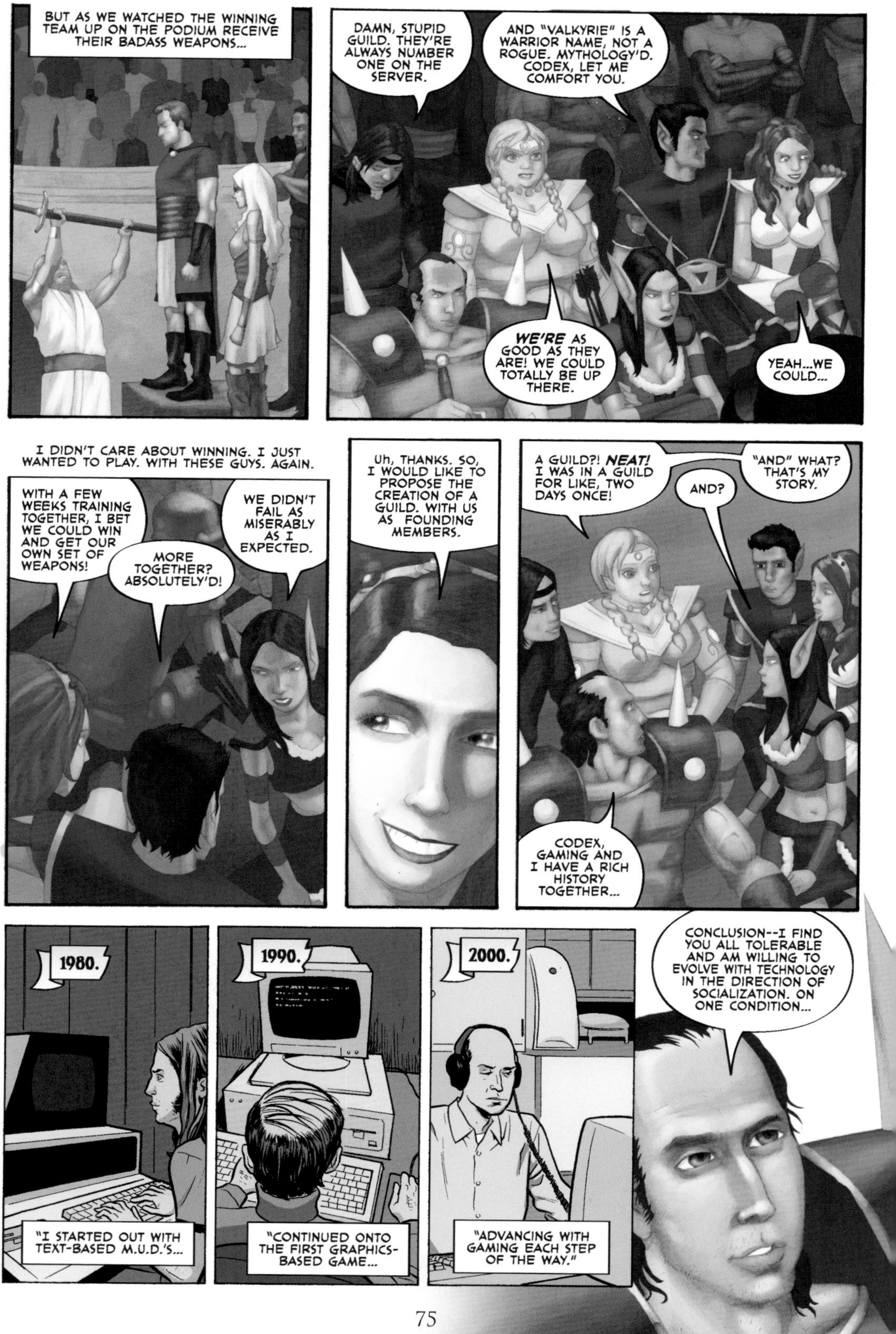

BUT AS WE WATCHED THE WINNING TEAM UP ON THE PODIUM RECEIVE THEIR BADASS WEAPONS...
DAMN, STUPID GUILD. THEY'RE ALWAYS NUMBER ONE ON THE SERVER.
AND "VALKYRIE" IS A WARRIOR NAME, NOT A ROGUE. MYTHOLOGY'D. CODEX, LET ME COMFORT YOU.
WE'RE AS GOOD AS THEY ARE! WE COULD TOTALLY BE UP THERE.
YEAH...WE COULD...
I DIDN'T CARE ABOUT WINNING. I JUST WANTED TO PLAY. WITH THESE GUYS. AGAIN.
WITH A FEW WEEKS TRAINING TOGETHER, I BET WE COULD WIN AND GET OUR OWN SET OF WEAPONS!
MORE TOGETHER? ABSOLUTELY'D!
WE DIDN'T FAIL AS MISERABLY AS I EXPECTED.
Uh, THANKS. SO, I WOULD LIKE TO PROPOSE THE CREATION OF A GUILD. WITH US AS FOUNDING MEMBERS.
A GUILD?! NEAT! I WAS IN A GUILD FOR LIKE, TWO DAYS ONCE!
AND?
"AND" WHAT? THAT'S MY STORY.
CODEX, GAMING AND I HAVE A RICH HISTORY TOGETHER...
1980.
"I STARTED OUT WITH TEXT-BASED M.U.D.'S...
1990.
"CONTINUED ONTO THE FIRST GRAPHICS-BASED GAME...
2000.
"ADVANCING WITH GAMING EACH STEP OF THE WAY."
CONCLUSION--I FIND YOU ALL TOLERABLE AND AM WILLING TO EVOLVE WITH TECHNOLOGY IN THE DIRECTION OF SOCIALIZATION. ON ONE CONDITION...

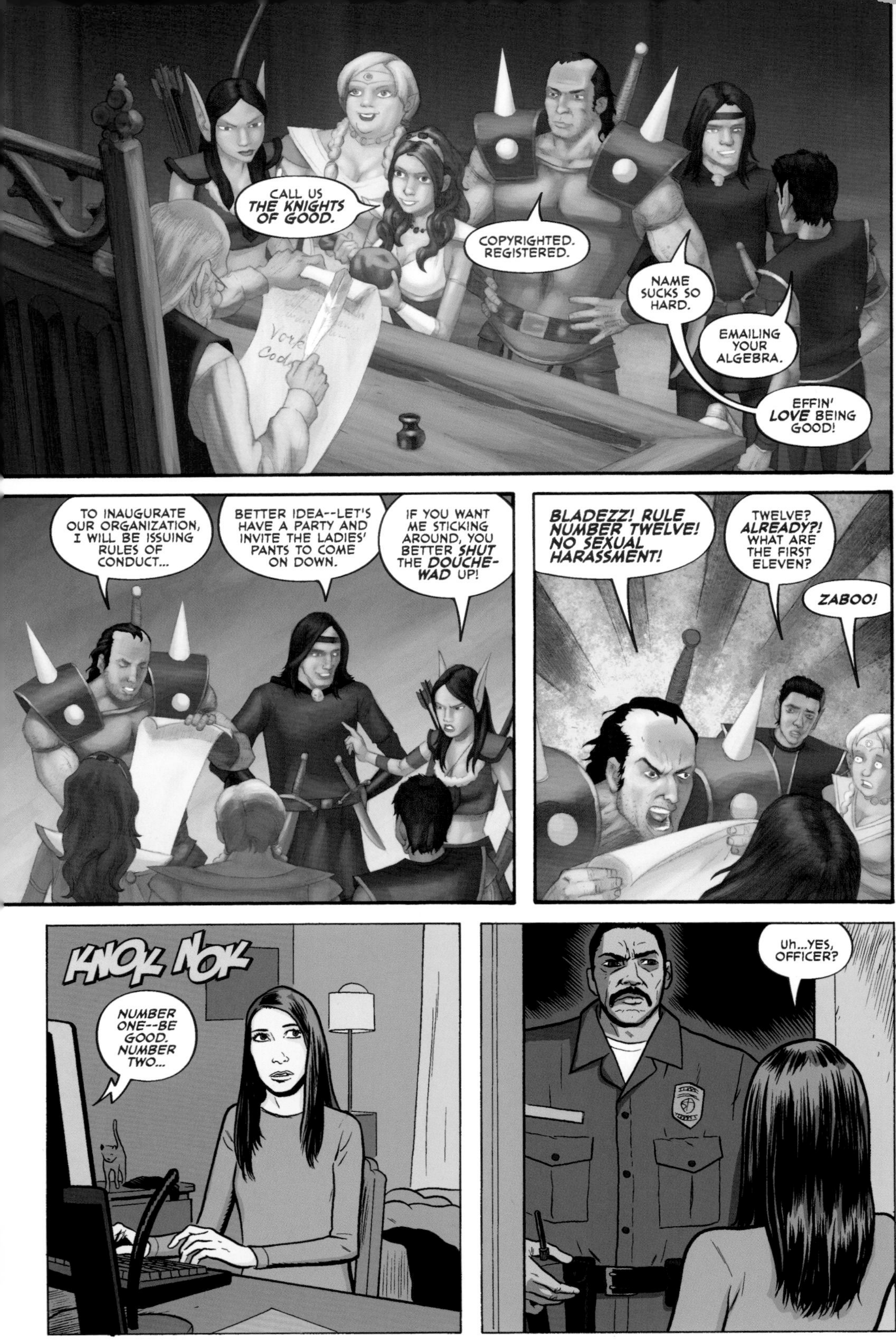
CALL US THE KNIGHTS OF GOOD.
COPYRIGHTED. REGISTERED.
NAME SUCKS SO HARD.
EMAILING YOUR ALGEBRA.
EFFIN' LOVE BEING GOOD!
TO INAUGURATE OUR ORGANIZATION, I WILL BE ISSUING RULES OF CONDUCT...
BETTER IDEA--LET'S HAVE A PARTY AND INVITE THE LADIES' PANTS TO COME ON DOWN.
IF YOU WANT ME STICKING AROUND, YOU BETTER SHUT THE DOUCHE-WAD UP!
BLADEZZ! RULE NUMBER TWELVE! NO SEXUAL HARASSMENT!
TWELVE? ALREADY?! WHAT ARE THE FIRST ELEVEN?
ZABOO!
KNOK NOK
NUMBER ONE--BE GOOD. NUMBER TWO...
Uh...YES, OFFICER?

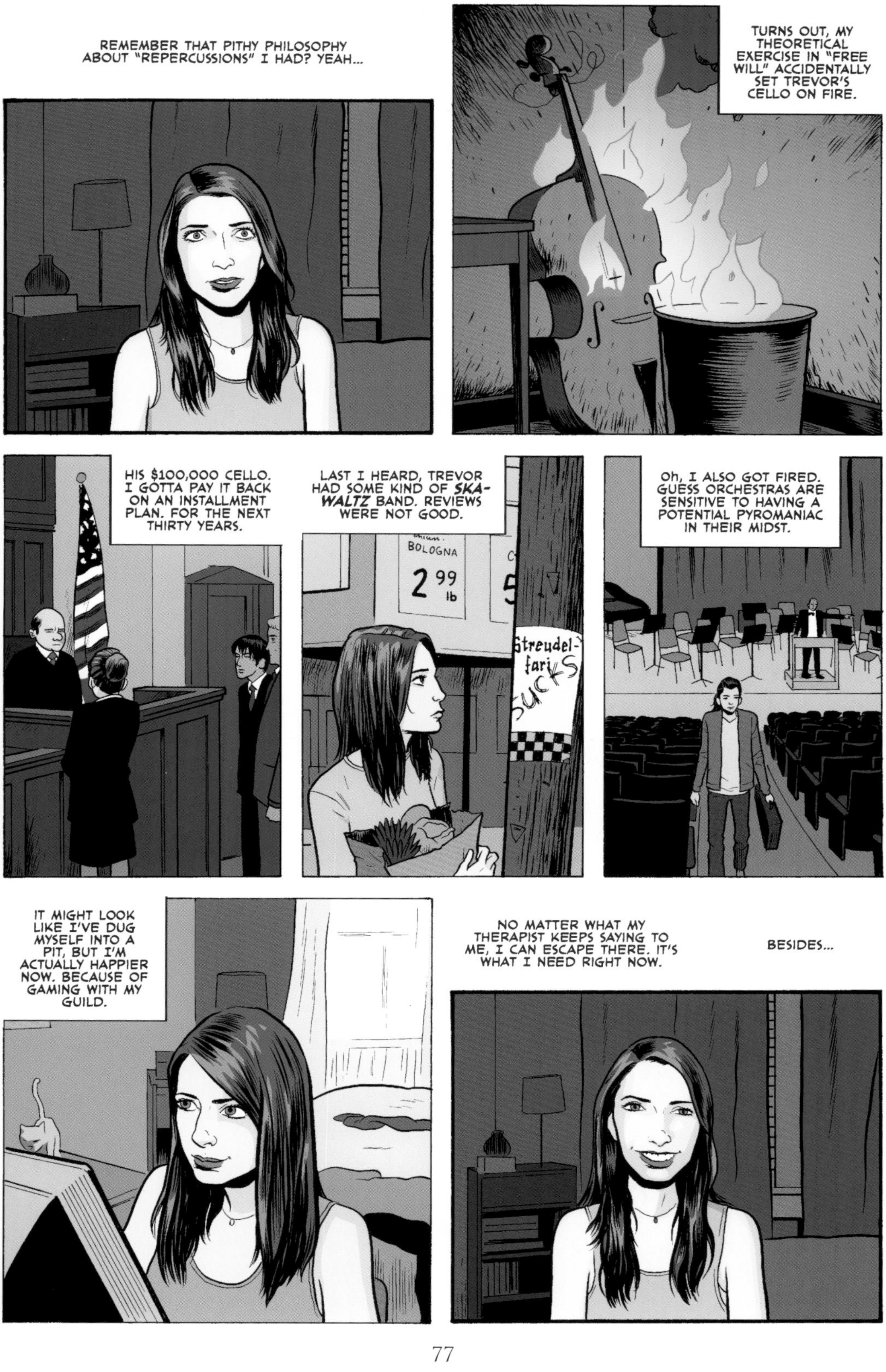
REMEMBER THAT PITHY PHILOSOPHY ABOUT "REPERCUSSIONS" I HAD? YEAH...
TURNS OUT, MY THEORETICAL EXERCISE IN "FREE WILL" ACCIDENTALLY SET TREVOR'S CELLO ON FIRE.
HIS $100,000 CELLO. I GOTTA PAY IT BACK ON AN INSTALLMENT PLAN. FOR THE NEXT THIRTY YEARS.
LAST I HEARD, TREVOR HAD SOME KIND OF SKA-WALTZ BAND. REVIEWS WERE NOT GOOD.
BOLOGNA
2.99 lb
Streudel-fari
SUCKS
Oh, I ALSO GOT FIRED. GUESS ORCHESTRAS ARE SENSITIVE TO HAVING A POTENTIAL PYROMANIAC IN THEIR MIDST.
IT MIGHT LOOK LIKE I'VE DUG MYSELF INTO A PIT, BUT I'M ACTUALLY HAPPIER NOW. BECAUSE OF GAMING WITH MY GUILD.
NO MATTER WHAT MY THERAPIST KEEPS SAYING TO ME, I CAN ESCAPE THERE. IT'S WHAT I NEED RIGHT NOW.
BESIDES...

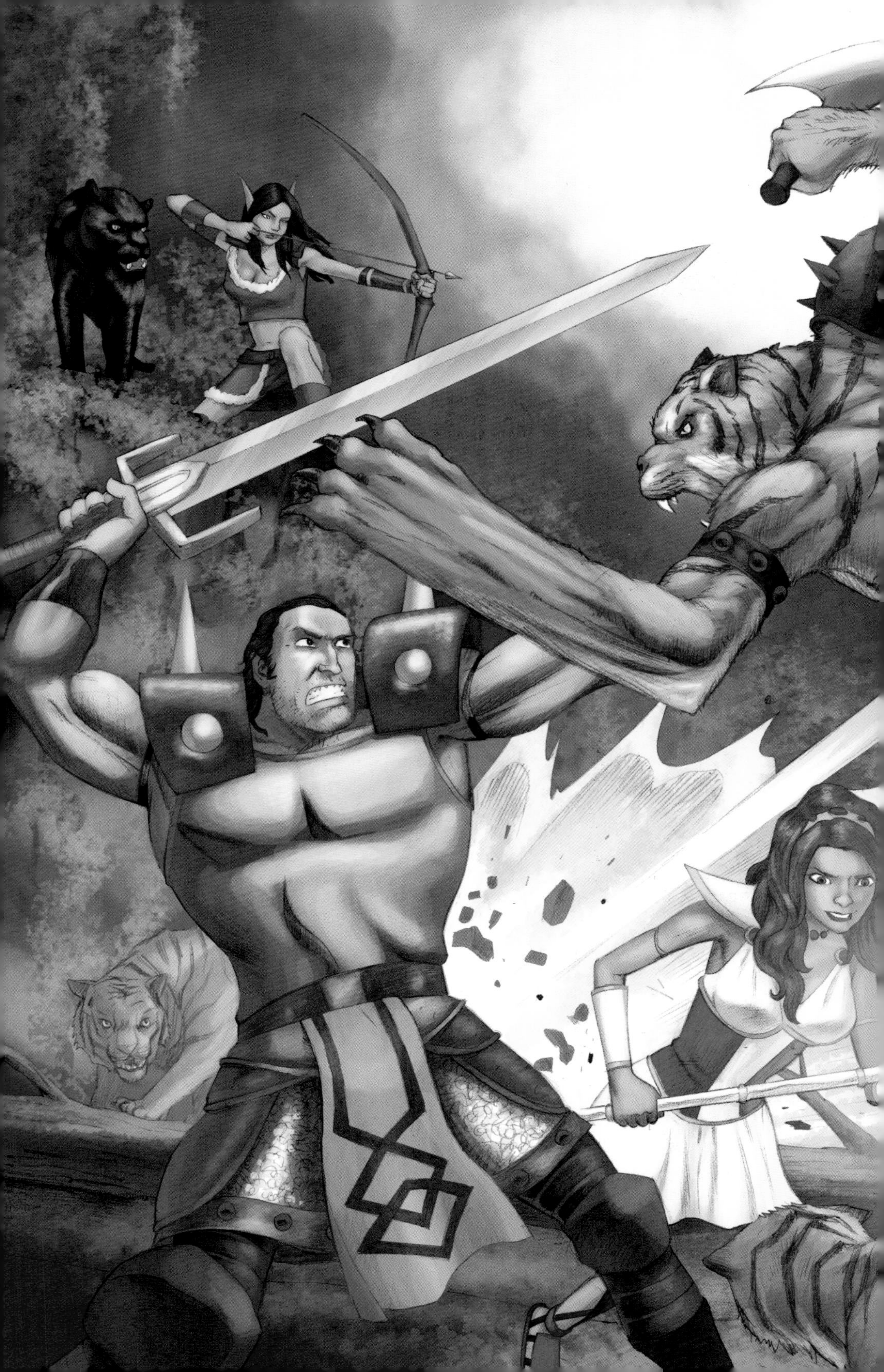

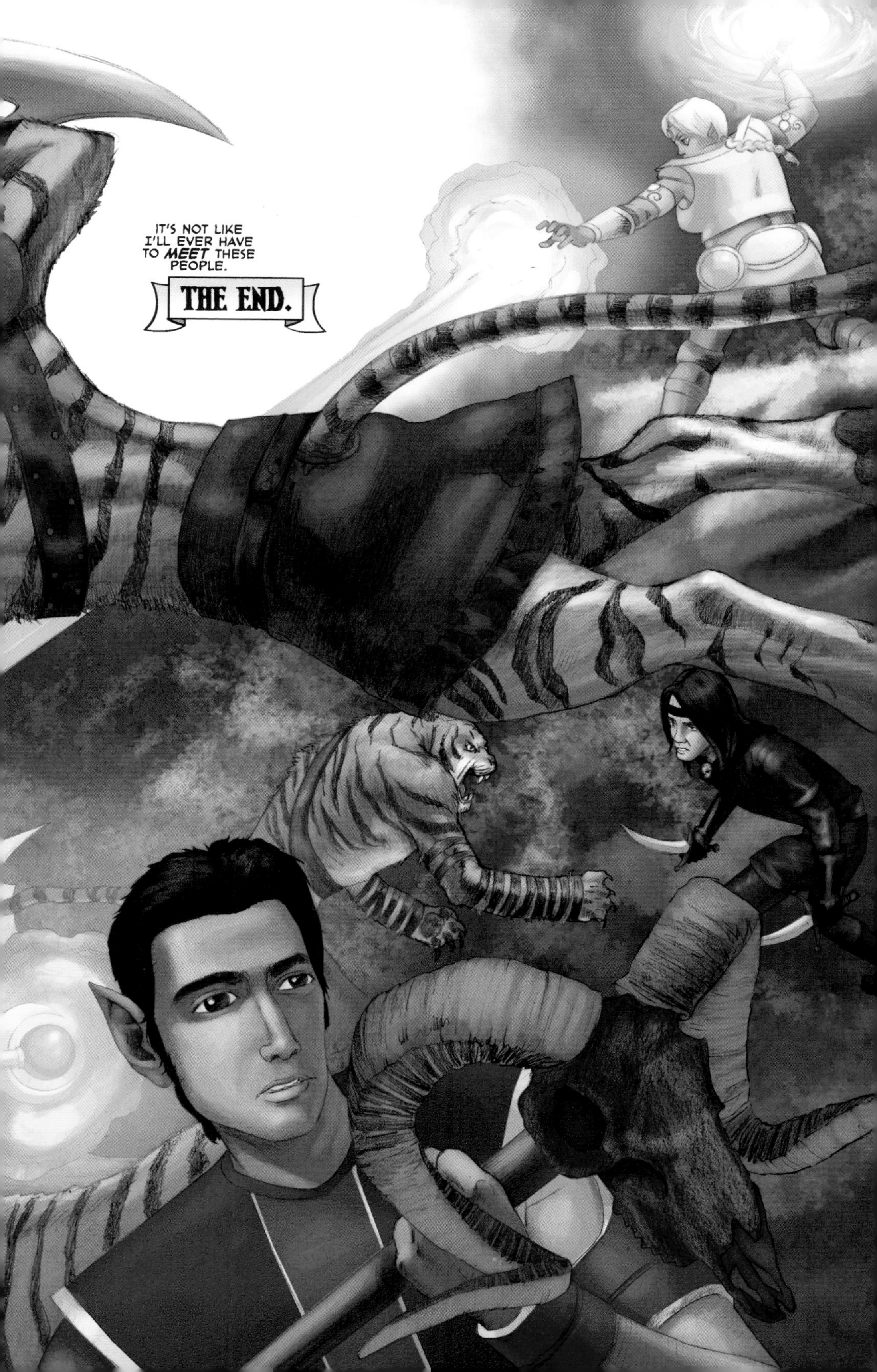
IT'S NOT LIKE I'LL EVER HAVE TO *MEET* THESE PEOPLE.
THE END.

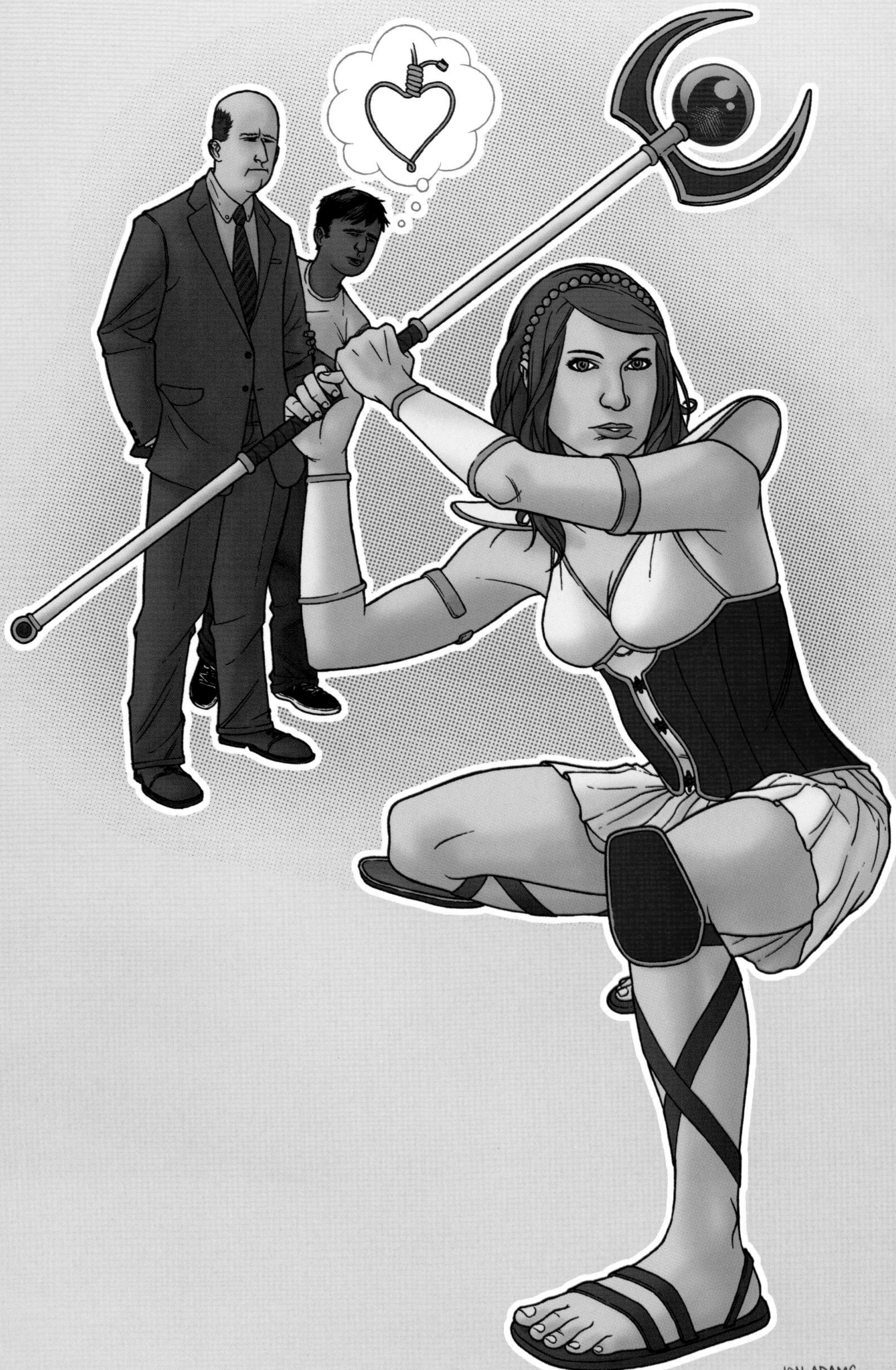
JON ADAMS
Illustration by Jon Adams

DEBUT STORY FROM

MYSPACE DARK HORSE PRESENTS

Script
FELICIA DAY

Art
JIM RUGG

Paints
JUAN FERREYRA

Colors
DAN JACKSON

Letters
BLAMBOT®'S NATE PIEKOS

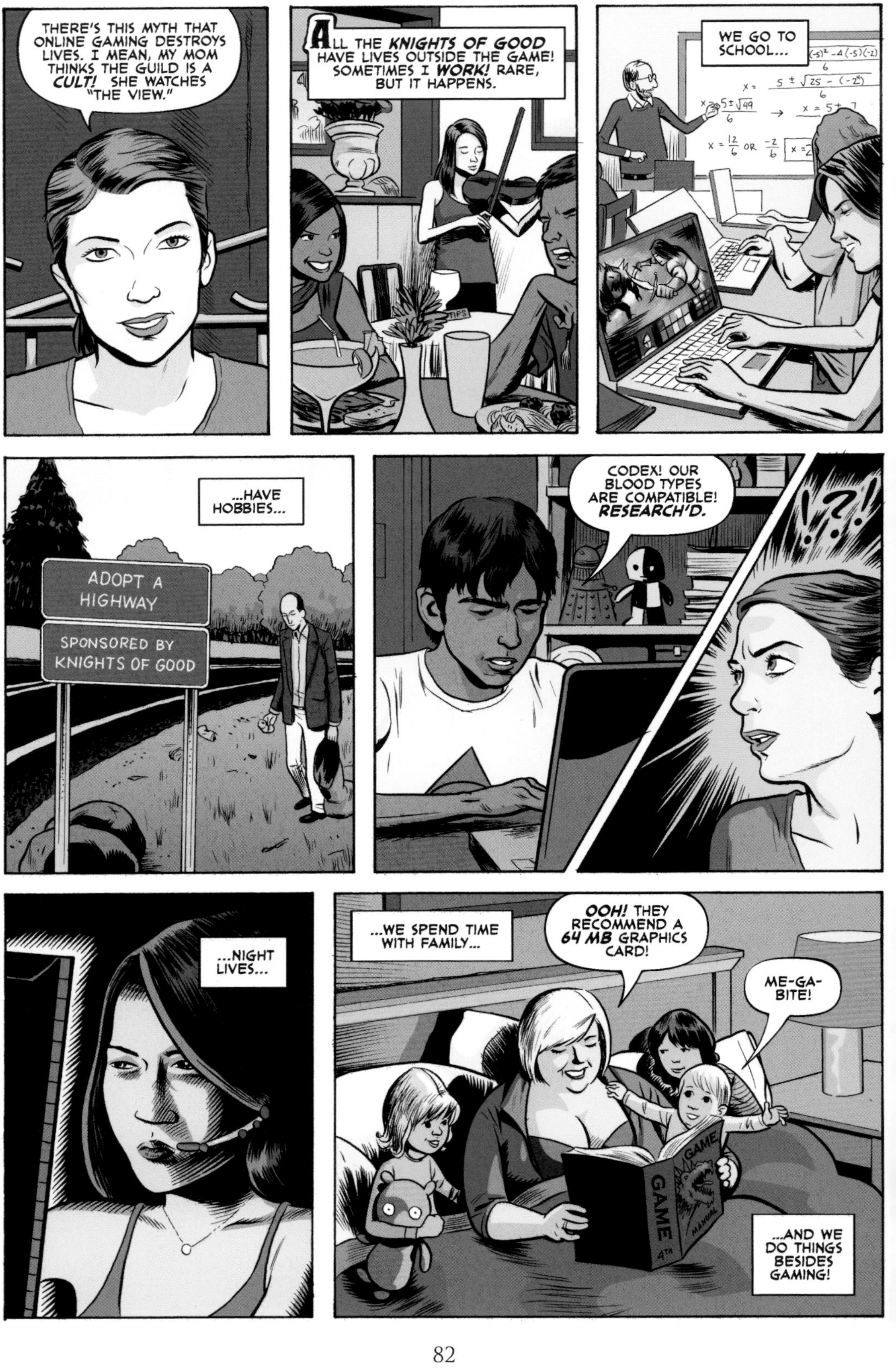
THERE'S THIS MYTH THAT ONLINE GAMING DESTROYS LIVES. I MEAN, MY MOM THINKS THE GUILD IS A CULT! SHE WATCHES "THE VIEW."
ALL THE KNIGHTS OF GOOD HAVE LIVES OUTSIDE THE GAME! SOMETIMES I WORK! RARE, BUT IT HAPPENS.
TIPS
WE GO TO SCHOOL...
...HAVE HOBBIES...
ADOPT A HIGHWAY
SPONSORED BY KNIGHTS OF GOOD
CODEX! OUR BLOOD TYPES ARE COMPATIBLE! RESEARCH'D.
!?!
...NIGHT LIVES...
...WE SPEND TIME WITH FAMILY...
OOH! THEY RECOMMEND A 64 MB GRAPHICS CARD!
ME-GA-BITE!
GAME
...AND WE DO THINGS BESIDES GAMING!

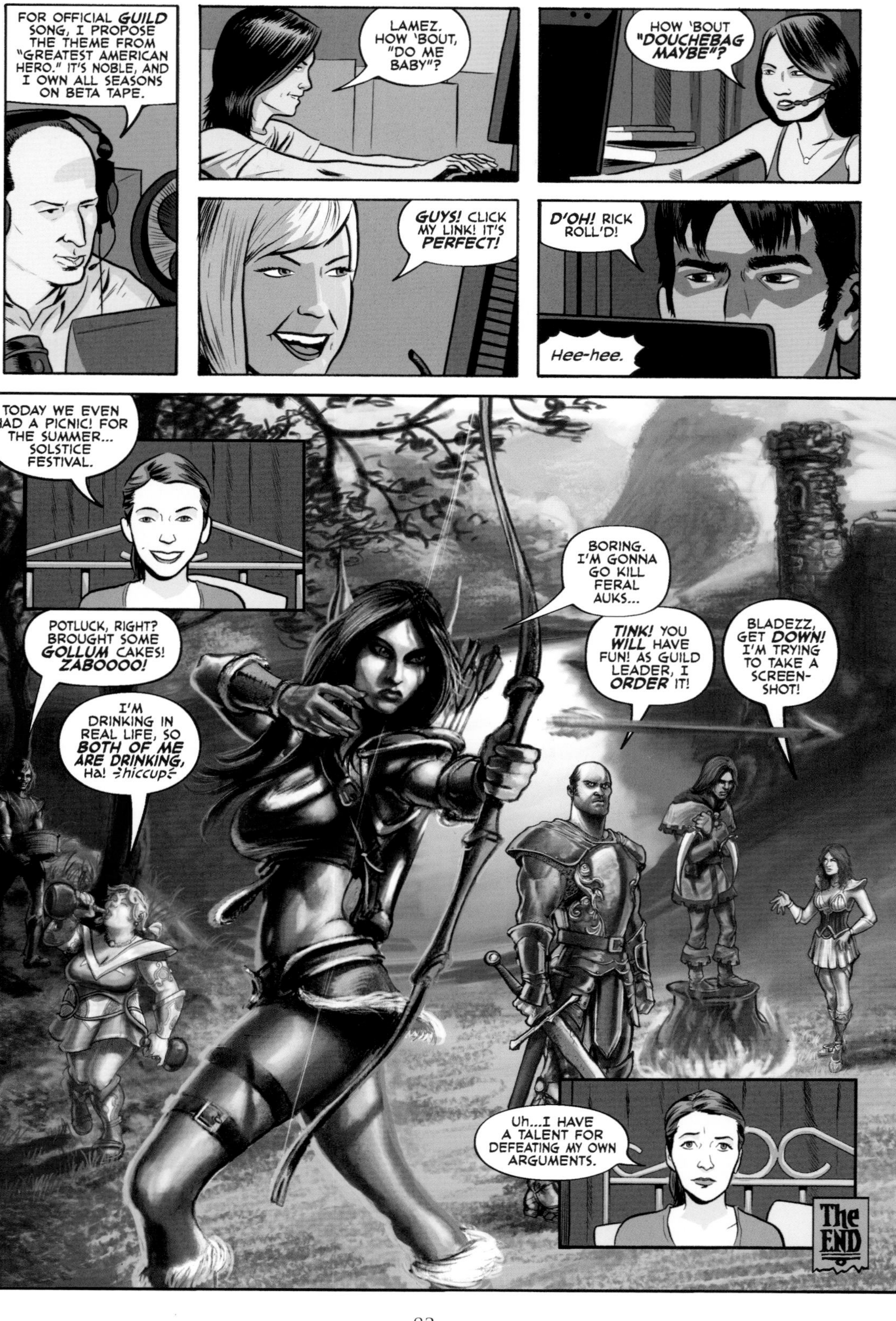
FOR OFFICIAL GUILD SONG, I PROPOSE THE THEME FROM "GREATEST AMERICAN HERO." IT'S NOBLE, AND I OWN ALL SEASONS ON BETA TAPE.
LAMEZ. HOW 'BOUT, "DO ME BABY"?
HOW 'BOUT "DOUCHEBAG MAYBE"?
GUYS! CLICK MY LINK! IT'S PERFECT!
D'OH! RICK ROLL'D!
Hee-hee.
TODAY WE EVEN HAD A PICNIC! FOR THE SUMMER... SOLSTICE FESTIVAL.
POTLUCK, RIGHT? BROUGHT SOME GOLLUM CAKES! ZABOOOO!
I'M DRINKING IN REAL LIFE, SO BOTH OF ME ARE DRINKING, Ha! *hiccup*
BORING. I'M GONNA GO KILL FERAL AUKS...
TINK! YOU WILL HAVE FUN! AS GUILD LEADER, I ORDER IT!
BLADEZZ, GET DOWN! I'M TRYING TO TAKE A SCREEN-SHOT!
Uh...I HAVE A TALENT FOR DEFEATING MY OWN ARGUMENTS.
The END

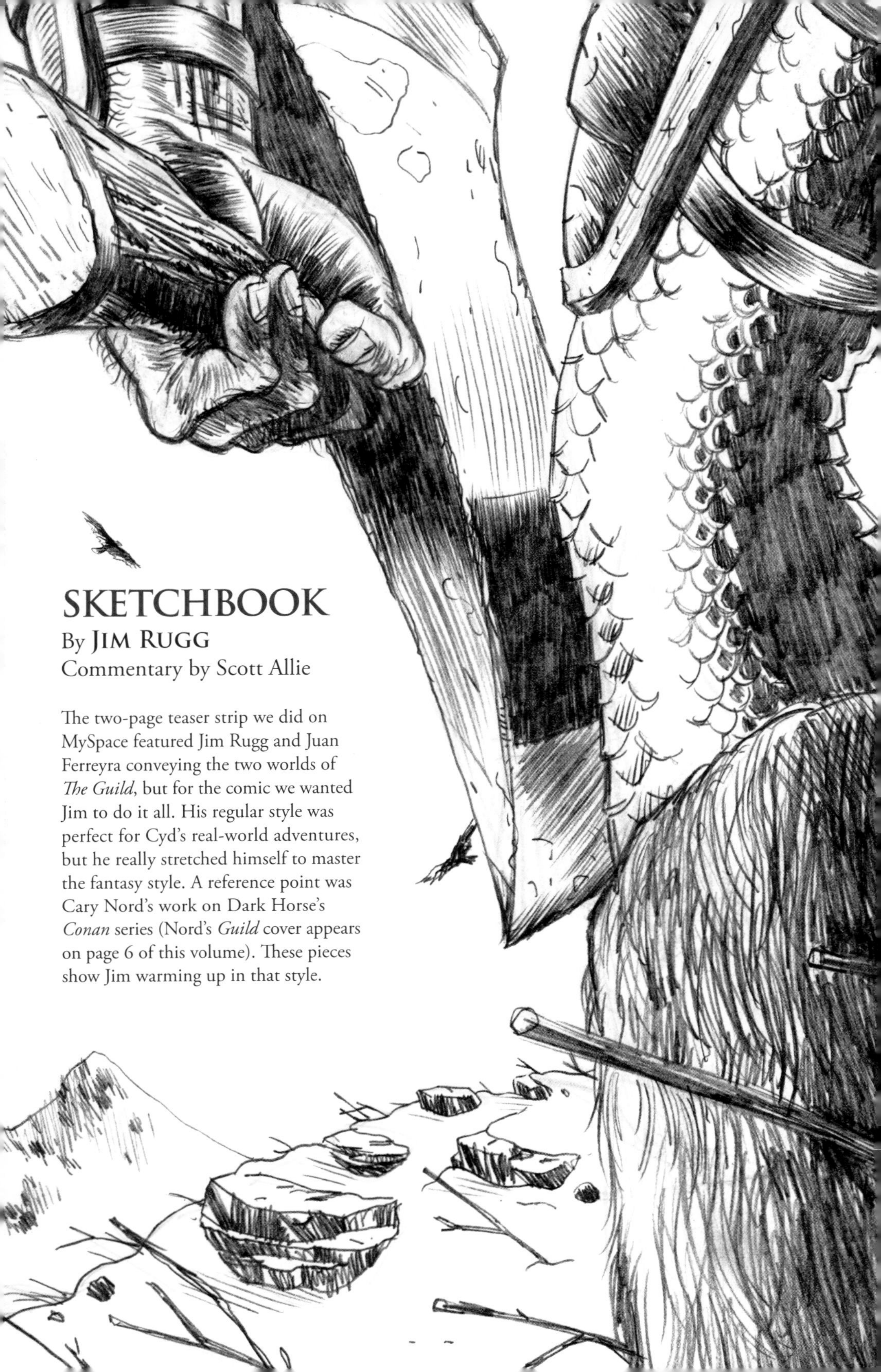

SKETCHBOOK

By **Jim Rugg**

Commentary by Scott Allie

The two-page teaser strip we did on MySpace featured Jim Rugg and Juan Ferreyra conveying the two worlds of *The Guild*, but for the comic we wanted Jim to do it all. His regular style was perfect for Cyd's real-world adventures, but he really stretched himself to master the fantasy style. A reference point was Cary Nord's work on Dark Horse's *Conan* series (Nord's *Guild* cover appears on page 6 of this volume). These pieces show Jim warming up in that style.

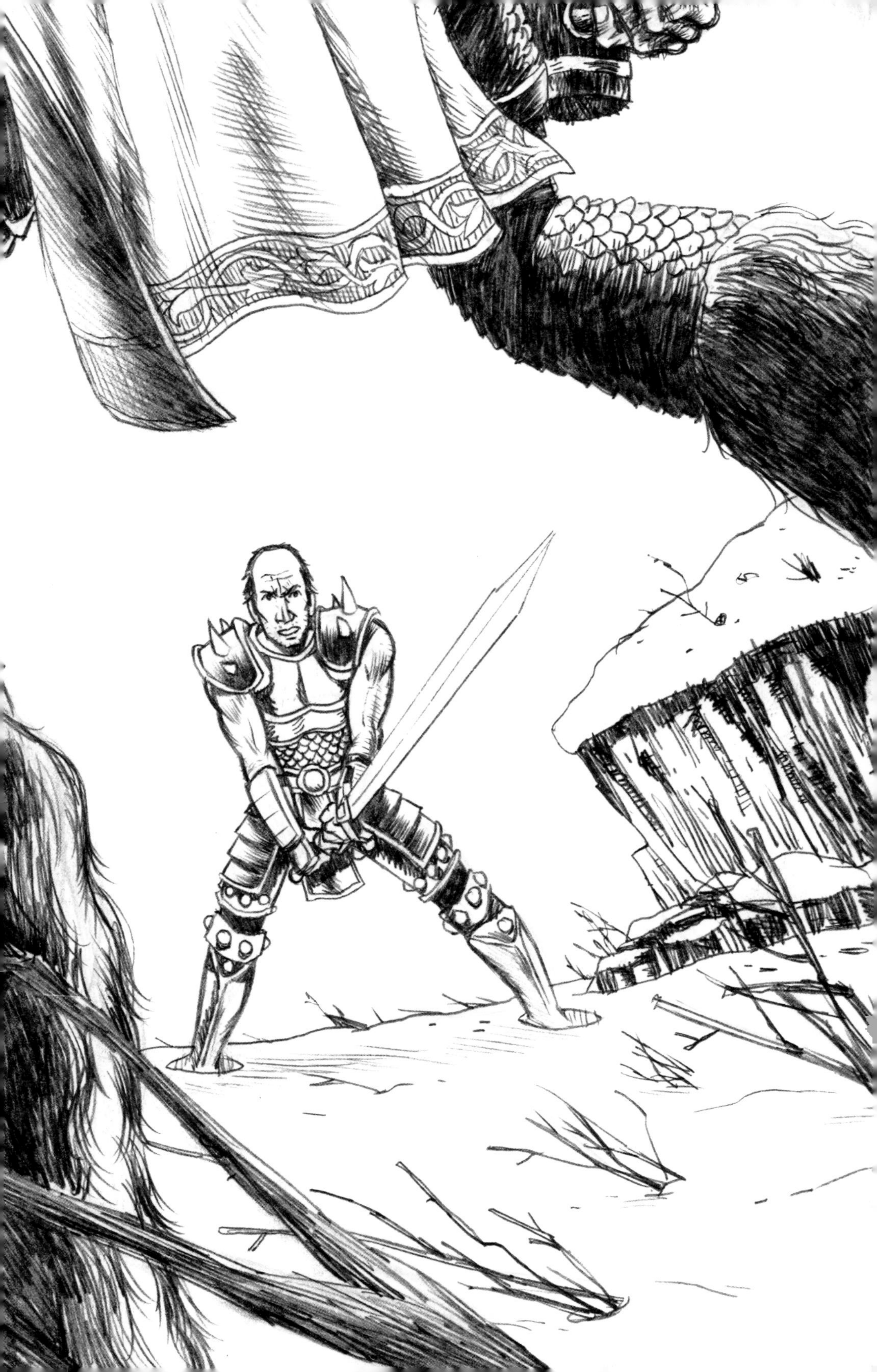

Jim's early warm-ups on Felicia's likeness. Below: Jim's take on the last panel of the MySpace strip, from which Juan based his version.

Facing: defining Codex's various looks, and a kitten. Also, cover sketches. See page 29 of this volume for the final piece.

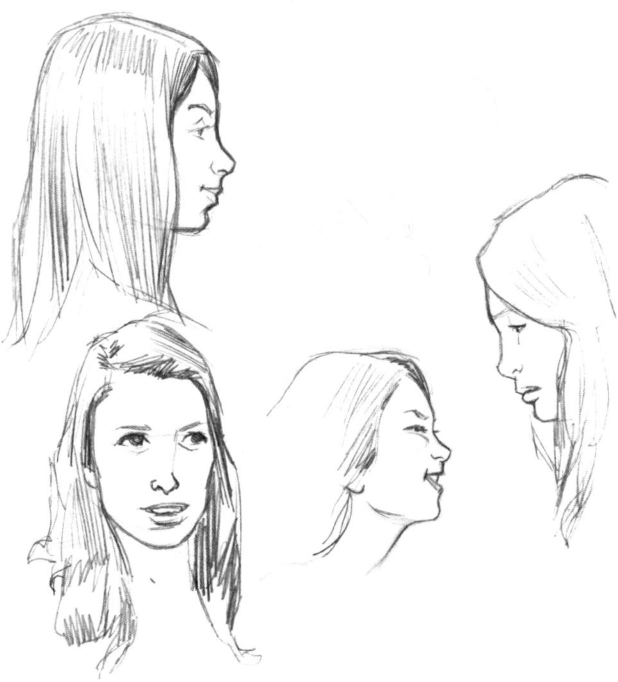

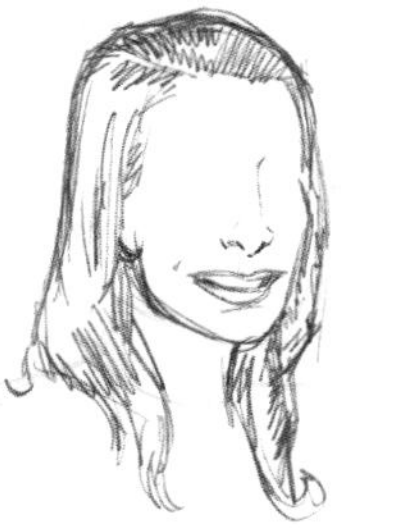

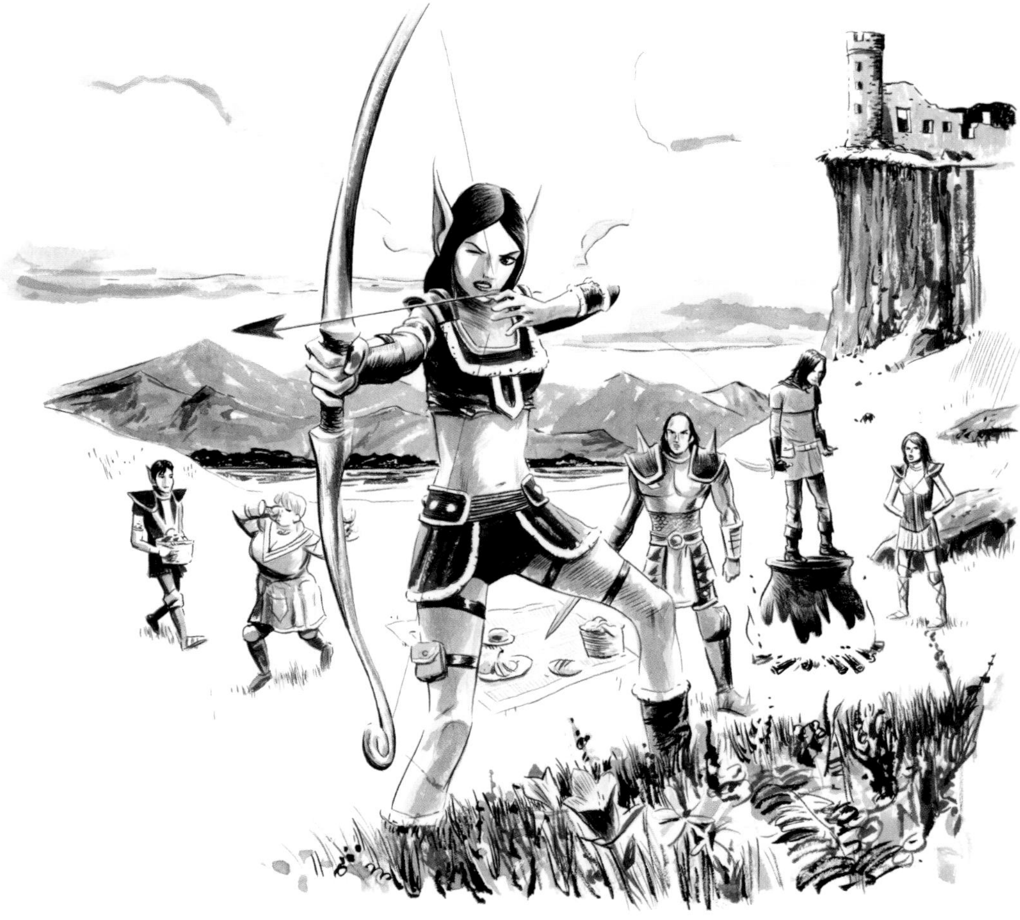

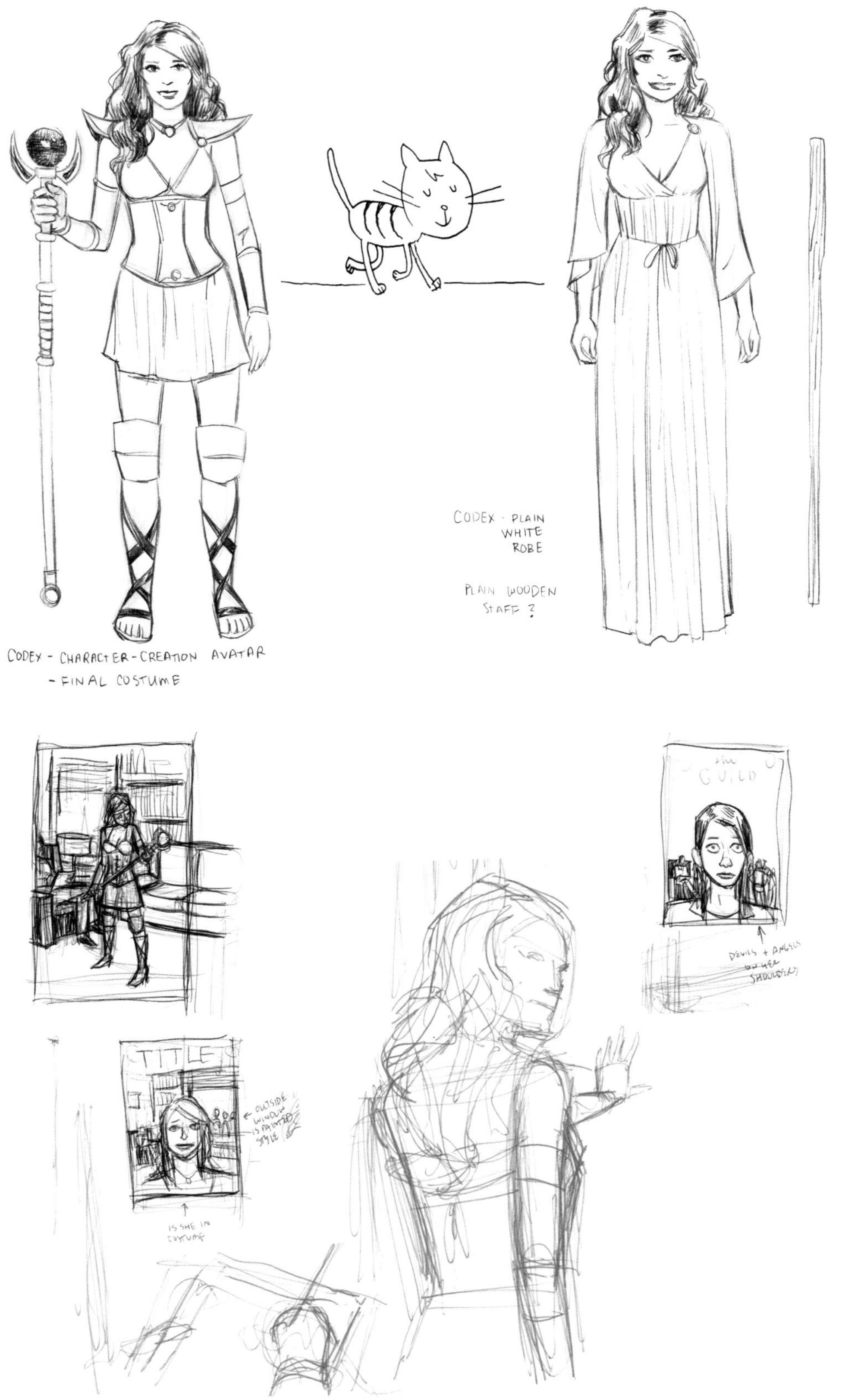
CODEX - CHARACTER-CREATION AVATAR
- FINAL COSTUME
CODEX - PLAIN
WHITE
ROBE
PLAIN WOODEN
STAFF ?
THE GUILD
DEVILS + ANGELS
ON HER
SHOULDERS
TITLE
OUTSIDE
WINDOW
IS PAINTED
STYLE
IS SHE IN
COSTUME

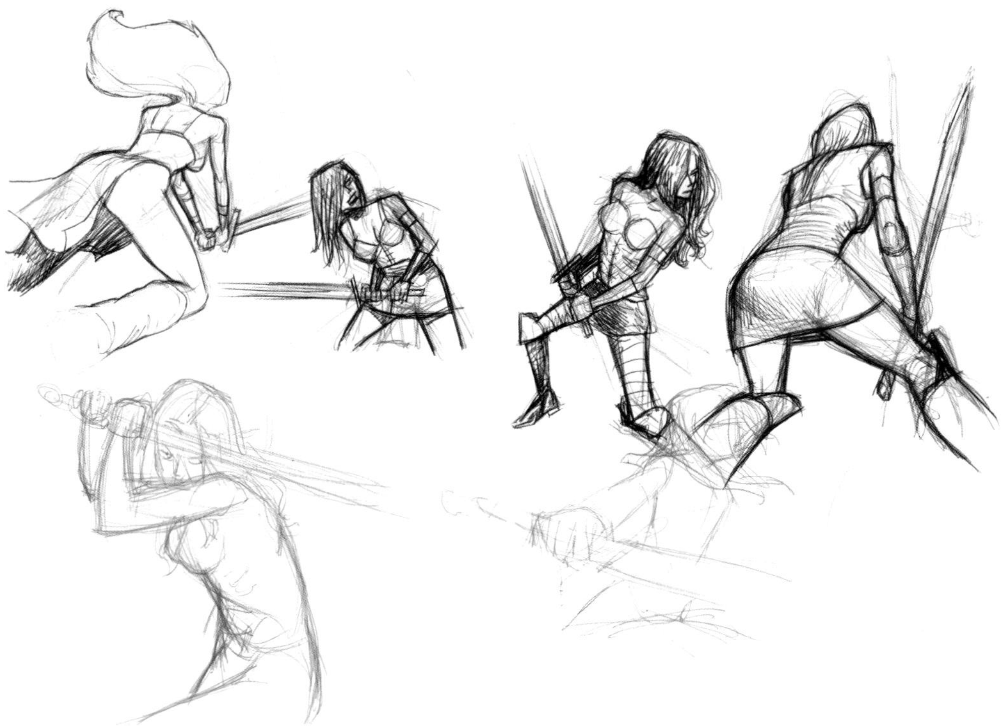

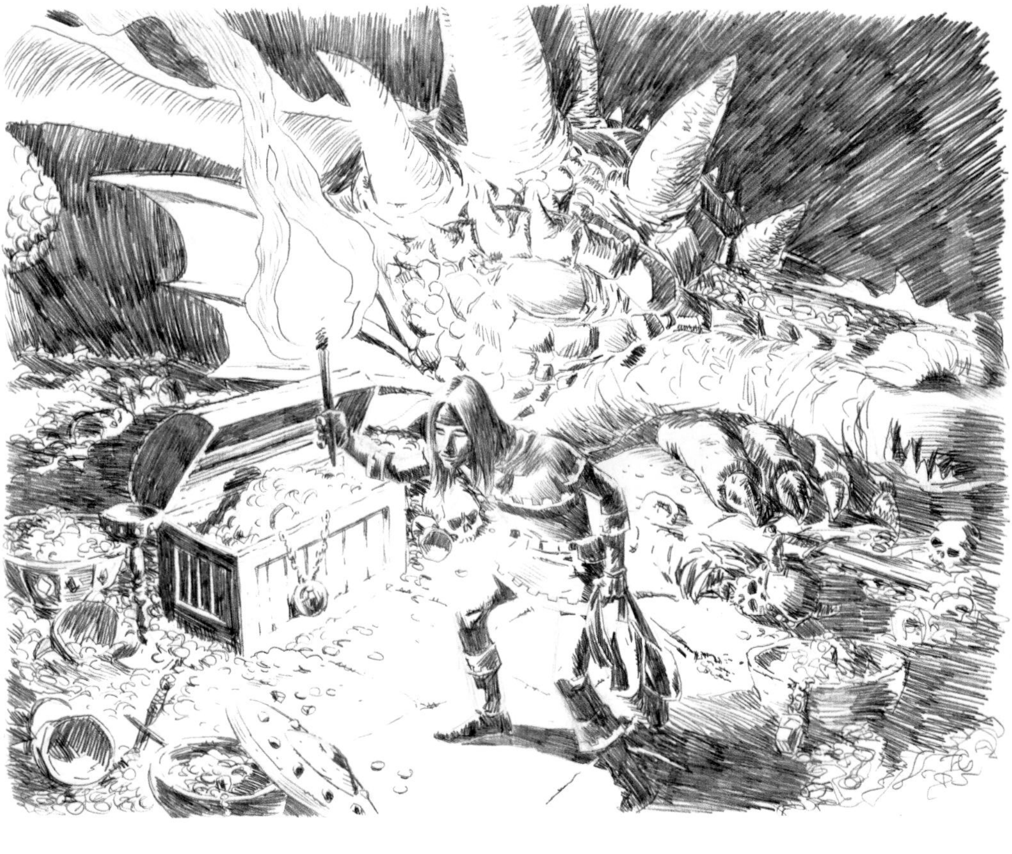

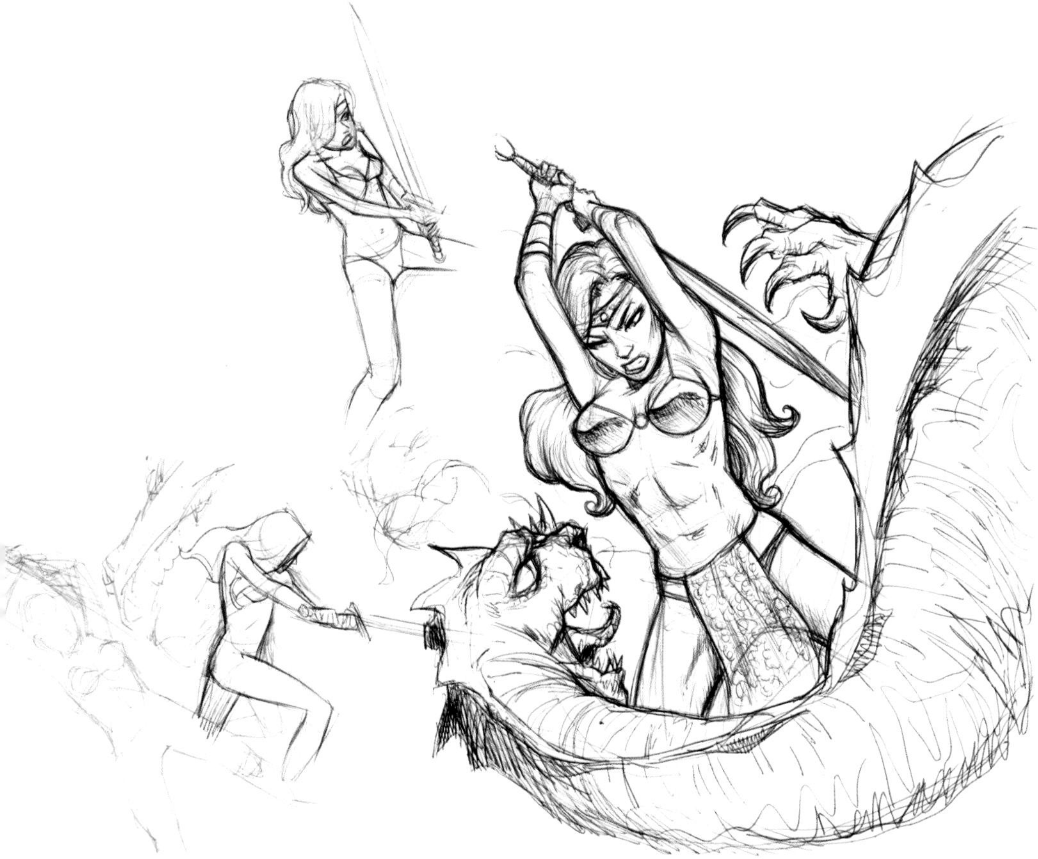

The game cover from Chapter 1 wound up being the first real test of Jim's fantasy style. He put a lot of work into getting that one right, as did colorist Dan Jackson, and they figured out a lot of the approach to the book in that one image.

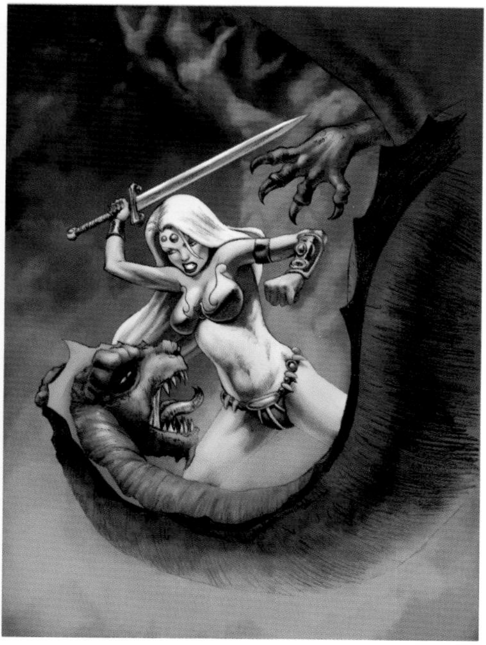

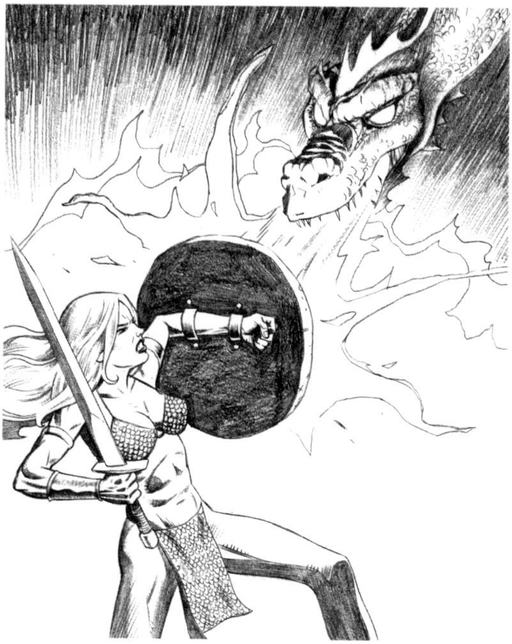

BONUS SECTION

When we approached Felicia about bringing *The Guild* to comics, we were already thinking of Jim Rugg, because of his excellent work on the Penny story for *Dr. Horrible*. However, we talked to a lot of artists, and their enthusiasm assured us there was a lot of crossover between the comics community and Guildies.

Zack Finfrock, *Warbot in Accounting*, nuklearpower.com.

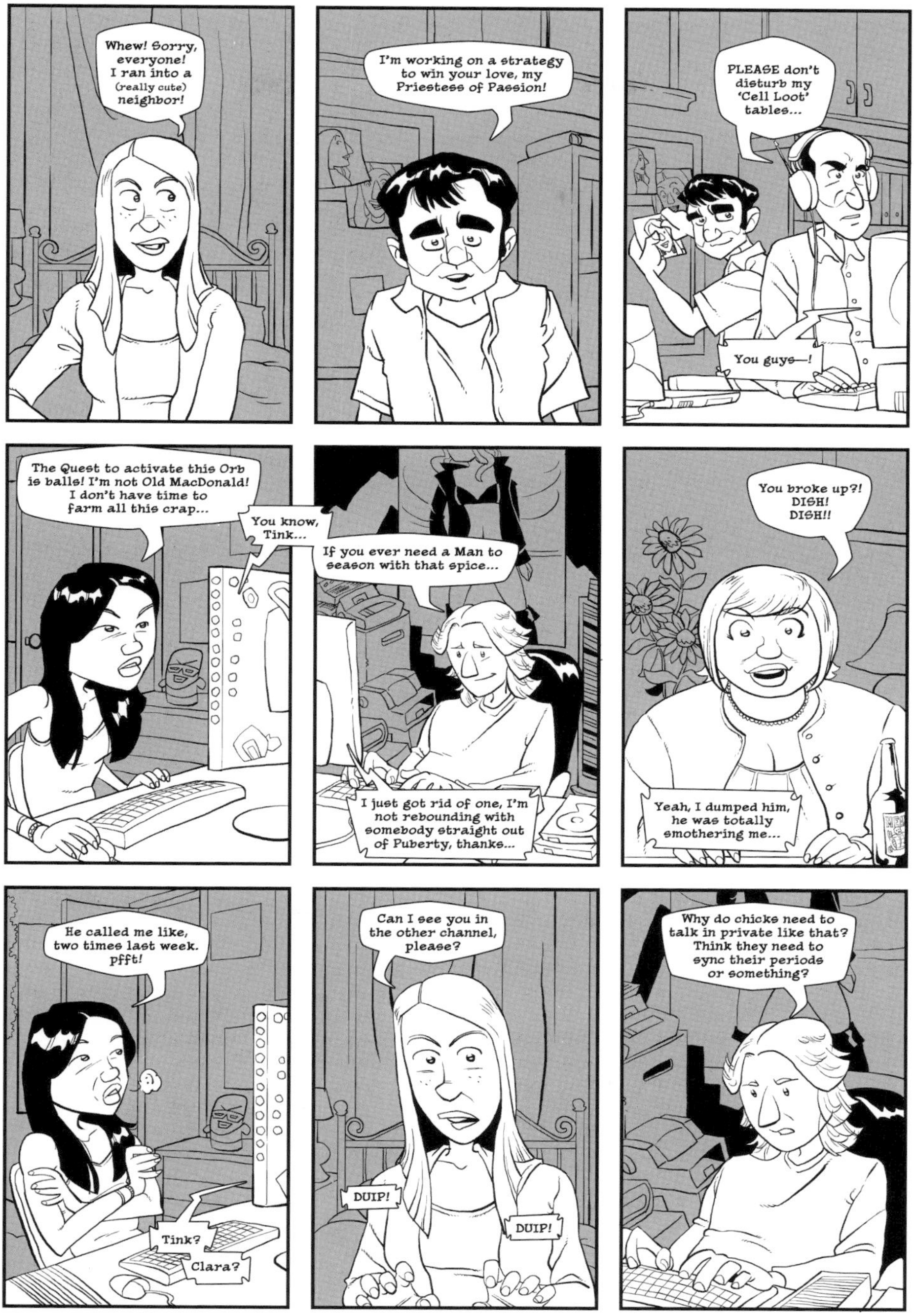
Whew! Sorry, everyone! I ran into a (really cute) neighbor!
I'm working on a strategy to win your love, my Priestess of Passion!
PLEASE don't disturb my 'Cell Loot' tables...
You guys—!
The Quest to activate this Orb is balls! I'm not Old MacDonald! I don't have time to farm all this crap...
You know, Tink...
If you ever need a Man to season with that spice...
I just got rid of one, I'm not rebounding with somebody straight out of Puberty, thanks...
You broke up?! DISH! DISH!!
Yeah, I dumped him, he was totally smothering me...
He called me like, two times last week. pfft!
Tink?
Clara?
Can I see you in the other channel, please?
DUIP!
DUIP!
Why do chicks need to talk in private like that? Think they need to sync their periods or something?

Indigo Kelleigh, lunarbistro.com.

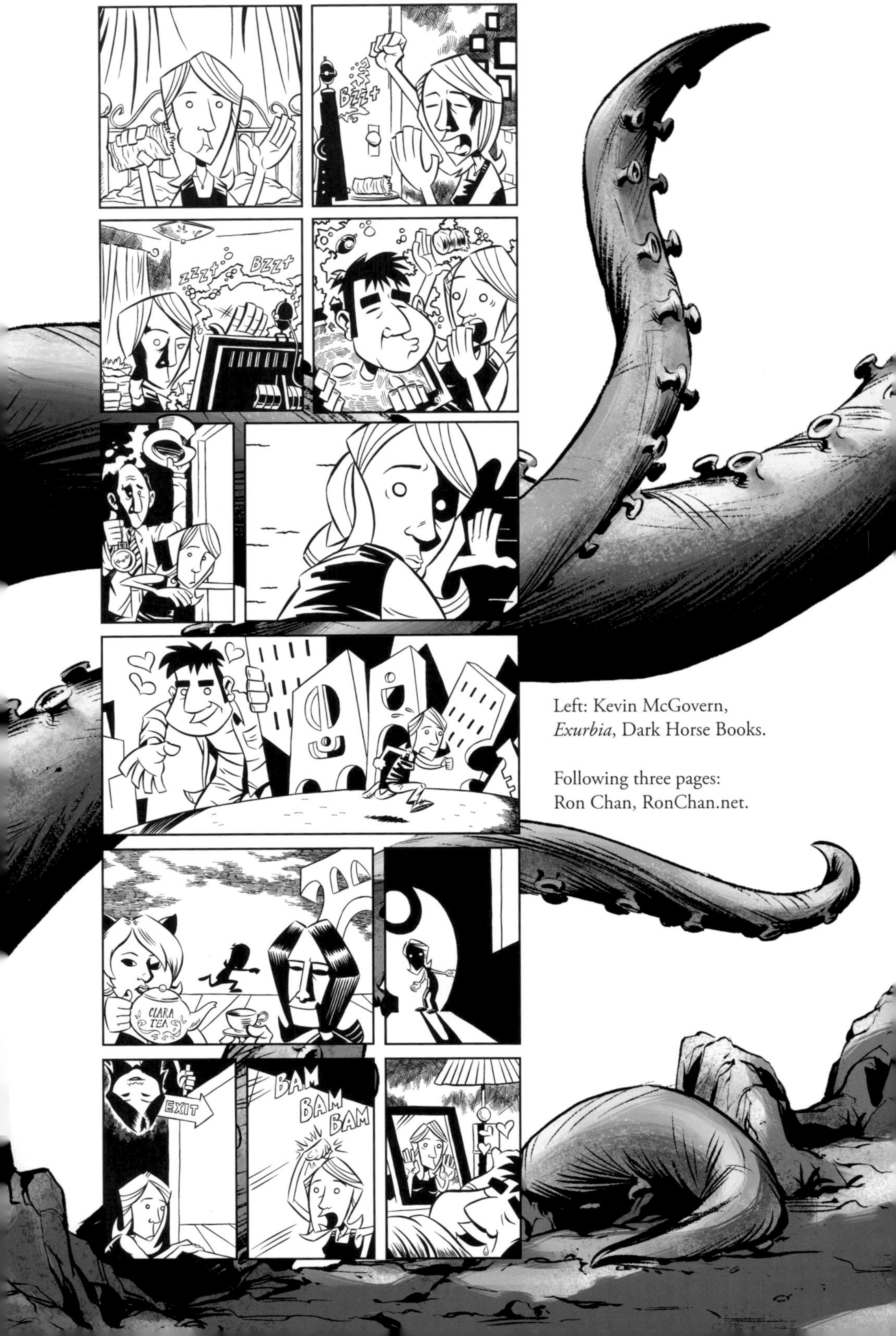
BZZZT
ZZZT
BZZT
CLARA TEA
EXIT
BAM
BAM
BAM

Left: Kevin McGovern, *Exurbia*, Dark Horse Books.

Following three pages: Ron Chan, RonChan.net.

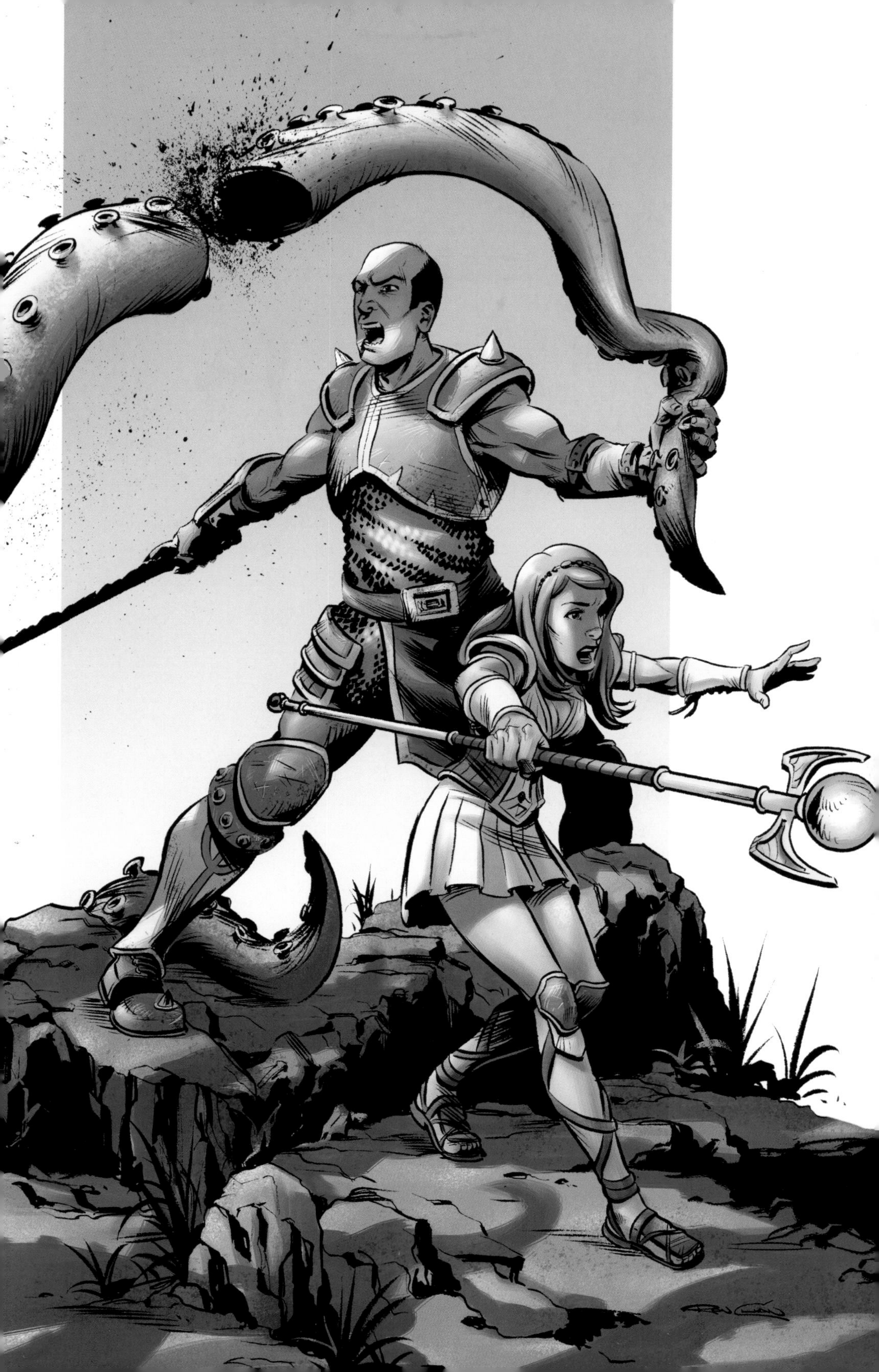

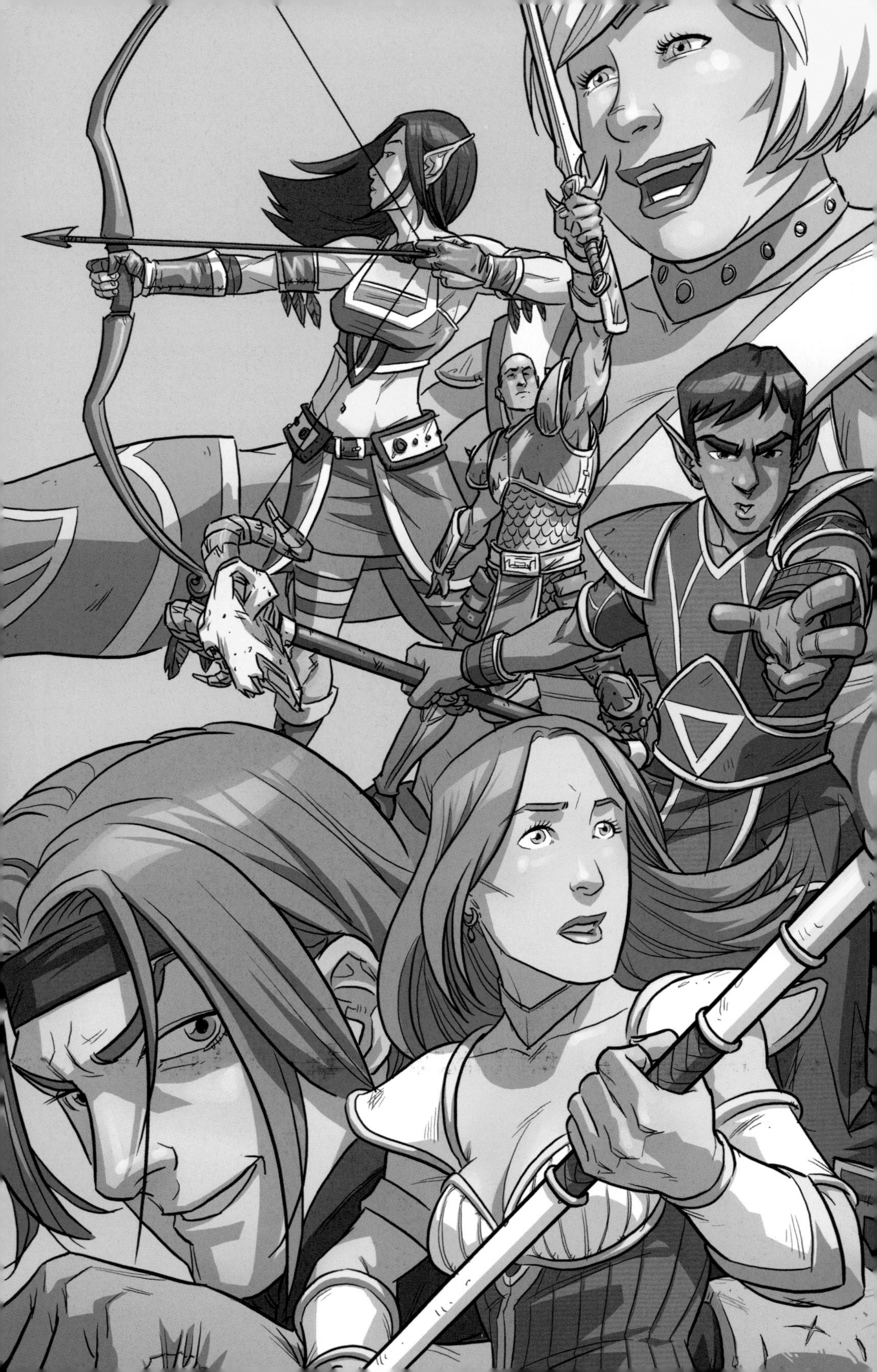

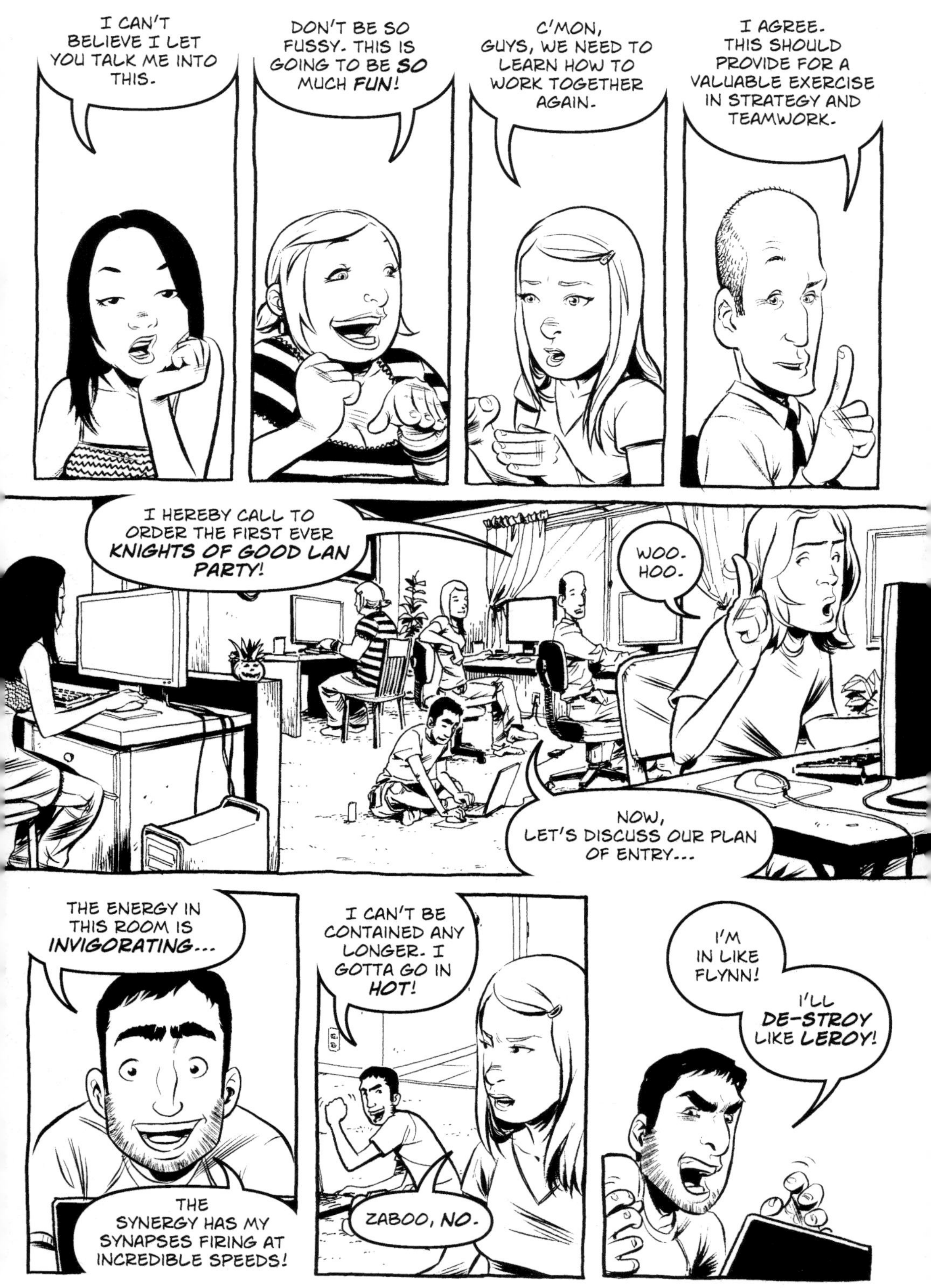

I CAN'T BELIEVE I LET YOU TALK ME INTO THIS.
DON'T BE SO FUSSY. THIS IS GOING TO BE **SO** MUCH **FUN**!
C'MON, GUYS, WE NEED TO LEARN HOW TO WORK TOGETHER AGAIN.
I AGREE. THIS SHOULD PROVIDE FOR A VALUABLE EXERCISE IN STRATEGY AND TEAMWORK.
I HEREBY CALL TO ORDER THE FIRST EVER **KNIGHTS OF GOOD LAN PARTY**!
WOO. HOO.
NOW, LET'S DISCUSS OUR PLAN OF ENTRY...
THE ENERGY IN THIS ROOM IS **INVIGORATING...**
THE SYNERGY HAS MY SYNAPSES FIRING AT INCREDIBLE SPEEDS!
I CAN'T BE CONTAINED ANY LONGER. I GOTTA GO IN **HOT**!
ZABOO, **NO**.
I'M IN LIKE FLYNN!
I'LL **DE-STROY** LIKE **LEROY**!

DARK HORSE BRINGS YOU THE BEST IN WEBCOMICS

These wildly popular cartoon gems were once only available online, but now can be found through Dark Horse Books with loads of awesome extras!

SINFEST
Volume One TPB
By Tatsuya Ishida

Sinfest is one of the most-read and longest-running webcomics out there, and explores religion, advertising, sex, and politics in a way fleen.com calls "both brutally funny and devastatingly on-target." The first volume collects the first six hundred *Sinfest* strips, introducing the full cast of characters and the opening installments of Ninja Theatre, beat poetry, calligraphy lessons, and the irresistible Pooch & Percival strips. If your comic-strip craving hasn't been satisfied since the nineties, deliverance is finally at hand.
ISBN 978-1-59582-319-9 | $14.99

WONDERMARK
Volume One: Beards of Our Forefathers HC
By David Malki

Dark Horse Comics is proud to present this handsome hardbound collection of David Malki's Ignatz-nominated comic strip *Wondermark*. Malki repurposes illustrations and engravings from nineteenth-century books into hilarious, collage-style comic strips. Beards are just the beginning.
ISBN 978-1-59307-984-0 | $14.99

MEGATOKYO
Volume One TPB
By Fred Gallagher and Rodney Caston

This reissue of the highly successful *Megatokyo* Volume One brings fans a new and revised version of the book with improved print quality and a larger trim size. This book will contain all of the comics from Chapter 0 as well as the running editorial comments featured in the original release. Exclusive to the Dark Horse reissue are additional drawings, historical notes, and selected rants from this first developmental year of the *Megatokyo* webcomic.
ISBN 978-1-59307-163-9 | $9.99

PENNY ARCADE
Volume One: Attack of the Bacon Robots! TPB
By Jerry Holkins and Mike Krahulik

Penny Arcade, the comic strip for gamers, by gamers, is now available in comic shops and bookstores everywhere. Experience the joy of being a hardcore gamer as expressed in hilariously witty vignettes of random vulgarity and mindless violence!
ISBN 978-1-59307-444-9 | $12.99